Ending the Physical Punishment of Children

Ending the Physical Punishment of Children

A Guide for Clinicians and Practitioners

Edited by
Elizabeth T. Gershoff and Shawna J. Lee

American Psychological Association
Washington, DC

Published by
American Psychological Association
750 First Street, NE
Washington, DC 20002
https://www.apa.org

Order Department
https://www.apa.org/pubs/books
order@apa.org

In the U.K., Europe, Africa, and the Middle East, copies may be ordered from Eurospan
https://www.eurospanbookstore.com/apa
info@eurospangroup.com

Typeset in Meridien and Ortodoxa by Circle Graphics, Inc., Reisterstown, MD

Printer: Sheridan Books, Chelsea, MI
Cover Designer: Nicci Falcone, Gaithersburg, MD

Library of Congress Cataloging-in-Publication Data

Names: Gershoff, Elizabeth T., editor. | Lee, Shawna J., editor.
Title: Ending the physical punishment of children : a guide for clinicians and practitioners / edited by Elizabeth T. Gershoff and Shawna J. Lee.
Description: Washington, DC : American Psychological Association, [2020] | Includes bibliographical references and index.
Identifiers: LCCN 2019022554 (print) | LCCN 2019022555 (ebook) | ISBN 9781433831140 (paperback) | ISBN 9781433831881 (ebook)
Subjects: LCSH: Corporal punishment of children. | Corporal punishment of children—Psychological aspects.
Classification: LCC HQ770.4 .E584 2020 (print) | LCC HQ770.4 (ebook) | DDC 649/.64—dc23
LC record available at https://lccn.loc.gov/2019022554
LC ebook record available at https://lccn.loc.gov/2019022555

http://dx.doi.org/10.1037/0000162-000

Printed in the United States of America

10 9 8 7 6 5 4 3 2 1

CONTENTS

CONTRIBUTORS

Amie F. Bettencourt, PhD, Johns Hopkins University School of Medicine, Baltimore, MD

Susan M. Breitenstein, RN, FAAN, PhD, The Ohio State University College of Nursing, Columbus

Deborah Bretl, RN, MSN, PPCNP-BC, Children's Hospital of Wisconsin, Milwaukee

Alan S. Brown, PhD, Southern Methodist University, Dallas, TX

Caitlin Canfield, PhD, New York University School of Medicine, New York

Ellen Chiocca, MSN, CPNP, RNC-NIC, PhD, DePaul University, Chicago, IL

Guadalupe Díaz, PhD, University of California, Irvine

Carrie Donnell, MSN, CPNP, Monroe Carell Jr. Children's Hospital at Vanderbilt, Nashville, TN

Katharine Doughty, RN, MS, CPNP-BC, Nationwide Children's Hospital, Columbus, OH

Howard Dubowitz, MS, FAAP, MD, University of Maryland School of Medicine, Baltimore

Joan E. Durrant, PhD, University of Manitoba, Winnipeg

Morgan Dynes, PhD, University of Toledo College of Medicine and Life Sciences, Toledo, OH

Maria M. Galano, PhD, University of Massachusetts, Amherst

Elizabeth T. Gershoff, PhD, University of Texas at Austin

Sandra A. Graham-Bermann, PhD, University of Michigan, Ann Arbor

Andrew Grogan-Kaylor, PhD, University of Michigan, Ann Arbor

Deborah Gross, DNSc, RN, FAAN, Johns Hopkins University School of Nursing, Baltimore, MD

George W. Holden, PhD, Southern Methodist University, Dallas, TX
Grant W. O. Holland, PhD, Dallas CBT, Dallas, TX
Gail Hornor, RNC, DNP, CPNP, Nationwide Children's Hospital, Columbus, OH
Kathryn H. Howell, PhD, University of Memphis, Memphis, TN
Michele Knox, PhD, University of Toledo College of Medicine and Life Sciences, Toledo, OH
Shawna J. Lee, PhD, University of Michigan, Ann Arbor
Bridget Marshall, DNP, CPNP, Colorado Mesa University, Grand Junction
Alan Mendelsohn, MD, New York University School of Medicine, New York
Cindy Miller-Perrin, PhD, Pepperdine University, Malibu, CA
Kristen Morris, DNP, RN, CPNP, Peyton Manning Children's Hospital at St. Vincent, Indianapolis, IN
Robin Perrin, PhD, Pepperdine University, Malibu, CA
Ronald J. Prinz, PhD, University of South Carolina, Columbia
Saribel Garcia Quinones, DNP, PNP-BC, New York University, New York
Stephanie M. Reich, PhD, University of California, Irvine
Erin Roby, PhD, New York University School of Medicine, New York
Seth Scholer, MPH, MD, Vanderbilt University Medical Center, Nashville, TN

Ending the Physical Punishment of Children

Introduction

The Rationale for Reducing Physical Punishment

Elizabeth T. Gershoff and Shawna J. Lee

Many parents use physical punishment because they hope it will make their children more compliant and better behaved. Yet several decades of research on parents' use of physical punishment have yielded a clear conclusion that physical punishment generally, and spanking specifically, is ineffective at improving children's behavior and in fact leads to a worsening of child behavior over time (Altschul, Lee, & Gershoff, 2016; Gershoff & Grogan-Kaylor, 2016; Gershoff, Lansford, Sexton, Davis-Kean, & Sameroff, 2012). The more children are physically punished, the more aggressive they are, the more behavior problems they have, the more mental health problems they have, and the worse they do on tests of cognitive ability (Gershoff & Grogan-Kaylor, 2016). Physical punishment is thus ineffective at achieving parents' goals of improving children's behavior and instead increases the risk that children will experience a range of negative side effects.

One such side effect is physical harm to the children. Despite common euphemisms such as "spanking" that minimize the fact that it involves violence, physical punishment involves hitting and hurting children (Gershoff, 2013). Adults are larger and stronger than children, and when they hit children with their hands or with objects, adults run the risk of causing physical harm. It is thus not surprising that parents who use physical punishment have an increased risk of physically abusing their children (Gershoff & Grogan-Kaylor, 2016; Lee, Grogan-Kaylor, & Berger, 2014).

http://dx.doi.org/10.1037/0000162-001
Ending the Physical Punishment of Children: A Guide for Clinicians and Practitioners,
E. T. Gershoff and S. J. Lee (Editors)

Indeed, physical punishment and physical abuse appear to be points along a single continuum of violence against children. Research studies that examined both physical punishment and physical abuse found that physical punishment is linked with the same detrimental outcomes for children as is physical abuse (Gershoff & Grogan-Kaylor, 2016). Research on adverse childhood experiences has also found that adults who recalled being spanked as children had more mental health and substance abuse problems than did adults who were not spanked as children, over and above whether they had experienced physical or emotional abuse (Afifi et al., 2017).

The strength of the evidence demonstrating physical punishment's risks has led increasing numbers of professional organizations serving children and families to strongly discourage physical punishment. For example, the American Psychological Association (2019), American Academy of Pediatrics (Sege, Siegel, Council on Child Abuse and Neglect, & Committee on Psychosocial Aspects of Child and Family Health, 2018), American Academy of Child and Adolescent Psychiatry (2012), American Professional Society on the Abuse of Children (2016), Canadian Paediatric Society (Durrant, Ensom, & Coalition on Physical Punishment of Children and Youth, 2004), Canadian Psychological Association (2004), and National Association of Pediatric Nurse Practitioners (2011) have each stated that physical punishment is harmful to children, that parents should avoid it, and that their members should help parents find alternative forms of discipline. The U.S. Centers for Disease Control and Prevention recently published a guidance document on the prevention of child maltreatment that called for educational and legislative interventions to reduce support for and use of physical punishment as a strategy to prevent child physical abuse (Fortson, Klevens, Merrick, Gilbert, & Alexander, 2016). This book documents a range of interventions, from the individual level to the community level, that can support the recommendations of these professional organizations to reduce parents' use of physical punishment.

Opposition to the physical punishment of children is not limited to U.S. and Canadian organizations; globally, an increasing number of international groups and nation states are taking action to reduce or eliminate physical punishment of children. The United Nations has unequivocally stated (United Nations Committee on the Rights of the Child, 2007) that all physical punishment, no matter how "mild," violates children's right to protection from violence under the Convention on the Rights of the Child (United Nations, 1989). The United Nations Committee on the Rights of the Child (2007) called for all countries that have ratified the Convention to legally ban and eliminate all physical punishment of children, including that by parents. As a result, 56 countries have heeded the United Nations' call and have legally prohibited all physical punishment of children (Global Initiative to End All Corporal Punishment of Children, 2019).

Although physical punishment can cause harm and does not improve children's behavior, it remains prevalent in the United States and around the world. In a large community-based study of urban American families, 53% of mothers and 44% of fathers of 3-year-olds reported that they had spanked their child at least once in the month before the survey (Lee, Altschul, & Gershoff, 2015). Lifetime prevalence of physical punishment in national studies tends to be more than 80% (Gershoff et al., 2012), meaning that the majority of children in the United States experience physical punishment at least once in their lifetimes. Prevalence around the world is similarly high: Nearly two thirds of 2- to 4-year-old children (63%) in a global survey had been physically punished in the previous month (UNICEF, 2017). With this book, we aim to change that.

THE PRESENT BOOK

The good news is that parenting behaviors are malleable and can be changed through education and training. A variety of approaches have been used successfully to prevent or reduce parents' use of physical punishment. However, there have been very few efforts to identify and synthesize these approaches. Indeed, a recent, purportedly comprehensive, review of parenting interventions by the National Academies of Sciences, Engineering, and Medicine (2016) neglected to include interventions aimed at reducing physical punishment. Therefore, professionals do not have a clear picture of the approaches available or of their levels of success.

The goal of this book is to identify and describe several of the leading evidence-based interventions that have successfully reduced parents' use of, or positive attitudes about, physical punishment. The authors describe 15 such interventions. This book is an in-depth follow-up to an article we published that provided narrative summaries of approaches to reduce physical punishment (Gershoff, Lee, & Durrant, 2017). To provide the detail we couldn't provide in the article, this book highlights each intervention in a separate chapter. Each chapter provides information about the evidence base for the intervention, its generalizability across populations and contexts, and how the intervention can be implemented in community and clinical settings.

To facilitate comparisons between interventions, each chapter follows the same general structure, first describing the intervention and its content that is relevant to physical punishment and how the intervention has been implemented to date. Next, authors review the evidence base regarding the intervention; most interventions have information from process evaluations, and all have evidence from outcome evaluations. Each chapter includes a discussion of limitations as well as suggested future uses of the program. The volume itself concludes with an afterword that summarizes common themes and discusses directions for future work in this area.

This book is targeted to clinicians, community practitioners, and policymakers who are interested in effective interventions to reduce and prevent physical punishment at the individual, group, or even societal level. The book includes information that interventionists require to decide which intervention to implement, including costs and how to obtain intervention materials.

We acknowledge that our list is not a comprehensive list of all interventions, but it is, we believe, illustrative of the range of interventions that have successfully reduced parents' positive attitudes about or use of physical punishment. We also note that the chapters are, in many cases, written by the program developers—a fact that both strengthens and limits the book, in different ways. Program developers are most familiar with their own programs and can thus provide the most authoritative program descriptions; however, the developers' attachment to their own work can also introduce bias when discussing research on their program's effectiveness. For this reason, each chapter discusses the limitations of the program as well as whether the program has been externally validated in online clearinghouses, which collect information about programs and rate the quality of the evidence supporting the program or that produce reports that recommend particular programs or types of intervention.

EMPIRICAL AND THEORETICAL BASES OF THE BOOK

Hundreds of studies on physical punishment have been conducted across disciplines (e.g., psychology, medicine, education) and across cultures and countries. The research consistently has shown that physical punishment increases the risk that children will engage in problem behavior and that they will experience other negative outcomes such as mental health problems (Gershoff & Grogan-Kaylor, 2016). Several prominent theories in psychology (e.g., social learning theory, hostile attribution bias theory, attachment theory, and coercive family process theory) explain the mechanisms whereby parents who physically punish their children tend to elicit negative outcomes from them, including increased aggression, increased antisocial behavior, and lower academic and cognitive outcomes (Gershoff, 2002).

The book also draws heavily from the field of prevention research. In a review of prevention and intervention research, the Institute of Medicine identified three levels of intervention: indicated interventions, selective interventions, and universal interventions (Mrazek & Haggerty, 1994). Figure 1 displays these three types of interventions in a typical pyramid diagram organized by the intensity and the size of the target population, with the specific populations for the prevention of physical punishment identified within each type. *Indicated intervention programs* have the goal of changing rates of an undesirable behavior among a population that either has already displayed the behavior or is at substantial risk for doing so. Because they are so targeted, they serve the fewest number of people, but they tend to involve intensive services, so are often the most expensive. *Selective prevention programs* are aimed at subgroups of the population that collectively have higher than average risk for the behavior of concern, either immediately or at some point in the individuals' lifetimes. *Universal prevention programs* target an entire population and are not based on any specific risk. They are the least intensive but have the widest reach and thus are, per capita, the least expensive interventions.

FIGURE 1. Levels of and Targets for Intervention to Prevent or Reduce Physical Punishment

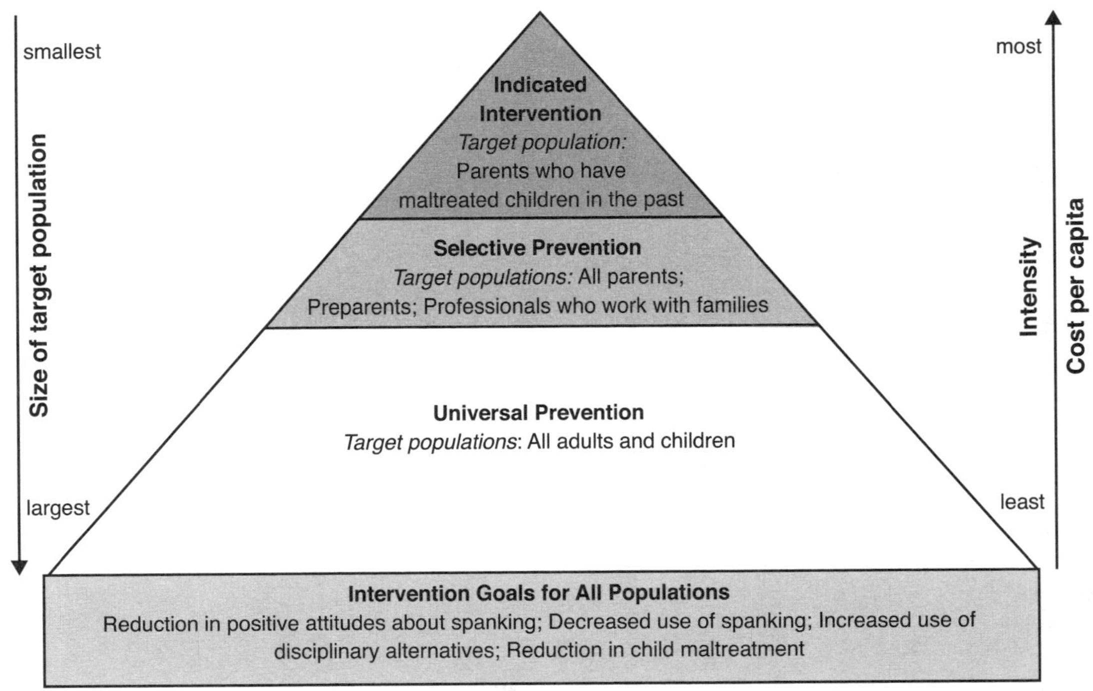

From “Promising Intervention Strategies to Reduce Parents’ Use of Physical Punishment,” by E. T. Gershoff, S. J. Lee, and J. E. Durrant, 2017, *Child Abuse & Neglect: The International Journal*, *71*, p. 10. Copyright 2017 by Elsevier. Reprinted with permission.

As with all interventions, the interventions in this book can each be categorized on the basis of one of these three levels of intervention. Thus, each chapter begins by noting whether the intervention it describes is indicated, selective, or universal as an indication of both the target population (e.g., everyone or a specific group of families) and how it might be implemented (e.g., an indicated intervention might be delivered one-on-one, whereas a universal intervention will need to be delivered to hundreds or thousands of people at a time). We hope these designations will be helpful to anyone deciding which intervention to reduce physical punishment fits best with their goals.

CONCLUSION

We are excited to be able to highlight these 15 interventions and are impressed by each program's demonstrated effectiveness at reducing approval of and use of physical punishment. We believe the interventions in this book will be useful to clinicians working with individual families or groups of families, community practitioners hoping to promote positive parenting broadly, and policymakers aiming to reduce all forms of violence against children at state and national levels. We hope that this book will also increase the dissemination and implementation of the interventions described herein.

REFERENCES

Afifi, T. O., Ford, D., Gershoff, E. T., Merrick, M., Grogan-Kaylor, A., Ports, K. A., . . . Peters Bennett, R. (2017). Spanking and adult mental health impairment: The case for the designation of spanking as an adverse childhood experience. *Child Abuse & Neglect: The International Journal, 71*, 24–31. http://dx.doi.org/10.1016/j.chiabu.2017.01.014

Altschul, I., Lee, S. J., & Gershoff, E. T. (2016). Hugs, not hits: Maternal warmth, not spanking, predicts positive child behaviors in the first five years of life. *Journal of Marriage and the Family, 78*, 695–714. http://dx.doi.org/10.1111/jomf.12306

American Academy of Child and Adolescent Psychiatry. (2012, July 30). *Policy statement on corporal punishment.* Retrieved from http://www.aacap.org/aacap/policy_statements/2012/Policy_Statement_on_Corporal_Punishment.aspx

American Professional Society on the Abuse of Children. (2016). *APSAC position statement on corporal punishment of children.* Retrieved from https://www.apsac.org/apsacpublications

American Psychological Association. (2019). *Resolution on physical discipline of children by parents.* Retrieved from https://www.apa.org/about/policy/physical-discipline.pdf

Canadian Psychological Association. (2004). *Policy statements: Physical punishment of children and youth.* Retrieved from https://cpa.ca/aboutcpa/policystatements/#physical

Durrant, J. E., Ensom, R., & Coalition on Physical Punishment of Children and Youth. (2004). *Joint statement on physical punishment of children and youth.* Retrieved from http://www.cheo.on.ca/en/physicalpunishment

Fortson, B. L., Klevens, J., Merrick, M. T., Gilbert, L. K., & Alexander, S. P. (2016). *Preventing child abuse and neglect: A technical package for policy, norm, and programmatic activities.* Atlanta, GA: National Center for Injury Prevention and Control,

Centers for Disease Control and Prevention. Retrieved from http://www.cdc.gov/violenceprevention/childmaltreatment/index.html
Gershoff, E. T. (2002). Corporal punishment by parents and associated child behaviors and experiences: A meta-analytic and theoretical review. *Psychological Bulletin, 128,* 539–579. http://dx.doi.org/10.1037/0033-2909.128.4.539
Gershoff, E. T. (2013). Spanking and child development: We know enough now to stop hitting our children. *Child Development Perspectives, 7,* 133–137. http://dx.doi.org/10.1111/cdep.12038
Gershoff, E. T., & Grogan-Kaylor, A. (2016). Spanking and child outcomes: Old controversies and new meta-analyses. *Journal of Family Psychology, 30,* 453–469. http://dx.doi.org/10.1037/fam0000191
Gershoff, E. T., Lansford, J. E., Sexton, H. R., Davis-Kean, P., & Sameroff, A. J. (2012). Longitudinal links between spanking and children's externalizing behaviors in a national sample of White, Black, Hispanic, and Asian American families. *Child Development, 83,* 838–843. http://dx.doi.org/10.1111/j.1467-8624.2011.01732.x
Gershoff, E. T., Lee, S. J., & Durrant, J. E. (2017). Promising intervention strategies to reduce parents' use of physical punishment. *Child Abuse & Neglect: The International Journal, 71,* 9–23. http://dx.doi.org/10.1016/j.chiabu.2017.01.017
Global Initiative to End All Corporal Punishment of Children. (2019). *Progress.* Retrieved from https://endcorporalpunishment.org/countdown
Lee, S. J., Altschul, I., & Gershoff, E. T. (2015). Wait until your father gets home? Fathers' and mothers' spanking and development of child aggression. *Children and Youth Services Review, 52,* 158–166. http://dx.doi.org/10.1016/j.childyouth.2014.11.006
Lee, S. J., Grogan-Kaylor, A., & Berger, L. M. (2014). Parental spanking of 1-year-old children and subsequent child protective services involvement. *Child Abuse & Neglect: The International Journal, 38,* 875–883. http://dx.doi.org/10.1016/j.chiabu.2014.01.018
Mrazek, P. J., & Haggerty, R. J. (Eds.). (1994). *Reducing risks for mental disorders: Frontiers for prevention intervention research.* Washington, DC: National Academies Press.
National Academies of Sciences, Engineering, and Medicine. (2016). *Parenting matters: Supporting parents of children ages 0–8.* Washington, DC: The National Academies Press. http://dx.doi.org/10.17226/21868
National Association of Pediatric Nurse Practitioners. (2011). NAPNAP position statement on corporal punishment. *Journal of Pediatric Health Care, 25*(6), e31–e32. http://dx.doi.org/10.1016/j.pedhc.2011.07.003
Sege, R. D., Siegel, B. S., Council on Child Abuse and Neglect, & Committee on Psychosocial Aspects of Child and Family Health. (2018). Effective discipline to raise healthy children. *Pediatrics, 142*(6), e20183112. http://dx.doi.org/10.1542/peds.2018-3112
UNICEF. (2017). *A familiar face: Violence in the lives of children and adolescents.* Retrieved from https://data.unicef.org/wp-content/uploads/2017/11/VAC-Brochure-FINAL-10-31-17.pdf
United Nations. (1989, November 20). Convention on the Rights of the Child, G. A. Res. 44/25, U. N. GAOR, 44th Sess., at 3, U. N. Doc. A/RES/44/25. Retrieved from http://www.unicef.org/crc
United Nations Committee on the Rights of the Child (CRC). (2007, March 2). *CRC General Comment No. 8 (2006): The right of the child to protection from corporal punishment and other cruel or degrading forms of punishment (CRC/C/GC/8).* Retrieved from https://www.refworld.org/cgi-bin/texis/vtx/rwmain?page=search&docid=460bc7772&skip=0&query=crc/c/gc/8

I

INDIVIDUAL- AND FAMILY-LEVEL INTERVENTIONS

1

Brief Online Education

George W. Holden and Alan S. Brown

THE INTERVENTION

George Holden, PhD, at Southern Methodist University developed the Brief Online Education About Physical Punishment intervention. The intervention is *universal* in that it can be used with most adult audiences, including parents and those without children. The program can be administered by professionals and nonprofessionals.

Background and Theory of Change

Parents acquire their attitudes about physical punishment from a variety of sources. Most commonly, they derive their attitudes from their own experiences with their parents' disciplinary practices (Simons & Wurtele, 2010). Individuals also develop their attitudes about spanking from their own cultural context and values, as well as their naïve beliefs about the efficacy of inflicting pain in reducing unwanted behaviors. Despite the large research literature base that has now been published, many individuals remain unaware of the potential negative consequences that physical punishment can have on children. Furthermore, although pediatricians are the single most trusted source of disciplinary advice (Taylor, Moeller, Hamvas, & Rice, 2013) and many parents want to get more information about discipline (Young, Davis, Schoen, & Parker, 1998), parents may not think to ask their pediatrician about child

http://dx.doi.org/10.1037/0000162-002
Ending the Physical Punishment of Children: A Guide for Clinicians and Practitioners,
E. T. Gershoff and S. J. Lee (Editors)

discipline during their child's doctor visits, and many family physicians do not often volunteer information on discipline (McCormick, 1992). In the absence of hearing about research on physical punishment from trusted sources, many parents may assume that physical punishment is not harmful to their children or that physical pain is an effective way to teach children how to behave.

When individuals form an attitude on a topic, if that belief is constructed upon a limited knowledge base, it is susceptible to change with new information. Therefore, providing education and information about findings from the scientific research on physical punishment may be potent enough to modify attitudes.

This approach of presenting counterattitudinal information to individuals has been successful in several prior studies of physical punishment. For instance, Robinson, Funk, Beth, and Bush (2005) showed that having subjects read a passage on how physical punishment is relatively ineffective in changing a child's behavior resulted in a reduction in favorable attitudes toward spanking. In addition, a pediatrician who developed a 20-minute video (*Play Nicely*; see Chapter 5, this volume) describing disciplinary techniques that do not involve physical punishment has shown that the *Play Nicely* video reduces parents' positive attitudes toward spanking when compared with the attitudes of those parents in a control condition (Hudnut-Beumler, Smith, & Scholer, 2018; Scholer, Hamilton, Johnson, & Scott, 2010).

Informing parents about the research findings on physical punishment via the Internet is another reasonable approach, given online access is widespread and has improved for families across all socioeconomic levels. Using the Internet or mobile technology has proven successful in modifying attitudes and behaviors regarding parenting and child well-being (e.g., Enebrink, Högström, Forster, & Ghaderi, 2012). Furthermore, recent research indicates that more effort should be invested in teaching parenting skills through Internet platforms because they are easy to access, are inexpensive to apply, and can be effective in changing behaviors (Breitenstein, Gross, & Christophersen, 2014; Jones et al., 2013; McGoron & Ondersma, 2015).

Main Goal of the Intervention

The main goal of this intervention is to provide brief psychoeducational information about the scientific research concerning the negative effects of physical punishment on children. Information is intended for both parents and nonparents. The assumption is that those with positive attitudes toward physical punishment will modify those views once they become aware of the research evidence about the problems linked to physical punishment.

Brief Description of the Intervention

This psychoeducational intervention can be administered by anyone. No specialized training is required. The intervention consists of reading through the information. On average it takes approximately 30 minutes to read the information. Typically, the mode of delivery is via computer to an individual. However, the information could also be delivered in a group setting by projecting the content onto a large screen. The materials needed to administer the intervention include a computer and access to the Internet. Alternatively, a hard copy (handout) of the program can be provided, but this mode of delivery may be less engaging.

Content Relevant to Spanking or Physical Punishment

To make the information more engaging, the person administering the intervention first asks participants to estimate to what extent the research has identified links between spanking (the most common form of physical punishment) and child behavior or family relationship problems. The choices were no relation, moderate relation, or strong relation. After selecting their rating, participants then read a summary of the research showing that spanking increases risk for child behavior problems as well as other family problems.

The information consisted of three sentences about how spanking was related to problems in seven domains (aggression, child abuse, depression, delinquency, moral values, partner abuse, and quality of parent–child relationship). Also included were five other domains (e.g., adult obesity, attention-deficit disorder, social phobia) where there is no evidence linking spanking with the problem. See Exhibit 1.1 for examples.

Implementation of the Intervention

A total of 638 parents and college students who participated in two research studies have used the program. To date, the settings have been computer-based

---

EXHIBIT 1.1

Examples of Evidence About Spanking in Educational Component

Spanking and aggression. Aggression is broadly defined as behaviors that are hostile, injurious, or destructive in nature. The research evidence is very clear that the children of parents who rely on spanking as a disciplinary technique are more aggressive with their peers than other children. This finding has been replicated in more than 25 studies.

Spanking and quality of parent–child relationship. The relationship between a parent and child is measured by such things as communication, trust, and affection. Fourteen research studies show very strong evidence that when a child is spanked by their parent, the bond between them is substantially weakened. The poor parent–child bonds that result from spanking mainly include an insecure attachment of the child to the mother and negative child–parent interactions.

(presumably people were in their homes) and on one college campus. One sample was university-based, and the second sample was community-based. Participants ranged in age from 18 to 52 years (Holden, Brown, Baldwin, & Croft Caderao, 2014). Of the parents who have used the program, their children ranged in age from 2 through 8 years old. Across the two samples, most participants were White (82%), but some were Hispanic (8%), African American (6%), Asian American (3%), or other. The college students came from a major metropolitan area in the Southwestern United States; parents participated from all across the country. The program is written in English but could readily be translated into other languages.

Evidence of Effectiveness From Outcome Evaluations

Holden and colleagues (2014) reported on two evaluations of the efficacy of the intervention. In their first study, participants were 118 college students (72% female; 64% White; M_{age} = 19.5 years) from a private, medium-sized southwestern university. In two sessions, approximately 1 week apart, attitudes toward physical punishment were measured using the Attitudes Toward Spanking (ATS) questionnaire (Holden, Coleman, & Schmidt, 1995). At the beginning of Session 2, all participants read a series of short three-sentence paragraphs about research findings showing the relationship between physical punishment and a particular problem behavior more likely to be exhibited in the child as a result of such punishment. Following this, they filled out the ATS questionnaire a second time. There was a significant reduction in positive attitudes toward spanking, and most participants (75%) reported that they had a less favorable attitude toward physical punishment as a result of reading the research summaries.

The first study used a nonparent sample, so a second study by Holden et al. (2014) examined whether the same attitudinal shift could be found with parents of young children (ages 3–8 years). A total of 414 parents were recruited (59% female; 78% White; $M_{education}$ = 10.5 years; M_{age} = 31 years) from MTurk. Participation consisted of a single session, with the ATS questionnaire given at the start and end of the session. Half of the participants (randomly selected) then read the research summaries on the relationships between physical punishment and child problem behaviors that were used in the first study. The other participants, in a control condition, read research findings related to child care. Similar to the results of the first study, parents who read the spanking-related research findings showed a reduction in positive attitudes about physical punishment, as measured by a significant decrease in ATS scores. Furthermore, this change was significantly greater than in the control group, suggesting that simply participating in an online study did not produce the behavior change. As in the first investigation, the overwhelming majority (79%) of participants in the physical punishment condition claimed that their attitudes had been changed as a result of reading the research findings. Furthermore, the positive change was greater for those who reported they had not been aware of the research on spanking.

Limitations

A limitation of this particular online education method was that it included no assessment concerning how the individual was processing or reacting to the information presented. Such process monitoring could be added to future versions of this computer-based education. Another limitation of the study was that although evidence emerged for attitude change, postintervention parental disciplinary responses were not assessed. Future research is needed to provide such a test.

SUGGESTED FUTURE USE OF THE PROGRAM

How Clinicians Can Use the Intervention

Clinicians can use the program as an educational tool in a variety of ways. For example, the program can be assigned to clients as homework and then be discussed during a session. Alternatively, the program can be used during a therapeutic session to elicit client attitudes and views about child punishment. A third option would be to use it in a group setting. For example, a volunteer could respond to the items in front of the group to stimulate group discussion.

How Community Practitioners Can Use the Intervention

Community practitioners can use it similarly to how clinicians use it.

How Policymakers Can Use the Intervention

This intervention could be used in a wide variety of ways to educate individuals. For example, it could be used in high school or college courses or in hospitals and other settings as a form of prenatal education. It could also be used in community settings for parent education or by professional organizations for continuing education credit.

INFORMATION ON OBTAINING THE PROGRAM

There is no cost to obtain the program. No training is required. For more information about how to obtain the intervention, contact George Holden (gholden@smu.edu).

REFERENCES

Breitenstein, S. M., Gross, D., & Christophersen, R. (2014). Digital delivery methods of parenting training interventions: A systematic review. *Worldviews on Evidence-Based Nursing, 11*, 168–176. http://dx.doi.org/10.1111/wvn.12040

Enebrink, P., Högström, J., Forster, M., & Ghaderi, A. (2012). Internet-based parent management training: A randomized controlled study. *Behaviour Research and Therapy, 50,* 240–249. http://dx.doi.org/10.1016/j.brat.2012.01.006

Holden, G. W., Brown, A. S., Baldwin, A. S., & Croft Caderao, K. (2014). Research findings can change attitudes about corporal punishment. *Child Abuse & Neglect: The International Journal, 38,* 902–908. http://dx.doi.org/10.1016/j.chiabu.2013.10.013

Holden, G. W., Coleman, S., & Schmidt, K. L. (1995). Why 3-year-old children get spanked: Parent and child determinants in a sample of college-educated mothers. *Merrill-Palmer Quarterly, 41,* 431–452.

Hudnut-Beumler, J., Smith, A., & Scholer, S. J. (2018). How to convince parents to stop spanking their children. *Clinical Pediatrics, 57,* 129–136. http://dx.doi.org/10.1177/0009922817693298

Jones, D. J., Forehand, R., Cuellar, J., Kincaid, C., Parent, J., Fenton, N., & Goodrum, N. (2013). Harnessing innovative technologies to advance children's mental health: Behavioral parent training as an example. *Clinical Psychology Review, 33,* 241–252. http://dx.doi.org/10.1016/j.cpr.2012.11.003

McCormick, K. F. (1992). Attitudes of primary care physicians toward corporal punishment. *JAMA, 267,* 3161–3165. http://dx.doi.org/10.1001/jama.1992.03480230053027

McGoron, L., & Ondersma, S. J. (2015). Reviewing the need for technological and other expansions of evidence-based parent training for young children. *Children and Youth Services Review, 59,* 71–83. http://dx.doi.org/10.1016/j.childyouth.2015.10.012

Robinson, D. H., Funk, D. C., Beth, A., & Bush, A. M. (2005). Changing beliefs about corporal punishment: Increasing knowledge about ineffectiveness to build more consistent moral and informational beliefs. *Journal of Behavioral Education, 14,* 117–139. http://dx.doi.org/10.1007/s10864-005-2706-9

Scholer, S. J., Hamilton, E. C., Johnson, M. C., & Scott, T. A. (2010). A brief intervention may affect parents' attitudes toward using less physical punishment. *Family and Community Health, 33,* 106–116. http://dx.doi.org/10.1097/FCH.0b013e3181d592ef

Simons, D. A., & Wurtele, S. K. (2010). Relationships between parents' use of corporal punishment and their children's endorsement of spanking and hitting other children. *Child Abuse & Neglect: The International Journal, 34,* 639–646. http://dx.doi.org/10.1016/j.chiabu.2010.01.012

Taylor, C. A., Moeller, W., Hamvas, L., & Rice, J. C. (2013). Parents' professional sources of advice regarding child discipline and their use of corporal punishment. *Clinical Pediatrics, 52,* 147–155. http://dx.doi.org/10.1177/0009922812465944

Young, K. T., Davis, K., Schoen, C., & Parker, S. (1998). Listening to parents: A national survey of parents with young children. *Archives of Pediatrics & Adolescent Medicine, 152,* 255–262.

2

Alternative Biblical Interpretations Intervention

Cindy Miller-Perrin and Robin Perrin

THE INTERVENTION

The Alternative Biblical Interpretations Intervention (ABII) was developed by Robin Perrin and Cindy Miller-Perrin at Pepperdine University. The intervention is *selective*, as it is targeted to adults, either preparents or parents, who have a conservative Protestant religious affiliation.

Background and Theory of Change

The ABII is based on the intuitive observation that parents learn how to parent by drawing on their own experiences as children and by looking to others—including peers and institutions—for further guidance. Given that most of these interpersonal and institutional forces promote and condone physical punishment, at least in the United States, physical punishment of children remains the norm.

These pro-physical-punishment norms are especially salient among conservative Protestants (i.e., evangelicals, fundamentalists, charismatic Christians). Empirical evidence consistently demonstrates that conservative Protestants, compared with U.S. adults more generally, are more pro–physical punishment in both their attitudes and behavior (Ellison, Bartkowski, & Segal, 1996; Ellison & Sherkat, 1993; Hoffmann, Ellison, & Bartkowski, 2017). The reasons for these differences, which are well documented and widely discussed (e.g., see Webb, 2011), can in part be traced to several Old Testament

http://dx.doi.org/10.1037/0000162-003
Ending the Physical Punishment of Children: A Guide for Clinicians and Practitioners,
E. T. Gershoff and S. J. Lee (Editors)

scriptures, primarily from the book of Proverbs (13:24, 22:15, 23:13–14, 20:30). Many conservative Protestants interpret these passages as an endorsement of physical punishment. Another contributing factor is that many conservative Protestants believe that children are, by nature, disobedient and that physical punishment is a necessary tool in "breaking the will" of the rebellious child (Dobson, 2017).

Recent research suggests that the attitudinal gap between conservative Protestants and U.S. adults in general has remained fairly stable over time, perhaps even becoming more pronounced (Hoffmann et al., 2017). However, there is evidence that younger and more educated conservative Protestants are amenable to change (Hoffmann et al., 2017). In addition, although it is well-established that conservative Protestant parents are likely to reject critiques of physical punishment offered by secular parenting experts (Holden, Miller, & Harris, 1999), it is reasonable to speculate that these same critiques offered from within the conservative Protestant community might be more effective (Perrin, Miller-Perrin, & Song, 2017).

Main Goal of the Intervention

The main goal of the ABII is to provide an alternative way of interpreting the Bible as it relates to the physical punishment of children. The ABII, although acknowledging that the Bible emphasizes the importance of discipline, argues that discipline does not have to take a physical form. Thus, the ultimate goal of the intervention is to decrease positive attitudes and intentions toward spanking and ultimately reduce the use of spanking as a disciplinary technique.

Brief Description of the Intervention

Administration of the ABII is conducted in person and takes approximately 30 minutes. The participants (1) read the ABII script, (2) listen to a verbal summary of the script presented by the researchers, and (3) ask clarifying questions of the script content (but are not allowed to engage in discussion or debate on the issue of spanking). The ABII can be delivered one-on-one or in a group setting with teachers, clinicians, community practitioners, or clergy serving as instructors. The only required material is a copy of the ABII script, originally available in Perrin et al. (2017) and reprinted here with permission in Appendix 2.1.

Content Relevant to Spanking or Physical Punishment

The ABII script (see Appendix 2.1) articulates the argument that the relevant biblical passages, and in particular, the passages in Proverbs, must be read with an understanding of the cultural context in which they were written.

Two specific contextual observations are relevant. First, it is important to understand the low status of children in the ancient world. As de Mause (1974) reminded us, "childhood," as we understand it in the modern world, was yet to be discovered in the ancient world. Rather than being nurtured and protected as they are today, children in the ancient world were often devalued, abused, and sometimes abandoned or killed (infanticide, particularly for girl infants, was not uncommon). Second, it is important to understand that the ancient world understood violence as the only way to discipline and that violence was often brutal and severe. Given the lowly status of children in the ancient world and the fact that relevant Proverbs passages were written for a population who understood that "blows and wounds cleanse away evil" (Proverbs 20:30), it is not surprising that parents in the ancient world would have been advised to hit their children.

The ABII articulates the argument that if we interpret these passages in their cultural context and we fully understand the severity of the violence administered in the ancient world, these passages take on new meaning. The Proverbs passages are, according to New Testament scholar (and evangelical) William Webb (2011), actually "progressive" if we understand social context. The passages are meant to limit violence:

> In a world in which the weak and powerless, including women, children, ethnic minorities, and slaves, were sometimes violently mistreated, the various passages on violence and parenting in the Old Testament could be interpreted as encouraging a more humane and less violent treatment of others, including children. (Perrin et al., 2017, p. 8)

The ABII concludes by stating that child discipline is most certainly necessary. However, adults do not need to hit children to be effective disciplinarians:

> There is no question that children need discipline. But the Bible was written at a time when violence was understood as the only way to discipline. Today we know that there are other ways to discipline children, with many alternative methods scientifically supported as more effective than spanking. Considering the Bible's attempt to regulate and control physical violence during its time, it is likely that a modern day reading of the scriptures should not be interpreted as an endorsement of physical punishment. (Perrin et al., 2017, p. 9)

Implementation of the Intervention

The ABII has been implemented successfully with a total of 323 college students, adults, and parents. Perrin et al. (2017) and Miller-Perrin and Perrin (2017) implemented the ABII with two different samples of primarily White college students ages 18 to 25 years. The ABII has also been successfully implemented with a sample of nonparent Korean adults, ages 18 to 40 years, as well as a sample of Korean parents, ages 20 to 56 years (Perrin, Miller-Perrin, Bayston, & Song, 2018). The ABII was translated into Korean for this purpose and was administered in a conservative Christian church.

Evidence of Effectiveness From Outcome Evaluations

Perrin and colleagues (2017) examined the effectiveness of three intervention conditions in a sample of 121 college students (87% female, 34% male; M_{age} = 19) attending a private, Christian, liberal arts university. Participants were randomly assigned to one of three conditions: (a) a control condition group that received information on child development, (b) an intervention condition that focused on empirical evidence of the ineffectiveness and potential harm of spanking, or (c) an intervention that focused on the empirical evidence about spanking as well as the ABII, which provided alternative interpretations of biblical passages sometimes used to justify spanking. Four weeks prior to the control and intervention sessions, students completed a demographic form and the Attitudes Toward Spanking (ATS) Scale (Holden, Coleman, & Schmidt, 1995). Immediately following the control and intervention sessions, students completed the ATS Scale a second time. Repeated measures analysis of variance (ANOVA) yielded a significant interaction for ATS scores, indicating that ATS scores decreased over time in both of the intervention conditions but not in the control condition. Subsequent analyses indicated that ATS scores in both intervention conditions decreased compared with the control condition and that a greater decrease in favorable attitudes toward spanking was observed for the ABII plus empirical research condition compared with the empirical research condition.

Miller-Perrin and Perrin (2017) examined how interventions that include either empirical research evidence about spanking or the ABII, or both, affected attitudes and intentions about spanking while also examining the role of religious conservatism. A sample of 129 college students (70% female, 30% male; M_{age} = 19) attending a private, Christian university was randomly assigned to one of three intervention conditions. The first condition included an intervention that focused on empirical evidence of the ineffectiveness and potential harm of spanking. The second condition included the ABII only, and the third condition included a combination of both the empirical evidence about spanking and the ABII. Four weeks prior to the intervention sessions, students completed a demographic form, the Religious Fundamentalism Scale (Altemeyer & Hunsberger, 2004), and the ATS Scale (Holden et al., 1995). Following the intervention sessions, students completed the ATS Scale a second time. A two-way ANOVA yielded a significant main effect for the intervention condition and an interaction effect between the intervention condition and religious fundamentalism, indicating that positive spanking attitudes declined most significantly in the condition that combined empirical research and the ABII, with the greatest change in attitudes among those with high levels of religious fundamentalist beliefs. In addition, positive spanking attitudes declined most significantly for participants identifying with a conservative religious affiliation.

Perrin and colleagues (2018) examined an intervention to change attitudes toward spanking among a sample of 60 Korean adults attending a conservative Protestant church in West Covina, California. The sample consisted of

37 nonparent Korean adults, ages 18 to 37 years (M_{age} = 25.50, SD = 5.28) and 23 Korean parents, ages 37 to 52 years (M_{age} = 43.39, SD = 4.04). Participants completed the ATS Scale (Holden et al., 1995) 4 weeks before receiving an intervention, which focused on empirical research demonstrating the ineffectiveness and potential harm associated with spanking along with the ABII. Following the intervention, participants completed the ATS a second time. Results of repeated measures ANOVA indicated a significant main effect, suggesting that positive spanking attitudes declined over time equally for both parents and nonparents.

Limitations

Most of the research on the ABII was conducted with homogeneous samples of primarily White, conservative Christians rather than samples that included diversity in terms of race, ethnicity, socioeconomic status, education, and geographic location. In addition, the research on the ABII measured short-term attitude change rather than actual behavior and the durability and long-term stability of change. Finally, the ABII is limited to addressing interpretations of Old Testament scripture and could be expanded to include relevant scriptures in the New Testament.

SUGGESTED FUTURE USE OF THE INTERVENTION

How Clinicians Can Use the Intervention

Clinicians can use the ABII with individual parents or couples or in groups of parents to change attitudes and intentions about spanking. The ABII is likely most effective when combined with a summary of the empirical research evidence on spanking.

How Community Practitioners Can Use the Intervention

The ABII can be used by community practitioners in the same way as do clinicians—with individual parents or couples or in groups of parents to change attitudes and intentions about spanking. In addition, community practitioners might use the ABII to reach conservative Christian communities more broadly by targeting religious leaders because parents often seek advice about child discipline from religious leaders (Taylor, Moeller, Hamvas, & Rice, 2013). Attitude change interventions directed at these leaders could effect change not only in leaders' attitudes but also through their potential influence on the attitudes of their congregants.

How Policymakers Can Use the Intervention

One overlooked factor that contributes to cultural acceptance of spanking is the religious convictions of parents. Christians generally, and conservative

Protestants in particular, are significantly more likely than other parents to support and practice physical punishment (Vieth, 2014). However, the majority of psychologists do not believe that spanking is an appropriate or effective part of parenting, even if religious (or cultural) beliefs condone its use (Miller-Perrin & Rush, 2018). Therefore, it is important for policymakers to acknowledge, and be sensitive to, the important role of religious beliefs that create and maintain positive attitudes toward physical punishment of children. It is equally important that policymakers are aware of the empirical research evidence on the ineffectiveness of spanking and the potential effectiveness of interventions, such as the ABII, that are sensitive and respectful toward parents' religious views and values so that they can advocate for change.

INFORMATION ON OBTAINING THE INTERVENTION

The scripts are available in Perrin et al. (2017) and Appendix 2.1. Additional information about the information is available from either of the developers, Cindy Miller-Perrin (cindy.miller-perrin@pepperdine.edu) or Robin Perrin (robin.perrin@pepperdine.edu).

APPENDIX 2.1. ABII SCRIPT

A CHRISTIAN PERSPECTIVE ON DISCIPLINE

You should know something up front. As will quickly become obvious, we clearly have an opinion about spanking. We think children should never be spanked. Our opinion is based on a number of factors including our academic training, our reading of the research findings on spanking, our experience as parents, and our interpretation of Biblical teachings as Christians. Our opinion is not necessarily common in Christian settings, but Christians are increasingly beginning to believe that spanking may not be the best disciplinary alternative. Regardless of your own opinion, we ask that you keep an open mind about what we have to say today. After our discussions, we will ask you to fill out an anonymous questionnaire on your attitudes toward child discipline. Don't tell us what you think we want to hear. Tell us, at this stage of your life, what you think about child discipline and what you plan to do when/if you become a parent.

Note. From "Changing Attitudes About Spanking Using Alternative Biblical Interpretations," by R. Perrin, C. Miller-Perrin, and J. Song, 2017, *International Journal of Behavioral Development, 41*, pp. 520–522.

WHAT THE BIBLE SAYS: SPARE THE ROD, SPOIL THE CHILD

Does the Bible endorse spanking? When we read the following passages, which are probably the four most commonly cited verses that relate to spanking, we are tempted to answer yes:

> He who spares the rod hates his son, but he who loves him is careful to discipline him (Proverbs 13:24).
>
> Folly is bound up in the heart of a child, but the rod of discipline will drive it far away (Proverbs 22:15).
>
> Do not withhold discipline from a child; if you punish them with the rod, they will not die. Punish them with the rod and save them from death (Proverbs 23:13–14).
>
> Blows and wounds cleanse away evil, and beatings purge the inmost being (Proverbs 20:30).

CULTURAL CONTEXT

We would argue, however, that we must read these passages with an understanding of the cultural context in which they were written. With our contemporary understanding of the value of children, it is difficult to fathom the degree to which children were devalued and often abused in the ancient world. For example, Hammurabi's Code, an ancient Babylonian code of laws that dates to approximately 800 BCE, details a violent "eye for an eye" world in which fathers were instructed to cut off the tongue or hand of a disrespecting son. In ancient Rome, unwanted children (mostly girls) could be left to die with no legal or social penalties, and fathers were permitted to sell their sons into slavery to settle debts.

Given that the relevant Old Testament passages were written to a people who understood "blows and wounds" to "cleanse evil away" (Proverbs 20:30), it should not surprise us that in the ancient world parents would be advised to use the "rod of discipline." Some Christian scholars take this cultural explanation a step further, arguing that the overall message about violence in the Old Testament is actually meant to place limits on violence. Again, we must acknowledge context. In a world in which the weak and powerless, including women, children, ethnic minorities, and slaves, were sometimes violently mistreated, the various passages on violence and parenting in the Old Testament could be interpreted as encouraging a more humane and less violent treatment of others, including children. That is, the passages actually place limits on parental discipline.

Slavery serves as a comparative example. The Bible does not condemn slavery. In fact, many of the Old Testament passages on slavery are beyond troubling. For example, according to Exodus 21:20–21,

> Anyone who beats their male or female slave with a rod must be punished if the slave dies as a direct result, but they are not to be punished if the slave recovers after a day or two, since the slave is their property.

This is indeed a difficult passage for Christians to justify. However, in a world where slavery was unquestioned, and brutal and sometimes deadly methods of social control were often employed by slave owners, this passage, like the passages on childhood discipline, become regulatory—an attempt to move the people of Israel away from "the surrounding cultural context and toward something better."

OUR SOLUTION

According to Chip Ingram from the Christian organization Focus on the Family (n.d.), "Regardless of the method, the Bible's word on discipline clearly demands that parents be responsible and diligent in spanking. . . . Obviously, the biblical approach is balanced, reasonable, and controlled." We, and many other Christians, would disagree that the biblical approach is balanced, reasonable, and controlled. In fact, many of the relevant biblical verses on physical punishment of children are brutal and violent, and by today's standards, abusive! Indeed, if we were going to use the Bible as a "recipe" for how to discipline our children, we would "cleanse evil away" with multiple injurious lashes to the back with a stick.

Most Christians have, in fact, abandoned many of the most violent Biblical directives endorsing violence. Focus on the Family, for example, encourages parents to adopt a loving and nonabusive "two smacks max" approach to spanking. While we applaud this recommendation as a move in the right direction, it is important to recognize that this simply is not a guideline found in the Bible. We would argue that such interpretations do not go far enough and that children should never be spanked.

There is no question that children need discipline. But the Bible was written at a time when violence was understood as the only way to discipline. Today we know that there are other ways to discipline children, with many alternative methods scientifically supported as more effective than spanking. Considering the Bible's attempt to regulate and control physical violence during its time, it is likely that a modern day reading of the scriptures should not be interpreted as an endorsement of physical punishment.

REFERENCES

Altemeyer, B., & Hunsberger, B. (2004). Research: A revised religious fundamentalism scale: The short and sweet of it. *The International Journal for the Psychology of Religion, 14*, 47–54. http://dx.doi.org/10.1207/s15327582ijpr1401_4

de Mause, L. E. (1974). *The history of childhood*. New York, NY: Psychohistory Press.

Dobson, J. C. (2017). *The new strong-willed child*. Carol Stream, IL: Tyndale House Publishers.

Ellison, C. G., Bartkowski, J. P., & Segal, M. L. (1996). Conservative Protestantism and the parental use of corporal punishment. *Social Forces, 74*, 1003–1028. http://dx.doi.org/10.1093/sf/74.3.1003

Ellison, C. G., & Sherkat, D. E. (1993). Conservative Protestantism and support for corporal punishment. *American Sociological Review, 58,* 131–144. http://dx.doi.org/10.2307/2096222

Hoffmann, J. P., Ellison, C. G., & Bartkowski, J. P. (2017). Conservative Protestantism and attitudes toward corporal punishment, 1986–2014. *Social Science Research, 63,* 81–94. http://dx.doi.org/10.1016/j.ssresearch.2016.09.010

Holden, G. W., Coleman, S. M., & Schmidt, K. L. (1995). Why 3-year-old children get spanked: Parent and child determinants as reported by college-educated mothers. *Merrill-Palmer Quarterly, 41,* 431–452.

Holden, G. W., Miller, P. C., & Harris, S. D. (1999). The instrumental side of corporal punishment: Parents' reported practices and outcome expectancies. *Journal of Marriage and the Family, 61,* 908–919. http://dx.doi.org/10.2307/354012

Ingram, C. (n.d.). *The biblical approach to spanking.* Retrieved from http://www.raisinggodlychildren.org/2012/10/the-biblical-approach-to-spanking.html

Miller-Perrin, C., & Perrin, R. (2017). Changing attitudes about spanking among conservative Christians using interventions that focus on empirical research evidence and progressive biblical interpretations. *Child Abuse & Neglect: The International Journal, 71,* 69–79. http://dx.doi.org/10.1016/j.chiabu.2017.03.015

Miller-Perrin, C., & Rush, R. (2018). Attitudes, knowledge, practices, and ethical beliefs of psychologists related to spanking: A survey of American Psychological Association division members. *Psychology, Public Policy, and Law, 24,* 405–417. http://dx.doi.org/10.1037/law0000184

Perrin, R., Miller-Perrin, C., Bayston, L., & Song, J. (2018, June). *Changing attitudes about spanking using alternative biblical interpretations among adult Korean conservative Protestants.* Paper presented at the 25th Annual APSAC Colloquium, New Orleans, LA.

Perrin, R., Miller-Perrin, C., & Song, J. (2017). Changing attitudes about spanking using alternative biblical interpretations. *International Journal of Behavioral Development, 41,* 514–522. http://dx.doi.org/10.1177/0165025416673295

Taylor, C. A., Moeller, W., Hamvas, L., & Rice, J. C. (2013). Parents' professional sources of advice regarding child discipline and their use of corporal punishment. *Clinical Pediatrics, 52,* 147–155. http://dx.doi.org/10.1177/0009922812465944

Vieth, V. I. (2014). From sticks to flowers: Guidelines for child protection professionals working with parents using scripture to justify corporal punishment. *William Mitchell Law Review, 40,* 907–942.

Webb, W. J. (2011). *Corporal punishment in the Bible: A redemptive-movement hermeneutic for troubling texts.* Downers Grove, IL: Intervarsity Press.

3

Baby Books

Stephanie M. Reich and Guadalupe Díaz

THE INTERVENTION

The Baby Books intervention was developed by Stephanie Reich, PhD, of the University of California, Irvine, and colleagues at Vanderbilt University. One randomized controlled trial of the intervention has been conducted (Baby Books 1, or BB1); a replication study, Baby Books 2 (BB2), is currently under way. This intervention is *selective* in that it targets first-time English- and Spanish-speaking mothers and fathers from low-income backgrounds.

Background and Theory of Change

Ample research has demonstrated that what parents know about child development influences how they interact with their children, the types of environments that they provide for them, and how their children develop (e.g., Huang, O'Brien Caughy, Genevro, & Miller, 2005; Jahromi, Guimond, Umaña-Taylor, Updegraff, & Toomey, 2014; Morawska, Winter, & Sanders, 2009; Scarzello, Arace, & Prino, 2016). Parents with accurate knowledge of typical child development tend to feel less stressed and more efficacious in parenting (Hess, Teti, & Hussey-Gardner, 2004; Huebner, 2002; Parush &

The development and evaluation of Baby Books 1 and Baby Books 2 has been supported by grants from the Eunice Kennedy Shriver National Institute of Child Health and Human Development (R01HD 447749 and R01HD078547).

http://dx.doi.org/10.1037/0000162-004
Ending the Physical Punishment of Children: A Guide for Clinicians and Practitioners,
E. T. Gershoff and S. J. Lee (Editors)

Hahn-Markowitz, 1997), provide more stimulating home environments (Benasich & Brooks-Gunn, 1996; Huang et al., 2005), and have children with improved cognitive, emotional, social and physical development (Albarran & Reich, 2013; Fewell & Wheeden, 1998).

In contrast, parents with inappropriate expectations of typical child development often overestimate the rate of development of their children, which contributes to impatience with and intolerance of their children's behavior (de Lissovay, 1973; Morawska et al., 2009), harsh discipline (Scarzello et al., 2016), and an increased risk for child maltreatment (Azar, Robinson, Hekimian, & Twentyman, 1984; McMillin et al., 2016; Peterson, Gable, Doyle, & Ewigman, 1997). Further, impatience and intolerance affect infant attachment (Schmidt & Eldridge, 1986; Ward, Kessler, & Altman, 1993), with harsh, inconsistent, and disengaged parenting behavior being highly correlated with poor attachment and future child psychopathology (e.g., Coyl, Roggman, & Newland, 2002; Erickson, Sroufe, & Egeland, 1985; Greenberg, Speltz, & DeKlyen, 1993).

In the United States, parent education about typical child development and optimal parenting practices is often provided by pediatric health care providers in the form of pediatric anticipatory guidance during typical well-child visits (American Academy of Pediatrics, Committee on Psychosocial Aspects of Child and Family Health, 1998; Hagan, Shaw, & Duncan, 2008; McMillin et al., 2016). However, mounting research indicates that little time during these visits is dedicated to parent education (Reisinger & Bires, 1980; Schuster, Duan, Regalado, & Klein, 2000), and when providers do discuss educational content, parents remember little of the content afterwards (Barkin et al., 2005; Morrongiello, Hillier, & Bass, 1995).

The Baby Books Project was based on the premise that parental education is important for parents of young children, but the traditional methods for parental education are inadequate. Thus, we decided to embed educational information into baby books, that is, books intended for parents to read to young children. Because books for young children are written in simple language, have pictures to supplement content, and are typically read more than once, we reasoned that books would be an ideal intervention platform.

Further, book sharing provides opportunities for parent–child interaction. Because parents know more about child development and parenting, they should engage in more developmentally appropriate practices during these interactions. In addition, children should demonstrate the developmental skills that the books are teaching during these interactions, reinforcing parents' knowledge gain and further improving both the quality and quantity of the parent–child interactions. Importantly, the books provide educational information about a range of developmental processes and parenting strategies, including nonphysical methods for disciplining children, the developmental underpinnings for why spanking is not effective, and why nonphysical corrections and positive responses for optimal behavior would be more appropriate.

Main Goals of the Intervention

The primary goals of the Baby Books Project were to (a) increase parental knowledge of typical child development and parenting practices recommended by developmental scientists and healthcare providers (Hagan et al., 2008); (b) change parental beliefs to be supportive of reading, emphasize nonphysical discipline strategies, responsive parenting, and stimulating interactions, and improve parenting practices (e.g., injury prevention, more language exposure); (c) increase the quality of parent–child interactions; and (d) promote parental and child health and well-being (e.g., reduced stress, improved mood, increased language skills, reduced preventable injuries). Our initial study, BB1, targeted these outcomes with just mothers and their babies from pregnancy through 18 months of age, and our second study (currently collecting data), BB2, targets these outcomes for English- and Spanish-speaking mothers, fathers, and children with an additional aim of improving the mother–father coparenting relationship as a way to promote positive and consistent discipline among both parents.

Brief Description of the Intervention

The primary mode of delivery is at the individual level. The Baby Books intervention relies on educational baby books provided to first-time parents at the same intervals as well-baby checkups as recommended by the American Academy of Pediatrics. The first set of baby books was developed by Dr. Reich and colleagues at Vanderbilt University. The second set of baby books was developed by Dr. Reich in partnership with Natasha Cabrera at the University of Maryland. For BB1, women were enrolled in their third trimester of pregnancy and given books during pregnancy and when their baby was 2, 4, 6, 9, and 12 months of age, for a total of six books. For BB2, books were provided to both mothers and fathers when babies were 9, 12, 15, 18, and 24 months, for a total of five books. Both BB1 and BB2 included data collection at each book distribution point, with an additional follow-up wave 6 months after the last book was delivered. For BB1, families were followed until the child was 18 months old. Families in the BB2 study are being followed until the children are 30 months old.

In the Baby Books intervention, parents both receive the intervention and deliver the intervention. That is, parents read the baby book that was created by the research team to the child, thus serving as recipients and deliverers of the intervention content. Because the intervention is delivered via books, no training is needed. The intervention is designed to be implemented in parents' homes.

Content Relevant to Spanking or Physical Punishment

This selective intervention targeted low-income families with only one child, in hopes of improving parenting knowledge, beliefs, and practices prior to them already being established. One specific aim of BB1 was to change beliefs about the use of spanking and physical forms of punishment. BB2 additionally seeks to change these beliefs and reduce physical punishment practices.

Content of the books explicitly addresses developmental reasons for why children might engage in behaviors that parents may view as misbehaving and why hitting will not correct that behavior. Books also describe how to ignore tantrums and emphasize the benefit of praise, redirection, and distraction. Figures 3.1 and 3.2 provide example text and illustrations that provide messages promoting positive and nonphysical discipline and coparenting strategies around discipline.

Implementation of the Intervention

The initial Baby Books Project used a three-group randomized design to test the impact of educational books in comparison with noneducational books (same images but noneducational text) or no books at all. For this evaluation, 198 primiparous women were recruited from clinics and randomly assigned to one of the three conditions during pregnancy. Because some mothers left the study as a result of miscarriage, infant death, moving, or disinterest, 168 women completed the first data-collection episode after random assignment and 145 were retained until their child was 18 months of age. These women lived in the southern United States, were all low-income, and were predominately African American (63%). According to the gestational age at recruitment, none of the babies were premature. Eighty percent of their pregnancies were unplanned. All books were delivered in person during home-based data collection visits.

BB2 replicates and expands BB1 by including mothers and fathers, targeting coparenting, providing books in English and in Spanish, and following children until 30 months of age. For this newer study, books were written specifically for mothers or fathers, and each family is assigned to one of four groups: books for fathers, books for mothers, books for both fathers and mothers, or commercial, noneducational books. This four-group randomized design allows for comparison of the similar or different effects of maternal education and paternal education and the potential additive or multiplicative effects of both maternal and paternal parenting education. This study of 240 families (480 parents) is currently under way. To date, two thirds of the families from two sites (Washington, DC, and Orange County, CA) have been enrolled. These families are ethnically and racially diverse, but predominately (71%) Latino. Family incomes are all less than $70,000 per year with a mean income of about $37,000 per year. Three of the books are delivered in person during home-based data collection, and two are sent by mail with corresponding phone interviews.

The Baby Books intervention has been used with families from the prenatal stage through the children's 30th month and with families from African American, White, and Hispanic/Latino cultural backgrounds, as well as with small numbers of Asian American and Native American families. The program is available in English and Spanish and has been tested in California, Tennessee, and the Washington, DC, area.

FIGURE 3.1. Sample Pages From the Baby Books Project

(a)

Papá fija límites y la cuida,
si su bebé se porta como debe,
la felicita, y con besos la premia,
asi aprende las reglas que puede.

(b)

FIGURE 3.1. Sample Pages From the Baby Books Project (*Continued*)

Praising good behavior and good choices too,
ignoring screams and tantrums until you are through.
You learn what to do by watching me.
So I need to think about what you see.

Felicito tus buena conducta y decisiones,
ignoro tus berrinches en todas situaciones.
Tú aprendes viendo lo que hago,
por eso darte buen ejemplo es mi trabajo.

(c)

Examples of nonphysical discipline content from (a) the 9-month book, (b) the 12-month book, and (c) the 18-month book. Panel A is from *Daddy's Growing Baby (El bebé del papa está creciendo)* (pp. 12–13), by K. Worley, S. Reich, and N. Cabrera. Spanish version by W. Ochoa, N. Alfaro, L. Peña, D. Aldoney, and G. Espino. Copyright 2016 by the Regents of the University of California. Panel B is from *Mommy, I'm 1! Look at All the Things I Can Do! (¡Mamá, tengo año 1! ¡Mira todo lo que puedo hacer!)* (p. 9), by K. Worley, S. Reich, N. Cabrera, and C. Kuhns. Spanish version by W. Ochoa, N. Alfaro, D. Aldoney, G. Espino, and N. Cabrera. Copyright 2016 by the Regents of the University of California. Panel C is from *All Kinds of Dads, Moms and Babies (Todo tipo de papás, mamas y bebés)* (p. 11), by S. Reich, R. Black, and N. Cabrera. Spanish version by W. Ochoa, D. Aldoney, N. Alfaro, N. Cabrera, and G. Espino. Copyright 2016 by the Regents of the University of California. Reprinted with permission.

FIGURE 3.2. Sample Pages From the Baby Books Project

(a)

(b)

Examples of coparenting advice on inside covers of (a) the 18-month book and (b) the 24-month book. Panel A is from *All Kinds of Dads, Moms and Babies (Todo tipo de papás, mamas y bebés)* (p. 17), by S. Reich, R. Black, and N. Cabrera. Spanish version by W. Ochoa, D. Aldoney, N. Alfaro, N. Cabrera, and G. Espino. Copyright 2016 by the Regents of the University of California. Panel B is from *Daddy, I'm 2! Look at All the Things I Can Do! (¡Papá, tengo 2 años! ¡Mira todo lo que puedo hacer!)* (p. 17), by S. Reich and N. Cabrera. Spanish version by W. Ochoa, N. Alfaro, N. Cabrera, and G. Espino. Copyright 2016 by the Regents of the University of California. Reprinted with permission.

EVIDENCE OF FEASIBILITY FROM PROCESS EVALUATIONS

Evidence That Training of Program Staff Was Successful

Because the intervention is delivered via books, no staff training is needed. However, BB1 confounds researcher presence with book delivered. That is why BB2 tests whether the impacts are equivalent when books are mailed or when books are delivered in person. This will shed light on the potential effectiveness of this type of intervention when scaled to other delivery systems (e.g., mail, book giveaway programs at clinics or preschools).

Evidence That Staff Had Buy-In and Like the Program

Mothers in BB1 reported being aware that the books were meant for them, rather than just their babies, but reported enjoying the books. Videotaped reading interactions with the books indicated that the mothers were familiar with the stories, demonstrating fidelity of implementation.

Evidence That Families Enjoy or Appreciate the Program

Data to address this question are being collected as part of the research study but are not currently available for analysis. As part of data collection for BB2, during each wave of data collection mothers and father report on aspects of the books that they like or dislike and number of times they had read the book in an average week, which allows a formal assessment of enjoyment and implementation fidelity.

Evidence of Effectiveness From Outcome Evaluations

BB1 was effective in increasing maternal knowledge of typical child development and recommended parenting practices (Reich, Bickman, Saville, & Alvarez, 2010), changing parenting beliefs (e.g., Auger, Reich, & Penner, 2014; Reich, Penner, Duncan, & Auger, 2012) and practices in the home (e.g., Reich, Penner, & Duncan, 2011), and improving maternal and child outcomes (e.g., Albarran & Reich, 2013; Khalessi & Reich, 2013; McManus, Khalessi, Lin, Ashraf, & Reich, 2017).

In addition to having more accurate knowledge of developmental timing and recommended parenting practices based on knowledge assessments at all waves of data collection (Reich et al., 2010), women in the educational book group also reduced their support for spanking and likelihood to report inappropriate expectations for their children (Reich et al., 2012). Using the five subscales of the Adult–Adolescent Parenting Inventory (AAPI; Bavolek & Keene, 2001) at the 2-, 6-, 12-, and 18-month home visits, we assessed mothers' inappropriate expectations of children, support of physical punishment, lack of empathy, reversal of parent–child role responsibilities, and oppression of children's power and independence. From the content of the book, we anticipated between-group differences on support of spanking and inappropriate expectations.

Across all waves, mothers who received educational books had higher AAPI scores, which indicated more developmentally appropriate and positive attitudes toward parenting. In contrast to both comparison conditions (noneducational-book and no-book groups), the intervention books statistically reduced mothers' endorsement of inappropriate expectations of children, support of physical punishment, parental lack of empathy, and reversal of parent–child role responsibilities. The impact of reducing support of physical punishment was strongest, with a 0.67 standard deviation effect size between the educational book and noneducational book and a 0.25 standard deviation effect size difference between the educational book and no-book groups. These effects were greater for African American mothers (effect sizes = 0.75 and 0.57) and those with low levels of educational attainment (high school diploma, general education diploma, or less: effect sizes = 0.78 and 0.49).

BB2 will additionally assess changes in parental knowledge and attitudes around discipline and spanking as well as measure self-reported discipline beliefs and practices over time and observational behavioral control strategies during playtime and cleanup tasks.

Cost–Benefit Analyses

Cost analyses have been conducted only for the impact on preventing injuries such as cuts, fall/dropping, and burns. This analysis included a sample of 167 mothers and their children participating in BB1 and involved retrospective medical chart audits of doctor office and emergency room visits and hospitalizations. Results comparing costs between groups found that mothers who received the educational books had children with fewer preventable injuries in the first 18 months of a child's life when compared with mothers who received a noneducational book or no books. Such a reduction in injuries corresponds to a predicted cost saving of $128,982 over the first 18 months (Reich, Andrade, & Tamman, 2019). These costs were based on Miller, Romano, and Spicer's (2000) cost estimates, calculated using inflation-adjusted data from their 1996 study of 22.2 million U.S. children. However, no cost–benefit analyses for changing parental attitudes about the use of spanking or physical discipline were conducted.

Limitations

Although the educational baby books hold promise, they have been used only with first-time parents, with the expectation that parenting practices are less established and more amenable to change. Their success with more experienced parents or other types of caregivers has not been tested. Further, the books have demonstrated effectiveness with reducing mothers' support of physical punishment but not their practices. The BB2 intervention will test their effectiveness in changing beliefs and practices for mothers and father of young children.

SUGGESTED FUTURE USE OF THE PROGRAM

How Clinicians Can Use the Intervention

These educational baby books could easily be added to clinical practice. For instance, they could be added to Reach Out & Read programs in pediatric clinics, delivered during nursing home visitations, or offered during Women, Infants and Children clinic visits. In addition, during well-baby visits, health care providers could use the books as a strategy to reinforce the information shared about pediatric anticipatory guidance.

How Community Practitioners Can Use the Intervention

The delivery of educational books does not need to be tied to clinical practice. The books could be made available through a variety of avenues such as public libraries, preschools, or even bookstores. These books could also be provided to parents who participate in parenting education classes as additional resources to take home and a way to emphasize information shared during parenting classes.

How Policymakers Can Use the Intervention

Policymakers could make funds available for the production and dissemination of these books to new families. Further, the Baby Books Project underscores the importance of parental education and, as such, policymakers should prioritize opportunities to provide education for parents in drafting and implementing policies.

INFORMATION ON HOW TO OBTAIN THE PROGRAM

Individuals can visit the program website at http://www.babybooks2.com or email the program developers, Stephanie Reich (smreich@uci.edu) or Natasha Cabrera (ncabrera@umd.edu), for more information on the project. As of this writing, the baby books used in the Baby Book Project are not yet publicly available.

REFERENCES

Albarran, A. S., & Reich, S. M. (2013). Using baby books to increase new mothers' self-efficacy and improve infant language development. *Infant and Child Development, 23*, 374–387. http://dx.doi.org/10.1002/icd.1832

American Academy of Pediatrics, Committee on Psychosocial Aspects of Child and Family Health. (1998). Guidance for effective discipline. *Pediatrics, 101*(4 Pt. 1), 723–728.

Auger, A., Reich, S. M., & Penner, E. K. (2014). The effect of baby books on mothers' reading beliefs and reading practices. *Journal of Applied Developmental Psychology, 35,* 337–346. http://dx.doi.org/10.1016/j.appdev.2014.05.007

Azar, S.-T., Robinson, D.-R., Hekimian, E., & Twentyman, C.-T. (1984). Unrealistic expectations and problem-solving ability in maltreating and comparison mothers. *Journal of Consulting and Clinical Psychology, 52,* 687–691. http://dx.doi.org/10.1037/0022-006X.52.4.687

Barkin, S. L., Scheindlin, B., Brown, C., Ip, E., Finch, S., & Wasserman, R. C. (2005). Anticipatory guidance topics: Are more better? *Ambulatory Pediatrics, 5,* 372–376. http://dx.doi.org/10.1367/A04-2131R1.1

Bavolek, S., & Keene, R. (2001). *Adult–adolescent parenting inventory AAPI-2: Administration and development handbook.* Park City, UT: Family Development Resources.

Benasich, A. A., & Brooks-Gunn, J. (1996). Maternal attitudes and knowledge of child-rearing: Associations with family and child outcomes. *Child Development, 67,* 1186–1205. http://dx.doi.org/10.2307/1131887

Coyl, D., Roggman, L., & Newland, L. (2002). Stress, maternal depression, and negative mother–infant interaction in relation to infant attachment. *Infant Mental Health Journal, 23*(1–2), 145–163. http://dx.doi.org/10.1002/imhj.10009

de Lissovay, V. (1973). Childcare by adolescent parents. *Children Today, 4,* 22–25.

Erickson, M.-F., Sroufe, L. A., & Egeland, B. (1985). The relationship between quality of attachment and behavior problems in preschool in a high-risk sample. *Monographs of the Society for Research in Child Development, 50*(1/2), 147–166. http://dx.doi.org/10.2307/3333831

Fewell, R. R., & Wheeden, C. A. (1998). A pilot study of intervention with adolescent mothers and their children: A preliminary examination of child outcomes. *Topics in Early Childhood Special Education, 18*(1), 18–25. http://dx.doi.org/10.1177/027112149801800105

Greenberg, M. T., Speltz, M. L., & DeKlyen, M. (1993). The role of attachment in the early development of disruptive behavior problems. *Development and Psychopathology, 5*(1–2), 191–213. http://dx.doi.org/10.1017/S095457940000434X

Hagan, J. F., Shaw, J. S., & Duncan, P. M. (2008). *Bright futures: Guidelines for health supervision on infants, children, and adolescents* (3rd ed.). Elk Grove Village, IL: American Academy of Pediatrics.

Hess, C., Teti, D., & Hussey-Gardner, B. (2004). Self-efficacy and parenting of high-risk infants: The moderating role of parent knowledge of infant development. *Journal of Applied Developmental Psychology, 25,* 423–437. http://dx.doi.org/10.1016/j.appdev.2004.06.002

Huang, K., O'Brien Caughy, M. O., Genevro, J. L., & Miller, T. L. (2005). Maternal knowledge of child development and quality of parenting among White, African-American and Hispanic mothers. *Applied Developmental Psychology, 26,* 149–170. http://dx.doi.org/10.1016/j.appdev.2004.12.001

Huebner, C. E. (2002). Evaluation of a clinic-based parent education program to reduce the risk of infant and toddler maltreatment. *Public Health Nursing, 19,* 377–389. http://dx.doi.org/10.1046/j.1525-1446.2002.19507.x

Jahromi, L. B., Guimond, A. B., Umaña-Taylor, A. J., Updegraff, K. A., & Toomey, R. B. (2014). Family context, Mexican-origin adolescent mothers' parenting knowledge, and children's subsequent developmental outcomes. *Child Development, 85,* 593–609. http://dx.doi.org/10.1111/cdev.12160

Khalessi, A., & Reich, S. M. (2013). A month of breastfeeding associated with greater adherence to pediatric nutrition guidelines. *Journal of Reproductive and Infant Psychology, 31,* 299–308. http://dx.doi.org/10.1080/02646838.2013.784898

McManus, M. A., Khalessi, A. A., Lin, J., Ashraf, J., & Reich, S. M. (2017). Positive feelings during pregnancy, early feeding practices, and infant health. *Pediatrics International, 59,* 593–599. http://dx.doi.org/10.1111/ped.13209

McMillin, S. E., Bultas, M. W., Zander, T., Wilmott, J., Underwood, S., Broom, M. A., & Zand, D. H. (2016). The role of maternal knowledge of child development in predicting risk for child maltreatment. *Clinical Pediatrics, 55,* 374–376. http://dx.doi.org/10.1177/0009922815586054

Miller, T. R., Romano, E. O., & Spicer, R. S. (2000). The cost of childhood unintentional injuries and the value of prevention. *The Future of Children, 10,* 137–163. http://dx.doi.org/10.2307/1602828

Morawska, A., Winter, L., & Sanders, M. R. (2009). Parenting knowledge and its role in the prediction of dysfunctional parenting and disruptive child behaviour. *Child: Care, Health and Development, 35,* 217–226. http://dx.doi.org/10.1111/j.1365-2214.2008.00929.x

Morrongiello, B. A., Hillier, L., & Bass, M. (1995). 'What I said' versus 'what you heard': A comparison of physicians' and parents' reporting of anticipatory guidance on child safety issues. *Injury Prevention, 1,* 223–227. http://dx.doi.org/10.1136/ip.1.4.223

Parush, S., & Hahn-Markowitz, J. (1997). The efficacy of an early prevention program facilitated by occupational therapists: A follow-up study. *The American Journal of Occupational Therapy, 51,* 247–251. http://dx.doi.org/10.5014/ajot.51.4.247

Peterson, L., Gable, S., Doyle, C., & Ewigman, B. (1997). Beyond parenting skills: Battling barriers and building bonds to prevent child abuse and neglect. *Cognitive and Behavioral Practice, 4*(1), 53–74. http://dx.doi.org/10.1016/S1077-7229(97)80012-0

Reich, S. M., Andrade, A. R., & Tamman, S. (2019). *Reducing injuries through educational baby books.* Manuscript in preparation.

Reich, S. M., Bickman, L., Saville, B. R., & Alvarez, J. (2010). The effectiveness of baby books for providing pediatric anticipatory guidance to new mothers. *Pediatrics, 125,* 997–1002. http://dx.doi.org/10.1542/peds.2009-2728

Reich, S. M., Penner, E. K., & Duncan, G. J. (2011). Using baby books to increase new mothers' safety practices. *Academic Pediatrics, 11*(1), 34–43. http://dx.doi.org/10.1016/j.acap.2010.12.006

Reich, S. M., Penner, E. K., Duncan, G. J., & Auger, A. (2012). Using baby books to change new mothers' attitudes about corporal punishment. *Child Abuse & Neglect: The International Journal, 36,* 108–117. http://dx.doi.org/10.1016/j.chiabu.2011.09.017

Reisinger, K. S., & Bires, J. A. (1980). Anticipatory guidance in pediatric practice. *Pediatrics, 66,* 889–892.

Scarzello, D., Arace, A., & Prino, L. E. (2016). Parental practices of Italian mothers and fathers during early infancy: The role of knowledge about parenting and child development. *Infant Behavior and Development, 44,* 133–143. http://dx.doi.org/10.1016/j.infbeh.2016.06.006

Schmidt, E., & Eldridge, A. (1986). The attachment relationship and child maltreatment. *Infant Mental Health Journal, 7,* 264–273.

Schuster, M. A., Duan, N., Regalado, M., & Klein, D. J. (2000). Anticipatory guidance: What information do parents receive? What information do they want? *Archives of Pediatrics & Adolescent Medicine, 154,* 1191–1198. http://dx.doi.org/10.1001/archpedi.154.12.1191

Ward, M.-J., Kessler, D. B., & Altman, S. C. (1993). Infant–mother attachment in children with failure to thrive. *Infant Mental Health Journal, 14,* 208–220. http://dx.doi.org/10.1002/1097-0355(199323)14:3<208::AID-IMHJ2280140306>3.0.CO;2-C

4

Motivational Interviewing

George W. Holden and Grant W. O. Holland

THE INTERVENTION

George Holden, PhD, and Grant Holland, PhD, from Southern Methodist University developed the Enhancing Motivation to Stop Spanking intervention. The intervention is *indicated* and/or *selective*, as it is targeted to parents, and may be especially useful for parents who are at risk of or who currently use physical punishment.

Background and Theory of Change

Attitudes toward physical punishment are one of the best predictors of whether and how often parents spank their children (e.g., Vittrup, Holden, & Buck, 2006). Consequently, targeting attitudes in favor of the use of physical punishment is a common strategy for those parenting interventions that attempt to reduce or eliminate parental harsh punishment. However, use of physical punishment can be a deeply entrenched practice that is difficult to change. Due to the intergenerational transmission of physical punishment, its widespread use in many communities, and multiple other influences on its use, many individuals have positive attitudes toward the use of physical punishment.

One clinical approach designed to address intransigent attitudes and behaviors is a technique called *motivational interviewing* (MI; Miller & Rollnick, 2002). Developed over the past few decades, MI has been widely applied to behaviors

http://dx.doi.org/10.1037/0000162-005
Ending the Physical Punishment of Children: A Guide for Clinicians and Practitioners,
E. T. Gershoff and S. J. Lee (Editors)

where resistance is expected and as a way of increasing individuals' desire to change. Part of MI's clinical appeal is that it has been found to be effective in producing change in as few as one to four sessions (Burke, Arkowitz, & Menchola, 2003).

Prior to the development of the present intervention, five studies had been published that showed attitudinal change indicating decreases in positive attitudes toward physical punishment (Griffin, Robinson, & Carpenter, 2000; Holden, Brown, Baldwin, & Croft Caderao, 2014; Reich, Penner, Duncan, & Auger, 2012; Robinson, Funk, Beth, & Bush, 2005; Scholer, Hamilton, Johnson, & Scott, 2010). However, the results from these studies indicated Cohen's *d*s ranged from 0.33 to 0.44 for change in individuals and 0.14 to 0.69 for the differences between the intervention and control groups. Although these findings were promising, effect sizes were only small to moderate.

The theory of planned behavior (Fishbein & Ajzen, 2011) offers a useful framework to guide efforts at changing attitudes and behavior. According to this theory, behavior is determined by attitudes regarding the utility of the behavior, beliefs about how others view the behavior (i.e., subjective norms), and views about the ease of engaging in the behavior. These three cognitions then determine the intention to use a behavior. Intentions, in turn, lead to action when there is the opportunity to engage in the behavior.

The Enhancing Motivation to Stop Spanking intervention addresses two of these three cognitions—attitudes and subjective norms—via psychoeducation. MI is particularly well-suited for changing parents' physical punishment attitudes and behaviors because the therapist does not dictate what the parent should do. Rather, the aim of MI is to get parents to create their own intention and motivation for changing their attitudes and behavior. Furthermore, parents are not told how they should discipline their children, an approach that is likely to elicit defensiveness. Instead, the MI approach consists of helping the parent to come to a recognition that there is a problem with the way that they are parenting and then to generate a solution.

Main Goal of the Intervention

The main goal of the Enhancing Motivation to Stop Spanking intervention is to change parental attitudes toward and intentions to use physical punishment through a customized psychoeducation dialogue. The intervention adapts an evidence-based approach, MI, to address parents' potential points of resistance to reducing their use of physical punishment.

Brief Description of the Intervention

The Enhancing Motivation to Stop Spanking intervention is a brief intervention consisting of one or more sessions, conducted by a clinician. The length of the session or sessions is flexible and can vary from about 20 minutes to an hour or longer. In the original study, the session averaged about 60 minutes and was delivered in a one-on-one format (clinician and parent). However, the intervention could also be conducted in a group. The authors recommend that the intervention be delivered by professionals, such as psychologists, counselors, social workers, pediatricians, and others in the helping or primary care professions, who have received some training in basic clinical interviewing skills and, preferably, additional training in the principles and techniques of MI. A private space to talk is needed. Some method of disseminating psychoeducation talking points and orienting the discussion (e.g., a handout) is preferable but not essential.

Content Relevant to Spanking or Physical Punishment

The intervention is designed to develop the parent's own motivation for change through a discussion of the effects of physical punishment. The intervention session consists of three phases: (1) engagement, (2) psychoeducation, and (3) evocation of new insights and behaviors. During the initial phase, the clinician engages the parent in an open-ended discussion to explore their values, childrearing goals, and disciplinary approach and practices. Without prompting, parents often discuss their use of physical punishment. Once this discussion has begun, the clinician requests the parent's permission to talk about physical punishment research. The parent is then shown a series of handouts that summarize the results of the Gershoff (2002) meta-analytic review.

The dialogue is tailored to each parent, with the clinician linking topics discussed earlier in the session and responding to the parent's questions and comments. Once the psychoeducation is completed, the clinician engages in MI "evoking" strategies. These include having the parent discuss their concerns regarding the information (e.g., "What concerns you the most?"), discussing how the research fits with the previously identified values and goals, and using other MI techniques (see Miller & Rollnick, 2002). The initial version of this intervention included only the psychoeducation component; the addition of an educational component on alternatives to physical punishment is a recommended direction for a next step in this area.

Implementation of the Intervention

The Enhancing Motivation to Stop Spanking intervention has been implemented successfully with a total of 43 parents. To date, the setting for delivery of the intervention has been limited to a psychology clinic on a university campus. The sample consisted of a racially and ethnically diverse group (African American [49%], Euro American [35%], and Hispanic [16%]) of English-speaking mothers living in a large metropolitan area in the southwest part of the United States. A total of 43 mothers participated. The mothers averaged 32 years old (range: 22 to 44 years old). The mothers included those who were married (49%), unmarried and not cohabiting (33%), divorced (12%), and cohabiting (6%). Their median family income was between $20,000 and $40,000. About half of the mothers had attended college. Their children ranged in age from 3 to 5 years old. The children did not have disabilities, and the mothers indicated no reports of child protective services involvement.

Evidence of Effectiveness From Outcome Evaluations

Evidence of this intervention's effectiveness is drawn from one randomized controlled trial with a waitlist control group (Holland & Holden, 2016). Mothers participated in one 60-minute intervention session with outcome measures assessed at three time points: baseline, immediately postintervention, and 1-month follow-up. The intervention had a significant effect on mothers' attitudes and intentions to use physical punishment, an effect that was replicated in the crossover group. Mothers reported significantly less favorable attitudes at postintervention and follow-up than at baseline. Mothers in the intervention group also showed greater reductions in their positive attitudes, compared with the control group. Similar results were found for intentions to spank. The effect sizes ranged from moderate to very large (ds = 0.67–2.72), and all were stronger than the previously published physical punishment intervention research, depending on the variable and analysis. Although the outcome evaluation did not include assessment of parents' responses to the program, informal comments by the participants indicated that the program was appreciated and, even in instances where parents were steadfast in their support for physical punishment, the tone of participants was respectful.

Limitations

The use of MI for changing attitudes and behavior is promising, but given its individualized delivery, is also a time-consuming and relatively expensive technique to administer. Consequently, it is not readily scalable. Options to address that limitation include using it in groups of parents or computerizing the approach. The primary limitation of the study is in the outcomes that were measured: Only attitudes and disciplinary behavioral intentions were collected after the intervention, not reports of behavior.

SUGGESTED FUTURE USE OF THE PROGRAM

How Clinicians Can Use the Intervention

To date, only one study (Holland & Holden, 2016) has used the MI technique in an effort to change attitudes toward physical punishment. However, one of the strengths of this intervention lies in its potential to be used and implemented in a range of settings. Though it was developed in a university and used by an individual trained to be a clinical psychologist, any professional trained in the principles of MI who is familiar with the physical punishment research could implement it.

This intervention may be thought of less as a stand-alone treatment than as a method of engagement that may be used when there is concern about physical punishment. It may be used as a component of, or complement to, programs or services provided to parents (e.g., parent education classes).

One of the strengths of this intervention is its potential to be used in many different settings and with diverse types of therapists. In fact, given that parents tend to have relatively low regard for university researchers when it comes to seeking advice about parenting practices (Taylor, Moeller, Hamvas, & Rice, 2013), stronger effect sizes may be found if the approach is used by medical professionals or religious leaders, the most trusted and influential sources of child-rearing information for parents (Taylor, Hamvas, Rice, Newman, & DeJong, 2011). With a modest amount of training, professionals can efficiently and effectively provide MI interventions. Though this intervention is already brief, it will be important to streamline this intervention even more to allow for its use in other settings where there are limits of time, space, and personnel.

How Community Practitioners Can Use the Intervention

Community practitioners can use the intervention in conjunction with therapists or other professionals who receive some training in MI. This intervention may also be appropriate for existing parent education programs in school or hospital settings or possibly through anticipatory guidance provided to parents by pediatricians, nurses, and other medical providers.

How Policymakers Can Use the Intervention

The MI approach could be a part of parent education programs for individuals at risk for, or with substantiated cases of, physical child abuse.

INFORMATION ON OBTAINING THE PROGRAM

There is no cost to obtain the program. No training is required. However, the individual who employs the approach should have a background as a clinical psychologist, a counselor, or a parent educator. For more information about how to obtain the intervention, contact George Holden (gholden@smu.edu).

REFERENCES

Burke, B. L., Arkowitz, H., & Menchola, M. (2003). The efficacy of motivational interviewing: A meta-analysis of controlled clinical trials. *Journal of Consulting and Clinical Psychology, 71*, 843–861. http://dx.doi.org/10.1037/0022-006X.71.5.843

Fishbein, M., & Ajzen, I. (2011). *Predicting and changing behavior: The reasoned action approach.* New York, NY: Taylor & Francis. http://dx.doi.org/10.4324/9780203838020

Gershoff, E. T. (2002). Corporal punishment by parents and associated child behaviors and experiences: A meta-analytic and theoretical review. *Psychological Bulletin, 128*, 539–579. http://dx.doi.org/10.1037/0033-2909.128.4.539

Griffin, M. M., Robinson, D. H., & Carpenter, H. (2000). Changing teacher education students' attitudes toward using corporal punishment in the classroom. *Research in the Schools, 7,* 27–30.

Holden, G. W., Brown, A. S., Baldwin, A. S., & Croft Caderao, K. (2014). Research findings can change attitudes about corporal punishment. *Child Abuse & Neglect: The International Journal, 38,* 902–908. http://dx.doi.org/10.1016/j.chiabu.2013.10.013

Holland, G. W. O., & Holden, G. W. (2016). Changing orientations to corporal punishment: A randomized, control trial of the efficacy of a motivational approach to psychoeducation. *Psychology of Violence, 6,* 233–242. http://dx.doi.org/10.1037/a0039606

Miller, W., & Rollnick, S. (2002). *Motivational interviewing: Preparing people for change* (2nd ed.). New York, NY: Guilford Press.

Reich, S. M., Penner, E. K., Duncan, G. J., & Auger, A. (2012). Using baby books to change new mothers' attitudes about corporal punishment. *Child Abuse & Neglect: The International Journal, 36,* 108–117. http://dx.doi.org/10.1016/j.chiabu.2011.09.017

Robinson, D. H., Funk, D. C., Beth, A., & Bush, A. M. (2005). Changing beliefs about corporal punishment: Increasing knowledge about ineffectiveness to build more consistent moral and informational beliefs. *Journal of Behavioral Education, 14,* 117–139. http://dx.doi.org/10.1007/s10864-005-2706-9

Scholer, S. J., Hamilton, E. C., Johnson, M. C., & Scott, T. A. (2010). A brief intervention may affect parents' attitudes toward using less physical punishment. *Family and Community Health, 33,* 106–116. http://dx.doi.org/10.1097/FCH.0b013e3181d592ef

Taylor, C. A., Hamvas, L., Rice, J., Newman, D. L., & DeJong, W. (2011). Perceived social norms, expectations, and attitudes toward corporal punishment among an urban community sample of parents. *Journal of Urban Health, 88,* 254–269. http://dx.doi.org/10.1007/s11524-011-9548-7

Taylor, C. A., Moeller, W., Hamvas, L., & Rice, J. C. (2013). Parents' professional sources of advice regarding child discipline and their use of corporal punishment. *Clinical Pediatrics, 52,* 147–155. http://dx.doi.org/10.1177/0009922812465944

Vittrup, B., Holden, G. W., & Buck, J. (2006). Attitudes predict the use of physical punishment: A prospective study of the emergence of disciplinary practices. *Pediatrics, 117,* 2055–2064. http://dx.doi.org/10.1542/peds.2005-2204

II

HOSPITAL- OR CLINIC-BASED INTERVENTIONS

5

Play Nicely

Seth Scholer

THE INTERVENTION

Play Nicely was developed by Seth Scholer, MD, at Vanderbilt University Medical Center. The intervention is *universal* and/or *selected*. To avoid stigmatizing parents, the intervention developer recommends implementing the program with all parents using a universal population-based approach. Another approach is to implement Play Nicely in a selected fashion, targeting parents who screen high on a parenting assessment tool.

Background and Theory of Change

Play Nicely is a video-based psychoeducational program designed to prevent child maltreatment by focusing on reducing unhealthy parenting practices (e.g., physical punishment) that constitute adverse childhood experiences (ACEs). ACEs can be categorized into two groups: household challenges (e.g., divorce, incarceration, mental illness, substance abuse, domestic violence) and child abuse and neglect. Some ACEs labeled as abuse and neglect are parenting-related. Examples of parenting-related ACEs include the use of physical punishment, threats, humiliation, yelling, and swearing. Exposure to these parenting behaviors led to the categorization of child abuse and neglect as an ACE. Research supports this, with studies showing that physical

http://dx.doi.org/10.1037/0000162-006
Ending the Physical Punishment of Children: A Guide for Clinicians and Practitioners,
E. T. Gershoff and S. J. Lee (Editors)

punishment and maltreatment are associated with poor health outcomes (Afifi et al., 2017).

Main Goals of the Intervention

The goals of the Play Nicely intervention are to provide an effective, efficient, and inexpensive method to educate parents about healthy discipline strategies and alternatives to physical punishment to avoid the incidence of ACEs. Features that differentiate Play Nicely from other parenting programs include its brevity, low cost, and ease of implementation.

Brief Description of the Intervention

The Play Nicely program educates parents about alternatives to physical punishment by asking the participant to consider the hypothetical situation of a young child hurting another. Participants are provided with a list of 20 options for how to respond (see Figure 5.1). Clicking on each option reveals feedback—"A great option," "A good option," or "There are better options"—along with 1 to 2 minutes of narrated feedback with explanatory bullet points. *Play Nicely: The Healthy Discipline Handbook* provides printed content that mirrors the narration from the multimedia program, providing tabbed pages labeled with each of the 20 options for learners to peruse (see Figures 5.2 and 5.3). Parents can learn how to respond to child aggression, one of the strongest risk factors for violence, and about healthy discipline options that can be used to address child aggression and other challenging child behaviors.

Viewing the Play Nicely multimedia program can take up to 50 minutes, depending on the sections viewed by the parent. Viewing one of the sections, "Recommendation 2"—the content that is most relevant to physical punishment—requires about 20 minutes, and each discipline option within Recommendation 2 takes approximately 1 minute to view. The Play Nicely handbook mirrors the content of the multimedia program, and the time needed to read the Play Nicely handbook content will vary depending upon reading level.

The Play Nicely program can be implemented with individuals or in a group setting. Because the person who introduces the program does not require any training, anyone can implement Play Nicely, including health care providers, educators, family members, and friends. Play Nicely can be introduced in 1 minute (see Figure 5.4); this is an important feature, especially for use in pediatric primary care where providers are often pressed for time.

The materials needed to implement the program vary depending upon the setting and the participants. With no materials, anyone can say to a parent, "I know about a great resource to fill your toolkit with lots of great options to discipline children when they have challenging behavior. The program is called Play Nicely and you can view it for free at playnicely.org."

FIGURE 5.1. Screenshot of Page Showing the 20 Options in the Play Nicely Multimedia Program

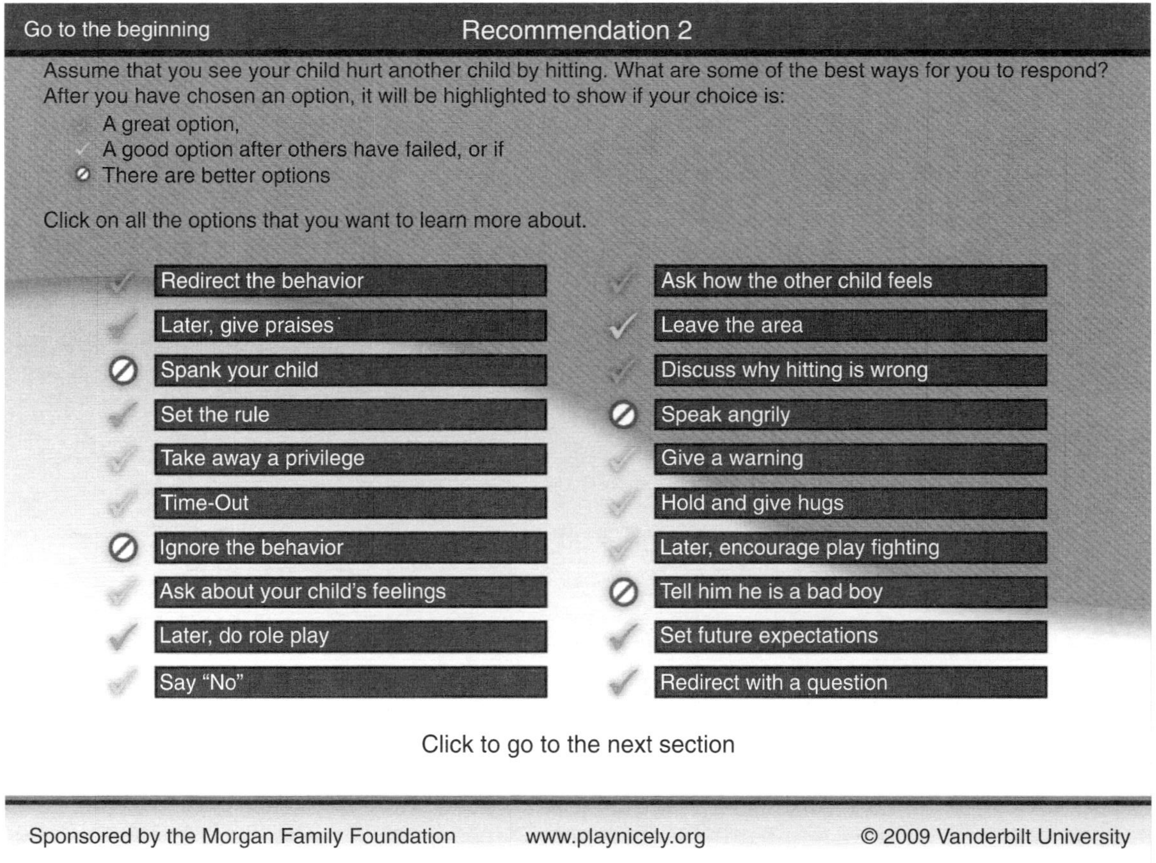

From *Play Nicely: The Healthy Discipline Program, Third Edition* [interactive multimedia program], by S. J. Scholer. Retrieved from http://www.playnicely.org. Copyright 2009 by Vanderbilt University. Reprinted with permission.

FIGURE 5.2. The "Spank Your Child" Page From the Handbook (Narrated in the Multimedia Program)

Play Nicely: The Healthy Discipline Handbook

Spank your child

X

There are better options

Spanking may seem to help in the short run, but it can actually make matters worse in the long run. Spanking may get a child's attention, but it does nothing to explain why the behavior is wrong. You are your child's role model. If you spank them, they will learn from you that physically hurting someone else is an acceptable way to deal with a challenging situation. It does not make sense to teach a child not to hit by hitting them. It is much better to use other ways such as redirecting to teach your child how not to hurt people. Because there are much better options to consider, spanking is not recommended as a form of discipline.

Some justify spanking by quoting the saying, "Spare the rod, you spoil the child." However, shepherds usually used a rod to guide sheep, not to hit them. Children should not be guided by hitting or spanking; rather they should be guided by setting the rule, redirecting, teaching why hurtful behavior is wrong, and getting them to think about the feelings of others. It is likely that if you spare the guidance, your child will develop behavior problems.

From *Play Nicely: The Healthy Discipline Handbook* (p. 9), by S. J. Scholer. Copyright 2015 by Vanderbilt University. Reprinted with permission.

FIGURE 5.3. The "Redirect Toward a Positive Behavior" Page From the Handbook (Narrated in the Multimedia Program)

Play Nicely: The Healthy Discipline Handbook

Redirect toward a positive behavior

✓

A great option

Redirecting toward a positive behavior is a great option. Redirecting means that you switch your child's hurtful behavior toward a useful behavior. Redirecting works really well for two reasons; it gives your child attention and it lets them know what they can do the next time, not just what they can't do. Redirecting should be used very often for children of all ages.

Examples:

For hitting/pushing/pulling hair, say "Use your hands to throw a ball, help me clean up the house, or build Legos."

For kicking, say "You can use your feet for walking."

For biting, say "Use your teeth to eat food."

For language that is hurtful, say "Let's think about better words to use the next time we are angry."

Redirecting is an important option because it helps children to learn that they have useful ways to use their bodies when they are frustrated or angry. Redirecting can help a child learn acceptable ways to respond to the many challenges they will meet throughout life.

FIGURE 5.4. How to Introduce the Play Nicely Intervention in 1 Minute

One Minute Clinic Intervention With the *Play Nicely* Handbook

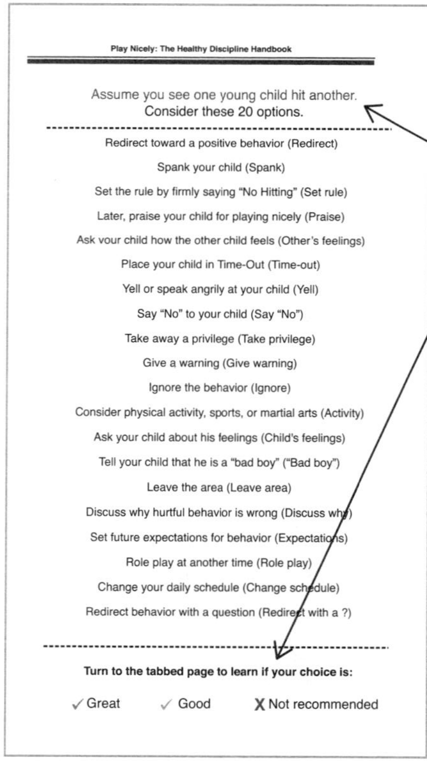

Play Nicely: The Healthy Discipline Handbook

Assume you see one young child hit another.
Consider these 20 options.

Redirect toward a positive behavior (Redirect)
Spank your child (Spank)
Set the rule by firmly saying "No Hitting" (Set rule)
Later, praise your child for playing nicely (Praise)
Ask your child how the other child feels (Other's feelings)
Place your child in Time-Out (Time-out)
Yell or speak angrily at your child (Yell)
Say "No" to your child (Say "No")
Take away a privilege (Take privilege)
Give a warning (Give warning)
Ignore the behavior (Ignore)
Consider physical activity, sports, or martial arts (Activity)
Ask your child about his feelings (Child's feelings)
Tell your child that he is a "bad boy" ("Bad boy")
Leave the area (Leave area)
Discuss why hurtful behavior is wrong (Discuss why)
Set future expectations for behavior (Expectations)
Role play at another time (Role play)
Change your daily schedule (Change schedule)
Redirect behavior with a question (Redirect with a ?)

Turn to the tabbed page to learn if your choice is:

✓ Great ✓ Good **X** Not recommended

Step 1: Turn to Page 7 in the Play Nicely Handbook.

"We want all parents to use healthy discipline strategies with their children. I would like to introduce you to the Play Nicely program.

"Assume you see one young child hit another. What are you going to do? Here is a list of 20 options."

"Some options are great, some are good after others have been tried, and some are not recommended. Turn the tabbed pages to learn why redirecting is a great option and why spanking is not recommended. The handbook fills your toolkit with lots of options so you can pull out the right strategy for the right circumstance."

[Advise parent about how to obtain the handbook (e.g. local resource center, library, clinic, through Vanderbilt, etc.)]

Step 2: Turn to the handbook's last page.

"Also, as another way to learn about discipline options, check out the free multimedia program on your computer, tablet, or smart phone by going to this website: www.playnicely.org."

"Show the program to everyone who takes care of your child. Your child will behave better if everyone is consistent with discipline."

"If you have ongoing concerns about your child's behavioral health, please make an appointment to come back and see me in 2-3 months."

From *Play Nicely: The Healthy Discipline Handbook* (p. 7), by S. J. Scholer.

Using a computer, tablet, or smartphone connected to the Internet, the person introducing the program can go to https://www.playnicely.org, click on "20 options" in the upper right corner, and show parents the screen with the 20 options (see Figure 5.1). Consider the following script to introduce the program:

> We would like all parents to learn healthy ways to discipline young children. Assume you see one young child hit another. What are you going to do? There is no one right answer, but some are better than others. Click on options that you want to learn more about. Each option takes 1 to 2 minutes to view. View as many as you like.

Printed material is also available for learners, especially those who prefer to read rather than view a multimedia program. The Play Nicely handbook is a tangible resource that can be shared with educators, trainees, and family members. Health care providers and other professionals can use the handbook to implement the Play Nicely program in 1 minute (see Figure 5.4).

Content Relevant to Spanking or Physical Punishment

The Play Nicely multimedia program contains multiple sections, and parents can select the content that they wish to view. For example, one section contains five recommendations; Recommendation 2 is the longest, requiring about 20 minutes to view. Recommendation 2 is especially relevant because it is an interactive part of the program that has been found to be related to physical punishment outcomes, even if parents view only 5 to 10 minutes of this section. In Recommendation 2, viewers see a list of 20 discipline options from which to choose for the hypothetical situation of one young child hitting another (see Figure 5.1). If they click on the spanking option, parents view bulleted text and hear narration that explains why spanking is not recommended; the content related to spanking is shared via an image of a page from the handbook (see Figure 5.2).

Play Nicely also provides parents with alternatives to physical punishment. Parents learn from the program that healthy discipline options to consider include redirecting, setting limits, setting future expectations, praising for good behavior, role-playing, changing your daily schedule, and explaining to the child why they should change their behavior. For example, one of the "great" discipline options is "redirect the behavior." The content related to redirecting is shared via an image of a page from the handbook (see Figure 5.3).

Implementation of the Intervention

Play Nicely has been implemented in pediatric clinics; medical schools; pediatric residency programs; Women, Infants and Children clinics; early education settings; and home-visiting programs. More than 1,000 parents of young children have viewed Play Nicely through research studies conducted in these settings (Burkhart, Knox, & Hunter, 2016; Burkhart, Knox, Hunter, Pennewitt, & Schrouder, 2018; Chavis et al., 2013; Hudnut-Beumler, Smith, &

Scholer, 2018; Scholer, Brokish, Mukherjee, & Gigante, 2008; Scholer, Hamilton, Johnson, & Scott, 2010; Scholer, Hudnut-Beumler, & Dietrich, 2010, 2012; Scholer, Hudnut-Beumler, Mukherjee, & Dietrich, 2015; Scholer, Mukherjee, Gibbs, Memon, & Jongeward, 2007; Scholer, Reich, Boshers, & Bickman, 2005, 2012; Scholer, Walkowski, & Bickman, 2008; Smith, Hudnut-Beumler, & Scholer, 2017). The total number of families who have viewed the program is unknown because the online multimedia program is free, an available CD-ROM can be viewed multiple times on one computer, and the handbook can be loaned.

At Vanderbilt University Medical Center, Play Nicely has been studied with low-income, English- and Spanish-speaking parents of children between the ages of 6 months and 10 years (Chavis et al., 2013; Hudnut-Beumler et al., 2018; Scholer, Hamilton, et al., 2010; Scholer, Hudnut-Beumler, & Dietrich, 2010, 2012; Scholer et al., 2007, 2015; Scholer, Walkowski, & Bickman, 2008; Smith et al., 2017). A study of the program has also been conducted with pediatric residents at the University of Toledo College of Medicine (Burkhart et al., 2018).

Evidence That Training of Program Staff Was Successful

Several studies have evaluated the impact of the program on health care trainees (Burkhart et al., 2016; Scholer, Brokish, et al., 2008; Scholer et al., 2005; Scholer, Reich, et al., 2012). Pediatric residents and students who viewed the program were more knowledgeable about how to educate parents about discipline, felt more confident in their skills, and were more likely to advise against using physical punishment when counseling parents.

In one study, pediatric residents and medical students were asked to consider the following vignette pre- and posttraining:

> Mrs. Smith is the mother of a 3-year-old child, Johnny, who is healthy and has normal development, including normal hearing. However, Mrs. Smith states that Johnny frequently hurts other children by hitting them and pushing them down. She seeks your advice about what, if anything, she should do. Please list ALL counseling points you might consider discussing with Mrs. Smith.

In response to this vignette, there was a significant increase posttraining in trainees' ability to describe healthy discipline strategies ($p < .001$, Cohen's $d = 0.97$). Compared with baseline, the researchers found a significant difference in the trainees' attitudes about spanking after viewing Play Nicely. The Attitude Toward Spanking (ATS) score, validated by Holden and colleagues, was 29 at pretraining and 21.4 at posttraining ($p < .001$; Cohen's $d = 1.00$; Burkhart et al., 2016; Holden, Coleman, & Schmidt, 1995).

Evidence That Staff Had Buy-In and Like the Program

At Vanderbilt, the Play Nicely program has become a first-line resource to educate parents and trainees about healthy discipline strategies. Health care providers (faculty, residents, and nurse practitioners) in the Vanderbilt

Pediatric Primary Care Clinic routinely recommend the Play Nicely program to parents of young children. The Junior League Family Resource Center at Vanderbilt has purchased copies of the handbook so that parents can borrow this resource for free. Another example of successful buy-in is that, over many years, health care providers at Vanderbilt have been interested in testing the program with parents.

Evidence That Families Enjoy or Appreciate the Program

Furthermore, research shows that parents seem to like the Play Nicely program. Parents report that Play Nicely is valuable to them and stimulates conversations with their health care provider (Scholer, Hudnut-Beumler, & Dietrich, 2012; Scholer et al., 2015). In a pediatric clinic, we asked English- and Spanish-speaking parents to view at least four of the interactive options and then asked parents if they valued the program as part of their clinic visit and if "Yes," why (Scholer, Hudnut-Beumler, & Dietrich, 2012). Almost all (128/129) parents reported that they valued the program. Most parents valued the program at a personal level, stating that the program was educational (76%), reinforced how they parent (8.6%), or helped spark a conversation with their physician (2%). A minority of parents valued the program because it might benefit others (16%). Of parents who had a conversation about discipline with their health care provider, more than 90% agreed that the program helped with the discussion (Scholer et al., 2015).

Play Nicely has been assessed for cultural sensitivity. After viewing at least four of the interactive options, parents rated several questions related to cultural sensitivity (Smith et al., 2017). More than 80% of parents in each racial or ethnic group reported that the program addressed their family needs, respected their family values, and was sensitive to their personal beliefs. One parent who reported the program was not culturally sensitive commented,

> I feel spanking is the best method. I feel this program is meant for Caucasian families, not Black families who spank their kids. I feel like the program is telling me that what I am doing is wrong, but if I don't spank my kids they will hit me.

Although it is important to take such concerns seriously, the goal of parenting programs should be to inform parents regarding best practices, even when it runs counter to strongly held, yet unhealthy, parenting beliefs held by a minority of parents (both White and Black). The fact that the program may provide education that runs counter to the beliefs of certain cultural groups, such as some African American parents or religious parents who endorse "spare the rod, spoil the child" beliefs, must be balanced with the health benefits to children of shifting norms related to physical punishment.

Evidence of Effectiveness From Outcome Evaluations

Studies demonstrate that Play Nicely is effective in improving outcomes related to the use of physical punishment for parents and health care trainees

(Chavis et al., 2013; Hudnut-Beumler et al., 2018; Scholer, Brokish, et al., 2008; Scholer, Hamilton, et al., 2010; Scholer, Hudnut-Beumler, & Dietrich, 2010; Scholer et al., 2007; Scholer, Reich, et al., 2012). Play Nicely was designed to educate parents, teachers, and health care providers about healthy discipline, especially in the context of responding to childhood aggression. Play Nicely decreases parents' plans to use physical punishment, their attitudes about physical punishment, and their use of physical punishment. Health care providers who view the program are more likely to counsel parents not to use physical punishment of their child. Other studies describe how the program works and whether the program is culturally sensitive for parents of different backgrounds.

One of the first indications that the Play Nicely program affects parents' planned use of physical punishment was a study of a convenience sample of 89 parents of 1- to 7-year-old children who viewed at least eight of the discipline strategies in the Play Nicely multimedia program (10–15 minutes) after a pediatric clinic visit (Scholer et al., 2007). After the intervention, parents answered an open-ended question regarding what, if anything, they planned to do differently to discipline their children at home. Ninety percent of parents planned to change how they discipline their children, and 30% verbalized that they planned to spank less.

This finding led to several randomized controlled trials (RCTs) that confirmed that the Play Nicely program can impact short-term outcomes related to physical punishment (Chavis et al., 2013; Scholer, Hamilton, et al., 2010; Scholer, Hudnut-Beumler, & Dietrich, 2010). Parents in a preschool and a pediatric clinic were randomized to view at least eight of the Play Nicely discipline options (Scholer, Hamilton, et al., 2010). Four months postintervention, parents in the intervention group had shifted their attitudes to be less favorable about physical punishments ($p < .01$), but parents in the control group had not (Smith et al., 2017).

In two RCTs, parents were randomized to an intervention and control group without their knowledge in order to take a population-based approach and decrease selection bias. Parents assigned to the intervention groups in both studies were more likely to have significant changes in outcomes related to spanking compared with the control groups (Chavis et al., 2013; Scholer, Hudnut-Beumler, & Dietrich, 2010). In the first study, parents of 1- to 5-year-old children randomized to the intervention group were asked to view at least four of the discipline options before the clinic visit (Scholer, Hudnut-Beumler, & Dietrich, 2010). After the clinic visit, all parents were asked what they planned to do differently to discipline their children. In the intervention group, 9% of parents stated that they planned not to spank their child compared with 0% in the control group ($p < .001$). In the other RCT, parents of 6-month-old to 2-year-old children were randomized to view at least four of the interactive options (Chavis et al., 2013). After the visit, parents completed the ATS, a validated scale that is associated with parents' actual use of physical punishment; higher scores have been found to be associated with an increased tendency of a parent to use spanking (Holden et al., 1995). Parents in the intervention group had an ATS score that was lower than that of parents in the control group ($p = .043$).

Independent studies of Play Nicely confirm its effect on health professionals and parents. At the University of Toledo College of Medicine, the program was viewed by pediatric residents, medical students, and parents; postexposure, all three groups demonstrated a decrease in attitudes toward using physical punishment (Burkhart et al., 2016, 2018).

Play Nicely works by offering parents alternatives to physical punishment (Hudnut-Beumler et al., 2018). Parents ($N = 197$) in clinic were asked to view at least four of the interactive options. The 9% of parents who spontaneously verbalized that they planned to use less spanking were asked what prompted this planned change in how they discipline. Most (63%) parents responded that they planned to use less discipline because the program taught them other options.

Limitations

Limitations of these studies include short-term follow-up and no measurement of parents' actual use of physical punishment. To address these limitations, a large RCT is in progress.

SUGGESTED FUTURE USE OF THE PROGRAM

How Clinicians and Community Practitioners Can Use the Intervention

The Play Nicely program is designed for anyone who cares for young children. In future projects, Play Nicely could be used for those who are not yet caring for children, such as with individuals in prenatal care and students in high school and college health education classes.

In health care settings, one approach is for health care providers to routinely recommend the program to parents (see Figure 5.4). Some parents need additional parenting education and support, whereas other parents may need little to no additional intervention. Therefore, health care providers may want to use the Play Nicely program in pediatric primary care in conjunction with a parenting assessment. Many parenting surveys have been developed to identify parents who are using healthy discipline strategies, but most are too long to be practically introduced into a well-child visit. In 2017 and 2018, the Play Nicely research team tested the Parenting and Childhood Stressors (PCS), an ACEs survey that includes a 12-item parenting assessment, with more than 1,000 parents of 6-month-old to 10-year-old children. On the basis of these data, the Play Nicely research team has incorporated the PCS into an ACEs algorithm to assist providers in responding to high scores regarding parenting and childhood stressors.

How Policymakers Can Use the Intervention

One of the benefits of Play Nicely is its widespread applicability to a variety of health care and community practice settings. Policymakers interested in preventing children's exposure to physical violence could recommend the use of Play Nicely on a large scale, for example, through home-visiting programs and through preschool programs such as Head Start.

INFORMATION ON OBTAINING THE PROGRAM

Play Nicely can be viewed online for free at http://www.playnicely.org. *Play Nicely: The Healthy Discipline Handbook* can be purchased for $14; bulk purchases receive a discounted price. The multimedia program is available at no cost in English and Spanish. The handbook is available in English, Spanish, and Arabic. The ACEs algorithm, designed to help health care providers identify parents who are using unhealthy discipline strategies and support them accordingly, is available for free. See https://www.playnicely.org for more information about how to view the multimedia program and obtain the handbook and the ACEs algorithm.

REFERENCES

Afifi, T. O., Ford, D., Gershoff, E. T., Merrick, M., Grogan-Kaylor, A., Ports, K. A., . . . Peters Bennett, R. (2017). Spanking and adult mental health impairment: The case for the designation of spanking as an adverse childhood experience. *Child Abuse & Neglect: The International Journal, 71*, 24–31. http://dx.doi.org/10.1016/j.chiabu.2017.01.014

Burkhart, K., Knox, M., & Hunter, K. (2016). Changing health care professionals' attitudes toward spanking. *Clinical Pediatrics, 55*, 1005–1011. http://dx.doi.org/10.1177/0009922816667313

Burkhart, K., Knox, M., Hunter, K., Pennewitt, D., & Schrouder, K. (2018). Decreasing caregivers' positive attitudes toward spanking. *Journal of Pediatric Health Care, 32*, 333–339. http://dx.doi.org/10.1016/j.pedhc.2017.11.007

Chavis, A., Hudnut-Beumler, J., Webb, M. W., Neely, J. A., Bickman, L., Dietrich, M. S., & Scholer, S. J. (2013). A brief intervention affects parents' attitudes toward using less physical punishment. *Child Abuse & Neglect: The International Journal, 37*, 1192–1201. http://dx.doi.org/10.1016/j.chiabu.2013.06.003

Holden, G. W., Coleman, S. M., & Schmidt, K. L. (1995). Why 3-year-old children get spanked—Parent and child determinants as reported by college-educated mothers. *Merrill-Palmer Quarterly, 41*, 431–452.

Hudnut-Beumler, J., Smith, A. E., & Scholer, S. J. (2018). How to convince parents to stop spanking their children. *Clinical Pediatrics, 57*, 129–136.

Scholer, S. J., Brokish, P. A., Mukherjee, A. B., & Gigante, J. (2008). A violence-prevention program helps teach medical students and pediatric residents about childhood aggression. *Clinical Pediatrics, 47*, 891–900. http://dx.doi.org/10.1177/0009922808319965

Scholer, S. J., Hamilton, E. C., Johnson, M. C., & Scott, T. A. (2010). A brief intervention may affect parents' attitudes toward using less physical punishment. *Family & Community Health, 33*, 106–116. http://dx.doi.org/10.1097/FCH.0b013e3181d592ef

Scholer, S. J., Hudnut-Beumler, J., & Dietrich, M. S. (2010). A brief primary care intervention helps parents develop plans to discipline. *Pediatrics, 125,* e242–e249. http://dx.doi.org/10.1542/peds.2009-0874

Scholer, S. J., Hudnut-Beumler, J., & Dietrich, M. S. (2012). Why parents value a brief required primary care intervention that teaches discipline strategies. *Clinical Pediatrics, 51,* 538–545. http://dx.doi.org/10.1177/0009922812439241

Scholer, S. J., Hudnut-Beumler, J., Mukherjee, A., & Dietrich, M. S. (2015). A brief intervention facilitates discussions about discipline in pediatric primary care. *Clinical Pediatrics, 54,* 732–737. http://dx.doi.org/10.1177/0009922815586049

Scholer, S. J., Mukherjee, A. B., Gibbs, K. I., Memon, S., & Jongeward, K. L. (2007). Parents view a brief violence prevention program in clinic. *Clinical Pediatrics, 46,* 724–734. http://dx.doi.org/10.1177/0009922807302508

Scholer, S. J., Reich, S. M., Boshers, R. B., & Bickman, L. (2005). A multimedia violence prevention program increases pediatric residents' and childcare providers' knowledge about responding to childhood aggression. *Clinical Pediatrics, 44,* 413–417. http://dx.doi.org/10.1177/000992280504400505

Scholer, S. J., Reich, S. M., Boshers, R. B., & Bickman, L. (2012). A brief program improves counseling of mothers with children who have persistent aggression. *Journal of Interpersonal Violence, 27,* 991–1004. http://dx.doi.org/10.1177/0886260511424501

Scholer, S. J., Walkowski, C. A., & Bickman, L. (2008). Voluntary or required viewing of a violence prevention program in pediatric primary care. *Clinical Pediatrics, 47,* 461–468. http://dx.doi.org/10.1177/0009922807311731

Smith, A. E., Hudnut-Beumler, J., & Scholer, S. J. (2017). Can discipline education be culturally sensitive? *Maternal and Child Health Journal, 21,* 177–186. http://dx.doi.org/10.1007/s10995-016-2107-9

6

Safe Environment for Every Kid (SEEK)

Howard Dubowitz

THE INTERVENTION

The Safe Environment for Every Kid (SEEK) model was developed by Howard Dubowitz, MS, FAAP, MD, and colleagues at the University of Maryland School of Medicine. SEEK is designed to be a *universal* intervention for all caregivers of children ages 0 to 5 years receiving pediatric primary care.

Background and Theory of Change

Several theories guided SEEK's development. Ecological–developmental theory (Belsky, 1993; Bronfenbrenner & Morris, 1998) recognizes the multiple and interacting systems surrounding a child. Pediatric care has mostly focused on the child; SEEK is based on understanding the strong influence of family and parental functioning on children's health, development and safety, and child maltreatment (CM). SEEK was also guided by the transtheoretical model (Prochaska & DiClemente, 1982, 1983; Prochaska, DiClemente, Velicer, & Rossi, 1992) that links an understanding of a person's stage of change (e.g., precontemplative) with an intervention tailored to the individual. Principles of motivational interviewing (MI) have also been incorporated (Miller & Rollnick, 2013; Williams & Wright, 2014). Prevention science, a multidisciplinary approach to addressing problems, also guided SEEK's development (Rubin, Lane, & Ludwig, 2001). The reduction of CM, with its multifactorial etiology,

http://dx.doi.org/10.1037/0000162-007
Ending the Physical Punishment of Children: A Guide for Clinicians and Practitioners,
E. T. Gershoff and S. J. Lee (Editors)

demands collaboration among disciplines. SEEK aims to effect change by enhancing the ability of pediatric primary care providers (PCPs) to address targeted problems, such as parental depression and harsh punishment, through collaborative work with professionals in other disciplines and agencies. The SEEK model also has been guided by social cognitive theory (Bandura, 2001). For example, role play is used to demonstrate how PCPs can address problems. Implementing these approaches and interacting with behavioral health professionals helps PCPs gain confidence and develop self-efficacy.

SEEK is premised on the amply documented link between psychosocial factors, such as parental depression, substance abuse, intimate partner violence, and harsh punishment, and greater risk for child abuse and neglect. Young children (ages 0–5) have frequent pediatric checkups, which fosters a trusting relationship between families and medical professionals, enabling the latter to inquire about sensitive issues, possible stressors, and challenges as well as strengths. Many of these professionals have not, however, been trained in how best to address the targeted problems, such as intimate partner violence. Thus, the SEEK model begins with online professional training to help PCPs enhance their level of comfort and competence with playing this role.

By addressing risk factors that impede parents' abilities to adequately nurture and optimally discipline their children, SEEK can support parents and parenting; strengthen families; promote children's health, development, and safety; and help prevent CM. Indeed, enough is known regarding the harm associated with harsh physical and psychological punishment that these can be considered forms of maltreatment.

Main Goals of the Intervention

Many daily stressors can impair parenting. Ameliorating stress while providing psychoeducation regarding children's behavior and constructive disciplinary approaches is incorporated in SEEK. The generally excellent rapport and trust between parents and PCPs offers a unique opportunity in a system of care that is already well-institutionalized.

Core components of the SEEK model are (a) training PCPs to identify and address targeted psychosocial problems that are prevalent risk factors for CM: parental depression and major stress, substance abuse, interpersonal violence, harsh discipline, and food insecurity; (b) the evidence-based SEEK Parent Questionnaire–Revised (PQ-R) to screen for risk factors at well-child visits (Dubowitz et al., 2007; Dubowitz, Prescott, Feigelman, Lane, & Kim, 2008; Feigelman et al., 2009; Kim, Dubowitz, Hudson-Martin, & Lane, 2008; Lane et al., 2007; Lane, Dubowitz, Feigelman, & Poole, 2014); (c) the SEEK algorithms with the Reflect–Empathize–Assess–Plan approach to help PCPs assess and address problems; (d) principles of MI; (e) SEEK Parent Handouts for each targeted problem, customized with local resources; and (f) a method for referring to community resources for identified problems—by the PCP or practice staff.

In health care practices implementing SEEK, after PCPs complete the initial online training, a decision is made regarding when to screen for the targeted problems. For example, this may occur at the 2-, 9-, 15-, 24-, 36-, 48-, and 60-month visits for all children regardless of risk status. The parent completes the SEEK PQ-R before or at the start of a regular checkup visit and gives it to their PCP. This is usually done in an exam room while waiting and takes 2 to 3 minutes. The PCP may then briefly assess positive screens and begin to address any identified problems; guidance is available to the PCP via the SEEK algorithms. Importantly, the approach incorporates principles of MI. This departs from traditional medical practice where patients and parents are simply told what to do. Instead, an effort is made to engage parents, understand their view of the issue, and together plan how best to address it. PCPs with access to a behavioral health professional, ideally on site, may opt to refer parents to this resource. The SEEK model is deliberately flexible in this regard. Some problems, such as harsh punishment, may be addressed in the practice, often involving follow-up visits. Other problems, such as substance use, require facilitation of referrals to community resources. The SEEK Parent Handouts or other similar materials are given to parents as adjuncts to what was conveyed during the visit.

Brief Description of the Intervention

SEEK is designed to be implemented by PCPs and delivered individually to one or both parents or to other primary caregivers. There is no set number of sessions; the number depends on the nature of a family's issues. SEEK is incorporated within pediatric primary care, using both regular checkup visits and additional ones scheduled as needed. PCPs have flexibility to assess the situation and determine how best to intervene and how to involve a behavioral health professional, ideally located on site. The SEEK PQ-R is used to screen parents for possible problems. The SEEK algorithms are recommended to guide the PCP's approach, especially initially. SEEK Parent Handouts should be customized with information on local resources and on the practice.

Content Relevant to Spanking or Physical Punishment

The targeted psychosocial risk factors for CM include parental difficulty with a child and physical punishment. SEEK has been carefully developed to provide a brief, efficient intervention with the premise that, with knowledge and skill, PCPs can play a pivotal role in reducing CM by identifying and addressing problems in a few strategic minutes. Of note, SEEK often involves primarily a triage function through the screening of problems and facilitation of referrals to community resources. Although SEEK probes possible physical punishment, there is no explicit content regarding CM. The SEEK PQ-R starts with this introduction:

> **Dear Parent or Caregiver:** Being a parent is not always easy. We want to help families have a safe environment for kids. So, we're asking everyone these

> questions about problems that affect many families. If there's a problem, we'll try to help. Please answer the questions about your child being seen today for a checkup. If there's more than one child, please answer "yes" if it applies to any one of them. This is voluntary. You don't have to answer any question you prefer not to. This information will be kept private, unless we're worried about your child's safety.

Two questions probe problems related to discipline and punishment: (1) Do you often feel your child is difficult to take care of? and (2) Do you sometimes find you need to slap or hit your child?

The SEEK training video for PCPs on physical punishment and discipline briefly provides the rationale for helping parents implement constructive forms of discipline. It demonstrates the PCP role modeling in case scenarios. The SEEK algorithm on discipline guides practitioners on how to briefly assess and initially address disciplinary challenges. It begins by asking about the child's most difficult behavior, whether the parent is getting help to address the behavior, and whether the parent would like help to address the behavior. For those declining help, possible barriers are probed, and guidance is offered on how PCPs can address barriers. The initial response ends with the professional offering to help or to facilitate a referral. Examples include approaching parents who believe hitting is needed and how to incorporate principles of MI.

Implementation of the Intervention

SEEK has been implemented in practices around the United States and in Sweden, mostly in primary health care settings serving children (pediatric and family medicine), but it has also been used in resident clinics (for trainees in pediatrics and in family medicine), child advocacy centers, an obstetric clinic providing prenatal care, and a clinic serving children with disabilities. We cannot estimate the number of families served, but it is likely more than 100,000. SEEK has been implemented with families with children ages 0 to 5 years from many different cultural backgrounds. Program materials are available in English, Spanish, Swedish, Chinese, and Vietnamese. In addition to general pediatric clinics, SEEK is being piloted in Virginia by the state health department in a clinic for children with disabilities and in Children's Advocacy Centers where children are evaluated for possible abuse or neglect.

Evidence That Training of Program Staff Was Successful

Two federally funded randomized controlled trials (RCTs) have been conducted on SEEK (Dubowitz, Feigelman, Lane, & Kim, 2009; Dubowitz, Lane, Semiatin, & Magder, 2012; Dubowitz et al., 2011; Feigelman, Dubowitz, Lane, Grube, & Kim, 2011). These trials are referred to as SEEK I and SEEK II.

Studies' Aims

There were two main aims: (a) to examine whether training in SEEK would significantly enhance PCPs' awareness, attitudes, level of comfort, perceived competence, and practice behavior with regard to addressing the targeted risk factors for CM; and (b) to examine whether SEEK would reduce the rate of CM, compared with standard pediatric primary care.

Studies' Samples

The SEEK I sample consisted of 558 high-risk, very low income, urban, mostly African American families (308 SEEK, 250 controls) served by pediatric resident clinics in West Baltimore and involved 95 physicians (Dubowitz et al., 2009; Feigelman et al., 2011). Approximately half of the children were male. Most of the parents were mothers, single, and unemployed, and they averaged 25 years of age. Families averaged 2.2 adults in the home, and most were receiving Medicaid.

SEEK II involved 105 pediatricians and nurse practitioners and 1,119 relatively low risk, mostly White, middle-income families recruited from 18 suburban private pediatric practices in central Maryland (Dubowitz et al., 2011, 2012). Mothers (595 SEEK, 524 controls) were mostly married and well-educated. The children averaged just over 2 years of age. Few (9%) were on Medicaid.

Studies' Design

Pediatric practices in both studies were randomized to implement either SEEK or standard care. Following baseline evaluations of the PCPs, those in practices randomized to SEEK received in-person training on how to briefly assess and initially address the targeted risk factors in a primary care visit. PCPs were evaluated at 18 to 36 months after the initial training. Parents were recruited from all practices with initial and follow-up assessments at 6 months (SEEK I) or 6 and 12 months (SEEK II).

Data regarding physical punishment were gathered from the parent self-report on the Conflict Tactics Scale, Parent–Child, describing how parents dealt with conflict and angry feelings in the family, including disciplinary approaches, during specified periods (Straus, Hamby, Finkelhor, Moore, & Runyan, 1998). There were five subscales: Nonviolent Discipline, Psychological Aggression, Corporal Punishment (minor physical assault), Severe Physical Assault, and Very Severe Physical Assault. Items such as "shook him (> 2 years old)," "spanked with a bare hand," and "slapped him on the face, head or ears" were considered minor physical assault. "Hit him or her with a fist or kicked him or her hard" represents severe physical assault, and "Beat him or her up, that is, you hit him or her over and over as hard as you could" indicates very severe physical assault. Few parents endorsed items indicating very severe physical assaults, so they were combined with severe assaults.

After approximately 3 years, data were gathered from the state agency on possible child protective services (CPS) involvement. Data were also abstracted from the children's medical records regarding CM-related diagnoses, before and after implementing SEEK. Measures included parents' satisfaction with the child's PCP. In SEEK II, medical students observed PCPs during three checkups at baseline and again at study end to observe their approach to and time spent on the targeted problems.

Impact on Primary Care Providers

In both studies, PCPs in SEEK practices reported significantly greater comfort and perceived competence in addressing the targeted risk factors, compared with controls (Dubowitz et al., 2009, 2011, 2012; Feigelman et al., 2011). Improvements were sustained for 18 to 36 months. Review of medical records revealed that PCPs in SEEK I practices were significantly more likely than controls to screen for the targeted risk factors. In SEEK II, this was confirmed by direct observation; screening increased on average across practices from less than 5% to 62% of visits. SEEK did not require significantly more time, on average, for PCPs to address psychosocial problems (Dubowitz et al., 2011). Having parents complete the PQ-R before visits saved time; this gain was offset when the PCPs addressed problems. Importantly, busy PCPs demonstrated they could effectively implement SEEK.

Evidence That Staff Had Buy-In and Like the Program

Staff buy-in has not been formally evaluated, but staff surveys completed during the two RCTs and ongoing informal feedback have revealed much appreciation of SEEK.

Evidence That Families Enjoy or Appreciate the Program

SEEK I parents reported more favorable views of their child's PCP compared with controls (Feigelman et al., 2011). In SEEK II, most parents initially regarded their PCP very highly, which limited room for improvement. Furthermore, concern that parents may view the screening as intrusive has not been borne out; rather, most appear grateful that concern extends beyond the child to the family as well. Over the past several years, formal and informal feedback from the increasing number of practices implementing SEEK have amply demonstrated that SEEK offers a practical model that can be readily implemented to improve pediatric primary care.

Evidence of Effectiveness From Outcome Evaluations

Measures from three sources assessed the effect of SEEK on CM: (a) parent self-report on the Parent–Child Conflict Tactics Scale (Straus et al., 1998), (b) review of children's medical records for abuse or neglect, and (c) CPS reports.

Parent Self-Report

SEEK I parents reported fewer severe physical assaults than did controls ($p = .04$; Dubowitz et al., 2009). SEEK II parents reported fewer instances of

Psychological Aggression (p = .02) and Minor Physical Assaults (p < .05), which included spanking with a bare hand, than did controls (Dubowitz et al., 2012). There were very few CPS reports in this relatively low risk sample and no significant differences between the groups.

Medical Records

Children in SEEK I practices experienced less medical neglect than did controls (Dubowitz et al., 2009). Results indicated less noncompliance with medical care (4.6% vs. 8.4%, p = .05) and fewer delayed immunizations (3.3% vs. 9.6%, p = .002).

CPS Reports

In SEEK I, fewer families were reported to CPS over a 3-year period (12% vs. 19.7%, p = .04; Dubowitz et al., 2009). Out of 248 total reports (a family could be reported more than once), 69% were for neglect, 21% were for physical abuse, and 6% were for sexual abuse. Of the 239 reports with outcome data, 56% were substantiated, 43% were unsubstantiated, and 2% were ruled out. One or more CPS reports were prevented in one of every 13 such families exposed to SEEK. Clearly, this was a high-risk sample.

Cost–Benefit Analyses

SEEK II costs $3.38 per child per year and $210 per CM experience prevented. On the basis of a conservative estimate of just the health care cost per case of CM at $2,908, providing SEEK to the estimated 29,610 children who were in the SEEK practices would have saved society between $1.6 and $5.0 million (Lane, Dubowitz, Frick, Semiatin, & Magder, 2011). Thus, overall, SEEK offers a model that appears to be significantly cost saving to society through prevention of CM.

Clearinghouse Registries

SEEK is listed in the following registries:

- *California Evidence-Based Clearinghouse for Child Welfare.* Top rating for SEEK as a primary prevention program for child abuse and neglect (1 = well supported by research evidence). http://www.cebc4cw.org/program/safe-environment-for-every-kid-seek-model/detailed
- *Implementing Child Maltreatment Prevention Programmes: What the Experts Say,* World Health Organization. SEEK is listed as an example program; no ratings or programs are provided. http://www.euro.who.int/__data/assets/pdf_file/0009/289602/Maltreatment_web.pdf?ua=1
- *Innovations Exchange,* U.S. Agency for Healthcare Research and Quality. The Exchange provides information on resources to improve health care quality and reduce disparities. SEEK received a "strong" evidence rating.

https://innovations.ahrq.gov/profiles/pediatrician-training-and-office-support-significantly-reduce-instances-child-maltreatment

- *Preventing Child Abuse and Neglect: A Technical Package for Policy, Norm, and Programmatic Activities*, Centers for Disease Control and Prevention. SEEK is listed under the category of "enhanced primary care." No ratings are provided. https://www.cdc.gov/violenceprevention/pdf/can-prevention-technical-package.pdf
- *Results First Clearinghouse Database*, Pew Charitable Trusts. SEEK has been given the "highest-rated program" designation. https://www.pewtrusts.org/pt/research-and-analysis/data-visualizations/2015/results-first-clearinghouse-database

In addition, the SEEK Parent Screening Questionnaire (now named the Parent Questionnaire–Revised or PQ-R) is included in the American Academy of Pediatrics' Bright Futures Tool and Resource Kit as an appropriate tool for parent and family assessment during health supervision visits (https://brightfutures.aap.org/materials-and-tools/tool-and-resource-kit/Pages/Developmental-Behavioral-Psychosocial-Screening-and-Assessment-Forms.aspx).

Limitations

The research presented has a few limitations. Even though the results from two large RCTs are very encouraging, the findings in the first study in a high-risk population were considerably stronger, and both studies were led by the developer of SEEK. It is recommended that the SEEK model be studied further by others and in different populations. Such a trial is underway in Sweden.

SUGGESTED FUTURE USE OF THE PROGRAM

How Clinicians Can Use the Intervention

Practitioners can implement SEEK independently via the online materials. They do need to sign a license agreement, and large organizations may need to pay a modest fee to help sustain dissemination of the model. The core components include the initial training and the SEEK PQ-R; the SEEK algorithms and SEEK Parent Handouts are recommended.

How Community Practitioners Can Use the Intervention

All settings providing primary health care to children, including residency training programs, are amenable to implementing SEEK. Although the model was not tested in other settings, some are piloting its use in prenatal clinics, child-care centers, and child advocacy centers.

How Policymakers Can Use the Intervention

It is recommended that policymakers facilitate SEEK's implementation. For example, some state health departments are using Centers for Disease Control and Prevention funding for this purpose. Another useful strategy available in several states is reimbursing medical professionals for their efforts with parents, including implementing SEEK; Current Procedural Terminology code 96161 covers care concerning parents in the context of pediatric checkups. Third, policymakers in health care systems can help by allocating more time for visits; a time crunch compromises the quality of care.

INFORMATION ON OBTAINING THE PROGRAM

Information about SEEK is available at http://www.SEEKwellbeing.org. Training materials are in English. The SEEK Parent Questionnaire is in English, Spanish, Chinese, Vietnamese, and Swedish. SEEK algorithms are in English and Spanish. SEEK Parent Handouts are in English and Spanish. Those seeking more information can contact Howard Dubowitz, MD (hdubowitz@som.umaryland.edu).

REFERENCES

Bandura, A. (2001). Social cognitive theory: An agentic perspective. *Annual Review of Psychology, 52*(1), 1–26. http://dx.doi.org/10.1146/annurev.psych.52.1.1

Belsky, J. (1993). Etiology of child maltreatment: A developmental-ecological analysis. *Psychological Bulletin, 114,* 413–434. http://dx.doi.org/10.1037/0033-2909.114.3.413

Bronfenbrenner, U., & Morris, P. A. (1998). The ecology of developmental processes. In W. Damon & R. M. Lerner (Eds.), *Handbook of child psychology: Theoretical models of human development* (pp. 993–1028). Hoboken, NJ: John Wiley & Sons.

Dubowitz, H., Feigelman, S., Lane, W., & Kim, J. (2009). Pediatric primary care to help prevent child maltreatment: The Safe Environment for Every Kid (SEEK) Model. *Pediatrics, 123,* 858–864. http://dx.doi.org/10.1542/peds.2008-1376

Dubowitz, H., Feigelman, S., Lane, W., Prescott, L., Blackman, K., Grube, L., . . . Tracy, J. K. (2007). Screening for depression in an urban pediatric primary care clinic. *Pediatrics, 119,* 435–443. http://dx.doi.org/10.1542/peds.2006-2010

Dubowitz, H., Lane, W. G., Semiatin, J. N., & Magder, L. S. (2012). The SEEK model of pediatric primary care: Can child maltreatment be prevented in a low-risk population? *Academic Pediatrics, 12,* 259–268. http://dx.doi.org/10.1016/j.acap.2012.03.005

Dubowitz, H., Lane, W. G., Semiatin, J. N., Magder, L. S., Venepally, M., & Jans, M. (2011). The safe environment for every kid model: Impact on pediatric primary care professionals. *Pediatrics, 127,* e962–e970. http://dx.doi.org/10.1542/peds.2010-1845

Dubowitz, H., Prescott, L., Feigelman, S., Lane, W., & Kim, J. (2008). Screening for intimate partner violence in a pediatric primary care clinic. *Pediatrics, 121,* e85–e91. http://dx.doi.org/10.1542/peds.2007-0904

Feigelman, S., Dubowitz, H., Lane, W., Grube, L., & Kim, J. (2011). Training pediatric residents in a primary care clinic to help address psychosocial problems and prevent child maltreatment. *Academic Pediatrics, 11,* 474–480. http://dx.doi.org/10.1016/j.acap.2011.07.005

Feigelman, S., Dubowitz, H., Lane, W., Prescott, L., Meyer, W., Tracy, J. K., & Kim, J. (2009). Screening for harsh punishment in a pediatric primary care clinic. *Child*

Abuse & Neglect: The International Journal, 33, 269–277. http://dx.doi.org/10.1016/j.chiabu.2008.09.011

Kim, J., Dubowitz, H., Hudson-Martin, E., & Lane, W. (2008). Comparison of three data collection methods for gathering sensitive and less sensitive information. *Ambulatory Pediatrics, 8,* 255–260. http://dx.doi.org/10.1016/j.ambp.2008.03.033

Lane, W. G., Dubowitz, H., Feigelman, S., Kim, J., Prescott, L., Meyer, W., & Tracy, J. K. (2007). Screening for parental substance abuse in pediatric primary care. *Ambulatory Pediatrics, 7,* 458–462. http://dx.doi.org/10.1016/j.ambp.2007.07.007

Lane, W. G., Dubowitz, H., Feigelman, S., & Poole, G. (2014). The effectiveness of food insecurity screening in pediatric primary care. *International Journal of Child Health and Nutrition, 3,* 130–138. http://dx.doi.org/10.6000/1929-4247.2014.03.03.3

Lane, W. G., Dubowitz, H., Frick, K., Semiatin, J. N., & Magder, L. S. (2011, October). *The Safe Environment for Every Kid (SEEK) Program: A cost-effective analysis.* Paper presented at the 139th Annual Meeting of the American Public Health Association, Washington, DC.

Miller, W. R., & Rollnick, S. (2013). *Motivational interviewing: Helping people change* (3rd ed.). New York, NY: Guilford Press.

Prochaska, J. O., & DiClemente, C. C. (1982). Transtheoretical therapy: Toward a more integrative model of change. *Psychotherapy: Theory, Research & Practice, 19,* 276–288. http://dx.doi.org/10.1037/h0088437

Prochaska, J. O., & DiClemente, C. C. (1983). Stages and processes of self-change of smoking: Toward an integrative model of change. *Journal of Consulting and Clinical Psychology, 51,* 390–395. http://dx.doi.org/10.1037/0022-006X.51.3.390

Prochaska, J. O., DiClemente, C. C., Velicer, W. F., & Rossi, J. S. (1992). Criticisms and concerns of the transtheoretical model in light of recent research. *British Journal of Addiction, 87,* 825–828. http://dx.doi.org/10.1111/j.1360-0443.1992.tb01973.x

Rubin, D., Lane, W., & Ludwig, S. (2001). Child abuse prevention. *Current Opinion in Pediatrics, 13,* 388–401. http://dx.doi.org/10.1097/00008480-200110000-00002

Straus, M. A., Hamby, S. L., Finkelhor, D., Moore, D. W., & Runyan, D. (1998). Identification of child maltreatment with the Parent–Child Conflict Tactics Scales: Development and psychometric data for a national sample of American parents. *Child Abuse & Neglect: The International Journal, 22,* 249–270. http://dx.doi.org/10.1016/S0145-2134(97)00174-9

Williams, A. A., & Wright, K. S. (2014). Engaging families through motivational interviewing. *Pediatric Clinics of North America, 61,* 907–921. http://dx.doi.org/10.1016/j.pcl.2014.06.014

7

The Video Interaction Project (VIP)

Caitlin Canfield, Erin Roby, and Alan Mendelsohn

THE INTERVENTION

The Video Interaction Project (VIP) has been developed by an interdisciplinary team at the NYU School of Medicine and New York City (NYC) Health + Hospitals/Bellevue, including researchers and practitioners in the fields of pediatrics, developmental psychology, and early childhood education. Development was initially led by Alan L. Mendelsohn, Benard P. Dreyer, and Virginia Flynn, with subsequent refinement by Samantha Berkule Johnson, Carolyn Cates, Adriana Weisleder, and Caitlin Canfield. This intervention is *universal* and can be delivered to all parents in primary health care settings regardless of their level of risk.

Background and Theory of Change

Studies have consistently shown that low-income children are less prepared for entry into school when compared with middle- and high-income children

The development and evaluation of the Video Interaction Project has been supported by grants from NIH/NICHD (1R01HD07639001A1, 5R01HD04774001-04, 2R01HD04774005-09), HRSA (1 T32HP22238 DHHS), NYU/H+H CTSI (1UL1RR029893), New York City Council (City's First Readers and council members Stephen Levin, Antonio Reynoso, Dan Garodnick, Rosie Mendez, and Carlina Rivera), Tiger Foundation, Marks Family Foundation, Rhodebeck Charitable Trust, New York Community Trust, Children of Bellevue, Inc., and KiDS of NYU Foundation, Inc.

http://dx.doi.org/10.1037/0000162-008
Ending the Physical Punishment of Children: A Guide for Clinicians and Practitioners,
E. T. Gershoff and S. J. Lee (Editors)

(Brooks-Gunn & Duncan, 1997; Duncan, Morris, & Rodrigues, 2011). These gaps in preparation for school become apparent early, as in the case of language development, and income-related disparities in achievement widen over time (Currie, 2005; Kuhfeld, Gershoff, & Paschall, 2018; Weisleder & Fernald, 2013). These widening disparities are problematic because early differences in developmental outcomes predict school readiness as well as long-term educational achievement (Belfield & Levin, 2007; Heckman, 2006; Tamborini, Kim, & Sakamoto, 2015), underscoring the need for effective interventions beginning in early childhood. Pediatric primary care has been increasingly recognized as an innovative and uniquely positioned platform for addressing these disparities because it is able to support population-wide, low-cost early childhood preventive interventions (High et al., 2014; Mendelsohn et al., 2011). The VIP capitalizes on this model by delivering parenting interventions in the context of pediatric primary care with the aim of preventing disparities in school readiness.

VIP is a strengths-based, relationship-based, family-centered intervention, which involves face-to-face interaction with a child development specialist (bachelor's level) at the time of well-child visits. The program is offered from birth to 5 years. At each session, for 3 to 5 minutes, the child development specialist video-records the parent and child playing/reading with a toy and/or book, then reviews the video with the parent to facilitate self-reflection and identifies and reinforces strengths. VIP promotes positive parenting and parent–child relationships through (a) enhancing self-efficacy and reducing parenting stress by reinforcing strengths and building on parent goals rather than imposing external goals, (b) facilitating planning/organization through goal setting and discussion of family contexts and needs using structured Parent Guides, (c) supporting interactional skills through self-reflection based on review of a video made of the parent and child playing/reading together, (d) enhancing interactional resources through provision of books and toys, and (e) engaging the extended family in caregiving through inclusion of multiple caregivers and provision of video to share at home.

Main Goal of the Intervention

The main goal of VIP is to reduce income-related disparities in school readiness. VIP does this through a brief intervention that trains parents in the use of positive parenting activities such as talking, playing, and reading and enhanced parent–child relationships and interactions (Cates et al., 2018).

Brief Description of the Intervention

VIP is administered in person. At each VIP session, the primary caregiver and child, as well as other family members as appropriate, meet one-on-one with a VIP facilitator for approximately 25 to 30 minutes. The mode of delivery is at the individual or family level. The VIP facilitator is a bachelor's level professional with a background in child development, public health, or a related field. There is required training for implementers, which includes a 3-day training course, followed by observation and continued supervision, with periodic meetings and session reviews after the training period.

VIP is delivered in the pediatric clinic and is designed to take place at the same time as well-child pediatric visits. VIP is delivered in two separate components, each of which consist of a number of sessions; the two components can be delivered in isolation or together. VIP 0–3 involves 14 sessions between birth and age 3, with six in the first year, four in the second year, and four in the third year. VIP 3–5 involves nine visits, one at each well-child visit at 36, 48, and 60 months, with additional visits every 3 months in between, capitalizing, where possible, on additional clinic visits by the families (e.g., camp/school physicals; sibling pediatric appointments; colocated services appointments, such as dental).

VIP materials for the facilitator include VIP visit-specific scripts, VIP intervention checklists, a video-recording device, a video monitor (for video playback), a laptop (for burning DVDs), and an instant camera (to take a picture of the parent and child at each visit that is attached to the Parent Guide that the parent takes home). VIP materials for the parent consist of VIP Parent Guides (with photo of parent and child attached), developmentally appropriate toys and/or books, and DVDs/USB drives containing a video copy of the parent–child interaction.

Content Relevant to Spanking or Physical Punishment

VIP does not directly address spanking or physical punishment as part of the intervention. Instead, it focuses on increasing positive parent–child interactions and strengthening parents' self-efficacy in handling their child's behavior, emotions, and development. By increasing positive interactions, VIP enhances the parent–child relationship and helps the parent be more in tune with their child's needs.

Each VIP session begins with a discussion of what the parent has noticed about the child and how the child has changed since their last visit, along with a discussion of relevant developmental milestones. The parent and interventionist sometimes secondarily discuss the child's social–emotional and behavioral competencies, including those that may be experienced negatively by the parent, such as tantrums, saying "no" and "mine," and independence-seeking behaviors. In this context, and in the context of discussions regarding reading, playing, and daily routines more broadly, the VIP interventionist seeks to emphasize the positive developmental stages that influence these behaviors and to share best practices for handling difficult situations. Discussions such as this serve to (a) lower stigmatization and parent self-consciousness regarding their child's behavior and development; (b) improve parent self-efficacy, as they leave the session with additional information on strategies to try; and (c) improve parent–child interactions by lowering stress.

Implementation of the Intervention

To date, VIP has been administered to approximately 2,000 families in pediatric primary care, including hospital clinics and community health centers. The intervention is also being piloted for use in association with Head Start programs. VIP is for families of children from 0 to 5 years old and has been used with parents from diverse racial and ethnic backgrounds (Hispanic/Latino, Black/African American, and White). VIP has been delivered to parents in the Mid-Atlantic region (New York, NY; Pittsburgh, PA) and the Midwest (Flint, MI). Preliminary pilot work has been conducted with children with biological developmental risks and disabilities (e.g., infants born premature, children with Down syndrome). VIP has also been used with at-risk families, such as families of children in foster care with both foster and biological parents.

Evidence That Training of Program Staff Was Successful

The VIP Center for Excellence has an extensive and ongoing supervisory process to maintain fidelity. Program staff are supervised, and fidelity to program components is assessed biweekly for the first 3 months of program implementation, monthly for the next 6 months, and periodically afterward. Although we have not systematically collected data on training and fidelity, training records and program monitoring indicate that each of the three main components of the program is delivered consistently and interventionist checklists and Parent Guides are completed appropriately.

Evidence That Staff Had Buy-In and Like the Program

Informal interviews with program interventionists indicate that they have substantial buy-in. Common themes expressed in these interviews include the desire to promote parent self-efficacy and pride in seeing families' growth emerge over time. VIP interventionists stay in their position for more than 2 years on average, indicating a degree of dedication to the program. In addition, clinic staff have generally been supportive of VIP and have worked with program staff to secure and continue funding.

Evidence That Families Enjoy or Appreciate the Program

Interviews with parents have indicated that they feel the VIP program has helped them appreciate shared moments with their children and has increased their reading and playing with their child. Furthermore, 78% of families enrolled in VIP 0–3 have continued in VIP 3–5 when the second component was available to them. These findings are consistent with those from a recent pilot study of an interventionist rating tool for engagement, in which VIP interventionists rated 90% of families as "mostly" or "very" engaged (Matalon, 2018). In addition, in a previous trial, families attended, on average, approximately 60% of VIP sessions from birth through age 5 and attended more than 70% of VIP sessions in the first 3 years of life, when sessions are more in accordance with well-child pediatric appointments (Canfield et al., 2019; Mendelsohn et al., 2011; Weisleder et al., 2016).

Evidence of Effectiveness From Outcome Evaluations

A secondary analysis of the impact of VIP on the use of harsh or physical punishment was conducted as part of a large longitudinal randomized controlled trial evaluating the efficacy of VIP versus a lower-intensity program called Building Blocks (BB) and a care-as-usual control (Canfield et al., 2015). Whereas VIP includes regular one-on-one meetings with an interventionist, BB involves mailed, age-appropriate information on child development and regular self-assessments for parents regarding children's milestones. Both interventions include the provision of toys and books. A total of 675 mothers (225 in each group) were recruited into the larger randomized controlled trial in the nursery of a large, urban public hospital between 2005 and 2008 and were followed until children reached second grade. Of those, 438 mothers (161 VIP, 113 BB, and 164 control) were assessed at child ages 14 months and 24 months. Mothers were interviewed at each of these time points about a variety of stressors, including maternal depressive symptoms and parenting stress, as well as about their interactions with their children and their discipline practices, including the use of physical punishment, using the Socolar Discipline Survey (Socolar, Savage, Devellis, & Evans, 2004).

The majority of the sample included in this analysis were Hispanic, born outside the United States, and low-income. VIP parents reported using fewer instances of physical punishment of the child in the past 3 months when the child was 24 months, with analysis indicating that this effect represented a reduced odds of using physical punishment (odds ratio = 0.59), with a significant linear effect of VIP over time (Cohen's $d = 0.24$). Mediation analysis indicated that VIP was related to reduced use of physical punishment through its impact on parenting and maternal well-being; that is, the relation was mediated by both increases in responsive parenting and decreases in maternal depression and parenting stress (see Figure 7.1). In summary, even though the VIP intervention does not directly address parents' use of physical punishment and discipline, the differences that emerged in this study suggested that the program played a role in parents' discipline strategies, which has important implications for the examination of program outcomes more broadly.

Clearinghouse Registries

Although not included in registries of evidence-based practice, the level of evidence for VIP was reported to be 1 (with 1 constituting the highest level of evidence), according to the Oxford Centre for Evidence-Based Medicine levels of evidence classification, in a systematic review of pediatric primary-care-based interventions (Howick et al., 2011). Furthermore, VIP has been recommended

FIGURE 7.1. Mediation of Impacts of the Video Interaction Project on Physical Punishment via Responsive Parenting and Maternal Psychosocial Risk

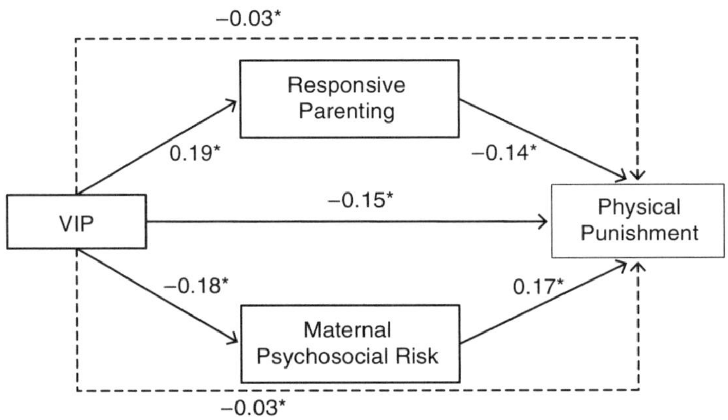

VIP = Video Interaction Project. * = $p < .05$

in the American Academy of Pediatrics' policy statement entitled "Poverty and Child Health in the United States" (American Academy of Pediatrics Council on Community Pediatrics, 2016) and was highlighted in the National Institute for Children's Health Quality (2016) summary report entitled *Promoting Young Children's (Ages 0–3) Socioemotional Development in Primary Care.*

Limitations

Because VIP is a universal program, it may not address the heterogeneity of needs for very high-risk parents and families. This issue is currently being addressed through the implementation and study of the Smart Beginnings initiative, which integrates VIP with a home-visiting program (Family Check-Up; Dishion & Stormshak, 2007) in a tiered model for families who are especially high-risk. It should also be noted, as stated earlier, that VIP does not specifically address physical punishment and therefore, physical punishment and harsh discipline have not been the primary outcomes under study in program research.

SUGGESTED FUTURE USE OF THE PROGRAM

VIP has developed protocols for scaling through the VIP Center of Excellence at NYU Langone Health/NYU School of Medicine and NYC Health + Hospitals/Bellevue. These protocols have included business and implementation plans as well as a curriculum and manual for training, supervision, and implementation. Programs have been implemented in New York City; Pittsburgh, Pennsylvania; and Flint, Michigan. The VIP Center of Excellence is interested in working with additional sites to scale the program broadly in health care as well as in other community-based locations and programs.

How Clinicians Can Use the Intervention

Clinicians interested in implementing VIP in their practice can work with the VIP Center of Excellence to develop a plan for funding and implementation.

How Community Practitioners Can Use the Intervention

Community practitioners are encouraged to make referrals to VIP, if it is available in their area. In addition, training in VIP is available for practitioners in a variety of settings; currently the VIP Center of Excellence is exploring partnerships with home-visiting programs and links with early childhood education; Women, Infants and Children; and other community-based services.

How Policymakers Can Use the Intervention

Research strongly supports a role for pediatric primary care in supporting positive parenting, enhancing the parent–child relationship, reducing parenting stress, and reducing physical punishment. In particular, studies of VIP suggest that enhancing positive parenting activities such as reading aloud and play may have a secondary impact on reducing physical punishment. Given the relatively low cost and potential scalability of VIP and similar programs (e.g., Reach Out and Read), findings support policies that facilitate reimbursement for and dissemination of these primary care programs. In addition, policies should support linkages across platforms, such as the New York City Council City's First Readers program, which links primary care to community-based programs, and the Smart Beginnings initiative linking VIP to home visiting through the Family Check-Up.

INFORMATION ON OBTAINING THE PROGRAM

For more information about how to obtain VIP, please visit the project website at http://www.videointeractionproject.org or email Dr. Alan Mendelsohn (alan.mendelsohn@nyulangone.org) or Dr. Anne Seery (Anne.Seery@nyulangone.org).

REFERENCES

American Academy of Pediatrics Council on Community Pediatrics. (2016). Poverty and child health in the United States. *Pediatrics, 137*(4), e20160339.

Belfield, C., & Levin, H. M. (2007). *The price we pay: Economic and social consequences of inadequate education*. Washington, DC: Brookings Institute Press.

Brooks-Gunn, J., & Duncan, G. J. (1997). The effects of poverty on children. *The Future of Children, 7*(2), 55–71. http://dx.doi.org/10.2307/1602387

Canfield, C. F., Weisleder, A., Cates, C. B., Huberman, H. S., Dreyer, B. P., Legano, L. A., . . . Mendelsohn, A. L. (2015). Primary care parenting intervention effects on the use of physical punishment among low-income parents of toddlers. *Journal of Developmental and Behavioral Pediatrics, 36*, 586–593. http://dx.doi.org/10.1097/DBP.0000000000000206

Canfield, C. F., Weisleder, A., Cates, C. B., Roby, E., Seery, A., & Mendelsohn, A. (2019). *Impacts of parent participation in preventive interventions on program outcomes.* Manuscript in preparation.

Cates, C. B., Weisleder, A., Berkule Johnson, S., Seery, A. M., Canfield, C. F., Huberman, H., . . . Mendelsohn, A. L. (2018). Enhancing parent talk, reading, and play in primary care: Sustained impacts of the Video Interaction Project. *The Journal of Pediatrics, 199,* 49–56.e1. http://dx.doi.org/10.1016/j.jpeds.2018.03.002

Currie, J. (2005). Health disparities and gaps in school readiness. *The Future of Children, 15*(1), 117–138. http://dx.doi.org/10.1353/foc.2005.0002

Dishion, T. J., & Stormshak, E. A. (2007). *Intervening in children's lives: An ecological, family-centered approach to mental health care.* Washington, DC: American Psychological Association. http://dx.doi.org/10.1037/11485-000

Duncan, G. J., Morris, P. A., & Rodrigues, C. (2011). Does money really matter? Estimating impacts of family income on young children's achievement with data from random-assignment experiments. *Developmental Psychology, 47,* 1263–1279. http://dx.doi.org/10.1037/a0023875

Heckman, J. J. (2006). Skill formation and the economics of investing in disadvantaged children. *Science, 312,* 1900–1902. http://dx.doi.org/10.1126/science.1128898

High, P. C., Klass, P., Donoghue, E., Glassy, D., DelConte, B., Earls, M., . . . Council on Early Childhood. (2014). Literacy promotion: An essential component of primary care pediatric practice. *Pediatrics, 134,* 404–409. http://dx.doi.org/10.1542/peds.2014-1384

Howick, J., Chalmers, I., Glasziou, P., Greenhalgh, T., Heneghan, C., Liberati, A., . . . Thornton, H. (2011). *Background document: Explanation of the 2011 Oxford Centre for Evidence-Based Medicine (OCEBM) Levels of Evidence.* Oxford, England: Oxford Centre for Evidence-Based Medicine. Retrieved from https://www.cebm.net/index.aspx?o=5653

Kuhfeld, M., Gershoff, E., & Paschall, K. (2018). The development of racial/ethnic and socioeconomic achievement gaps during the school years. *Journal of Applied Developmental Psychology, 57,* 62–73. http://dx.doi.org/10.1016/j.appdev.2018.07.001

Matalon, M. (2018). *The validity of the Interventionist Perception of Caregiver Engagement measure (IPCES) and predictors of parent engagement in a school readiness primary preventive intervention* (Unpublished master's thesis). New York University College of Global Public Health, New York, NY.

Mendelsohn, A. L., Huberman, H. S., Berkule, S. B., Brockmeyer, C. A., Morrow, L. M., & Dreyer, B. P. (2011). Primary care strategies for promoting parent-child interactions and school readiness in at-risk families: The Bellevue Project for Early Language, Literacy, and Education Success. *Archives of Pediatrics & Adolescent Medicine, 165,* 33–41. http://dx.doi.org/10.1001/archpediatrics.2010.254

National Institute for Children's Health Quality. (2016). *Promoting young children's (ages 0–3) socioemotional development in primary care.* Boston, MA: Author.

Socolar, R., Savage, E., Devellis, R. F., & Evans, H. (2004). The discipline survey: A new measure of parental discipline. *Ambulatory Pediatrics, 4,* 166–173. http://dx.doi.org/10.1367/A03-071R1.1

Tamborini, C. R., Kim, C., & Sakamoto, A. (2015). Education and lifetime earnings in the United States. *Demography, 52,* 1383–1407. http://dx.doi.org/10.1007/s13524-015-0407-0

Weisleder, A., Cates, C. B., Dreyer, B. P., Berkule Johnson, S., Huberman, H. S., Seery, A. M., . . . Mendelsohn, A. L. (2016). Promotion of positive parenting and prevention of socioemotional disparities. *Pediatrics, 137*(2), e20153239. http://dx.doi.org/10.1542/peds.2015-3239

Weisleder, A., & Fernald, A. (2013). Talking to children matters: Early language experience strengthens processing and builds vocabulary. *Psychological Science, 24,* 2143–2152. http://dx.doi.org/10.1177/0956797613488145

8

An Educational Intervention for Health Care Providers

Gail Hornor, Saribel Garcia Quinones, Deborah Bretl, Ellen Chiocca, Carrie Donnell, Katharine Doughty, Bridget Marshall, and Kristen Morris

THE INTERVENTION

The Educational Intervention for Health Care Providers was adapted from one originally developed by Lauren McAliley, CPNP, of Rainbow Babies and Children's Hospital in Cleveland, Ohio. It was revised by 10 pediatric nurse practitioners (PNPs) who were members of the National Association of Pediatric Nurse Practitioners Child Maltreatment and Neglect Special Interest Group (CMN SIG). This intervention is designed as a universal one to educate all health care providers.

Background and Theory of Change

Preventing the continued use of physical punishment in the United States will require changing parental attitudes and beliefs associated with the effectiveness and appropriateness of its use. Parents report that they listen to professionals, including health care professionals, regarding child discipline (Hornor et al., 2015; Taylor, Hamvas, Rice, Newman, & DeJong, 2011). However, although the use of physical punishment can contribute to numerous negative consequences for children, a significant number of pediatric health care providers continue to endorse the use of physical punishment (Hornor et al., 2015; Tirosh, Offer Shechter, Cohen, & Jaffe, 2003). Furthermore, pediatric health care professionals are not well trained to address these issues,

http://dx.doi.org/10.1037/0000162-009
Ending the Physical Punishment of Children: A Guide for Clinicians and Practitioners,
E. T. Gershoff and S. J. Lee (Editors)

and they do not consistently volunteer information about child discipline during visits with parents (Hornor et al., 2015, 2017; Regalado, Sareen, Inkelas, Wissow, & Halfon, 2004). The educational intervention was designed to provide pediatric health care providers with current scientific information related to the use of physical punishment, so that health care providers could communicate more effectively with parents. This approach proved to be effective in decreasing pediatric health care provider endorsement of the use of physical punishment (Hornor et al., 2015).

This intervention draws from Ajzen's (2002) theory of planned behavior (TPB) and builds on Ajzen and Fishbein's (1973) theory of reasoned action (TRA), which, together, posit three sets of beliefs that underlie motivation for a behavior: (a) behavioral beliefs that influence the attitude toward the behavior, (b) normative beliefs that influence the subjective norm, and (c) control beliefs, or the extent to which an individual perceives they can control their own behavior. Each of these areas has merit in describing individual attitudes and behaviors toward physical punishment as a form of discipline. In the case of physical punishment, the TRA suggests that the attitude toward childhood discipline may be a poor predictor of the behavior of physical punishment. Indeed, many caregivers may not want to use physical punishment as a form of discipline. TPB (Ajzen, 2002), as an extension of the TRA (Ajzen & Fishbein, 1973), included the construct of perceived control over performance of behavior. In other words, TPB poses the question: Does the caregiver feel they have a choice about whether or not to use physical punishment? Or, put another way: Does the caregiver feel they have the resources to discipline without using physical force?

Main Goals of the Intervention

The main goal of the educational intervention is to stimulate pediatric health care providers to evaluate their own attitudes and beliefs toward physical punishment and educate themselves about the research on physical punishment so that they can more effectively communicate that information to parents during health care visits.

Brief Description of the Intervention

The intervention is a 1-hour educational session that can be presented in person via a presentation to a group or individually through an online module. Continuing education credits for nurses, social workers, and physicians are available to those who complete the intervention. The intervention can be delivered by advanced practice nurses, nurses, physicians, social workers, or other health care professionals. The only materials needed are a 1-hour slide presentation entitled *What Can We Do to Help Children Behave? Alternatives to Corporal Punishment* or the equivalent presentation in an online format.

Content Relevant to Spanking or Physical Punishment

The educational intervention discusses child discipline in terms of defining the goals of effective discipline, the difference between discipline and punishment, and the difference between children behaving out of respect for a parent versus fear of a parent. The intervention explores potential influences upon individuals' beliefs regarding child discipline and the use of physical punishment, such as one's childhood experience with discipline and religious beliefs, as well as the policy and best practice position of health care organizations (e.g., No Hit Zones in the hospital, the American Academy of Pediatrics' statement advising parents against the use of physical punishment [Sege, Siegel, Council on Child Abuse and Neglect, & Committee on Psychosocial Aspects of Child and Family Health, 2018], and the National Association of Pediatric Nurse Practitioners' [2011] statement against the use of physical punishment under any circumstances). The slides also describe research that highlights the potential consequences to children from experiencing physical punishment. The presentation concludes with slides on alternatives to the use of physical punishment, as well as information regarding the global initiative to end the use of physical punishment.

Implementation of the Intervention

To date, 882 health care professionals have been exposed to the intervention, including registered nurses (n = 94; 10.7%), nurse practitioners (n = 104; 11.9%), social workers (n = 68; 7.8%), physicians (n = 5; 0.6%), medical assistants and nursing assistants (n = 16; 1.8%), child life specialists (n = 5; 0.6%), nursing students (n = 217; 24.8%), nurse practitioner students (n = 240; 27.4%), and other health care professionals (n = 126; 51.2%) working in the following regions of the United States: Northeast (n = 137; 15.5%), Southeast (n = 116; 13.2%), Midwest (n = 560; 63.4%), Southwest (n = 19; 2.2%), Northwest (n = 23; 2.6%), and West (n = 37; 4.2%). The intervention has been implemented in graduate and undergraduate nursing classes, professional nursing and multidisciplinary health care conferences, and multidisciplinary continuing education offerings for health care professionals.

Evidence of Effectiveness From Outcome Evaluations

The Corporal Punishment Attitude and Knowledge Surveys administered before and after the intervention were initially developed by Lauren McAliley, PNP, of Rainbow Babies and Children Hospital, Cleveland, Ohio, for use in their No Hit Zone project. The surveys were collaboratively reviewed and revised by the participating CMN SIG PNPs to ensure face validity; all were content experts in child maltreatment.

Hornor, Bretl, Chapman, Chiocca, et al. (2015) described the corporal punishment attitudes and beliefs of 882 pediatric health care providers who participated in the educational intervention. Less than one fifth (n = 126; 14.4%) of study participants who were also parents stated that their child's health care provider had ever discussed child discipline with them. Child discipline management was included in the health care education for less than half of participants (n = 365; 41.4%). Study participants' responses to only one spanking question, "spanking is never OK," differed significantly between those who had not received discipline education (n = 78; 15.6%) and those who had received discipline education(n = 83; 22.8%; p = .008) in their health care education.

This study then examined differences in study participants' responses to spanking questions before and after the educational intervention. Significantly fewer study participants felt that "spanking is sometimes necessary" after the educational intervention (n = 251; 28.9%) compared with before the educational intervention (n = 351; 39.88%; $p < .001$). More than two thirds of participants (n = 587; 67.4%) indicated that they felt nonphysical methods of discipline were more effective than spanking after the educational intervention, compared with approximately half of participants (n = 465; 52.8%; $p < .001$) before the intervention. Before the educational intervention 18.4% of participants (n = 162) endorsed the statement that "spanking is never OK." After the educational intervention, 22.6% of participants endorsed the statement. Significant changes in response to survey questions about spanking as a form of punishment before and after the educational intervention were noted for 10 survey questions (Hornor et al., 2015). After the intervention, the majority of participants (n = 679; 77%) stated that they were more likely to discuss child discipline with their patients/parents. Participants who stated that the educational intervention influenced their beliefs about child discipline also said they were more likely to discuss child discipline with their patients/parents (r = 0.22; $p < .0001$).

This study (Hornor et al., 2015) also indicated that participants' beliefs about the usefulness of spanking were shaped by whether they were spanked as a child. Participants who received little to no spanking as a child were significantly less likely to endorse the statement that "children who are never spanked are spoiled." Participants who were never spanked were the least likely to endorse "spanking is sometimes necessary." Participants who were frequently spanked were the most likely to endorse the need for spanking. Endorsement of nonphysical forms of discipline differed depending upon spanking history as a child. When compared with participants who were spanked, participants who were never spanked were most likely to state that nonphysical methods of discipline are more effective than spanking. Participants who were frequently spanked were the least likely to endorse nonphysical methods of discipline over spanking.

Limitations

Our intervention has some limitations. Geographic distributions of learners were not equally disbursed, with well over 50% of learners hailing from the

Midwest and fewer than 5% from the Southwest, Northwest, and West. A more even geographical distribution may have offered stronger statistical relationships between geographic regions. Nursing was the profession of three fourths of learners, which limited the ability to make comparisons among professions.

SUGGESTED FUTURE USE OF THE PROGRAM

How Clinicians Can Use the Intervention

This intervention provides health care professionals with a summary of the most recent research on how parents' use of physical punishment may impact children. It also discusses global efforts to eliminate the use of physical punishment and provides health care professionals some alternative methods of discipline that do not involve force or violence. Fewer than half of the health care professionals who received the educational intervention reported that they had received information or education on child discipline during their professional education. Child discipline techniques need to be included in health care providers' training curricula, as this is one of the most frequent questions that parents ask health care providers and such content is a critical part of caring for their pediatric patients. Health care professionals would benefit from information to educate parents about the devastating consequences of physical punishment and potential alternative techniques to deal with disciplinary issues. Health care providers who participated in the educational intervention reported that they were more likely to discuss child discipline with parents after this educational program, which highlights the importance of providing the knowledge of physical punishment consequences to providers.

How Community Practitioners Can Use the Intervention

The brief educational intervention used in this study can be used to educate health care providers and other community members to empower them to better advocate for the legal and cultural changes needed to eliminate the use of physical punishment in this country. In addition, basic positive parenting practices in this program should be reviewed by providers and incorporated in their daily practice particularly during primary care medical visits in the first few years of life. Multiple programs (including those summarized in this volume) are available to educate parents on positive parenting principles and teaching appropriate discipline.

INFORMATION ON OBTAINING THE PROGRAM

The educational intervention slide presentation entitled *Children Behave? Alternatives to Corporal Punishment*, is available via the website of the National Association of Pediatric Nurse Practitioners in the CMN SIG library. The pre- and postphysical punishment surveys are also available on the website at https://www.napnap.org/cmn.

REFERENCES

Ajzen, I. (2002). Perceived behavioral control, self-efficacy, locus of control, and the theory of planned behavior. *Journal of Applied Social Psychology, 32*, 665–683. http://dx.doi.org/10.1111/j.1559-1816.2002.tb00236.x

Ajzen, I., & Fishbein, M. (1973). Attitudinal and normative variables as predictors of specific behaviors. *Journal of Personality and Social Psychology, 27*, 41–57. http://dx.doi.org/10.1037/h0034440

Hornor, G., Bretl, D., Chapman, E., Chiocca, E., Donnell, C., Doughty, K., . . . Quinones, S. G. (2015). Corporal punishment: Evaluation of an intervention by PNPs. *Journal of Pediatric Health Care, 29*, 526–535. http://dx.doi.org/10.1016/j.pedhc.2015.04.016

Hornor, G., Bretl, D., Chapman, E., Herendeen, P., Mitchel, N., Mulvaney, B., . . . VanGraafeiland, B. (2017). Child maltreatment screening and anticipatory guidance: A description of pediatric nurse practitioner practice behaviors. *Journal of Pediatric Health Care, 31*, e35–e44. http://dx.doi.org/10.1016/j.pedhc.2017.05.006

National Association of Pediatric Nurse Practitioners. (2011). NAPNAP position statement on corporal punishment. *Journal of Pediatric Health Care, 25*(6), e31–e32. http://dx.doi.org/10.1016/j.pedhc.2011.07.003

Regalado, M., Sareen, H., Inkelas, M., Wissow, L. S., & Halfon, N. (2004). Parents' discipline of young children: Results from the National Survey of Early Childhood Health. *Pediatrics, 113*(Suppl.), 1952–1958.

Sege, R. D., Siegel, B. S., Council on Child Abuse and Neglect, & Committee on Psychosocial Aspects of Child and Family Health. (2018). Effective discipline to raise healthy children. *Pediatrics, 142*(6), e20183112. http://dx.doi.org/10.1542/peds.2018-3112

Taylor, C. A., Hamvas, L., Rice, J., Newman, D. L., & DeJong, W. (2011). Perceived social norms, expectations, and attitudes toward corporal punishment among an urban community sample of parents. *Journal of Urban Health, 88*, 254–269. http://dx.doi.org/10.1007/s11524-011-9548-7

Tirosh, E., Offer Shechter, S., Cohen, A., & Jaffe, M. (2003). Attitudes towards corporal punishment and reporting of abuse. *Child Abuse & Neglect: The International Journal, 27*, 929–937. http://dx.doi.org/10.1016/S0145-2134(03)00140-6

III

GROUP-BASED INTERVENTIONS

9

Positive Discipline in Everyday Parenting (PDEP)

Joan E. Durrant

THE INTERVENTION

Positive Discipline in Everyday Parenting (PDEP) was developed by Joan E. Durrant, PhD, University of Manitoba, in collaboration with Save the Children Sweden and the PDEP Program Development Team (Christine Ateah, Leslie Barker, Ashley Stewart-Tufescu, and Jean Tinling). PDEP is designed to be a *universal* intervention for all parents.

Background and Theory of Change

PDEP was created as part of Save the Children Sweden's response to the United Nations' *World Report on Violence Against Children* (Pinheiro, 2006), which documented the high global prevalence of punitive violence against children. The report called for parenting approaches that uphold children's rights to protection, dignity, and participation and that respect children's personhood and evolving capacities (Durrant, 2017; Durrant & Stewart-Tufescu, 2017). PDEP was developed in response to this call through a partnership between Save the Children Sweden (an international nongovernmental organization) and Joan Durrant, PhD (a developmental psychologist and academic). It is now a core program of Save the Children's Child Protection global theme.

PDEP is based on developmental theory and research. It aims to transform parents' views of their role from one of control and coercion to one of respectful mentorship and collaborative problem solving. Through a sequence of

http://dx.doi.org/10.1037/0000162-010
Ending the Physical Punishment of Children: A Guide for Clinicians and Practitioners, E. T. Gershoff and S. J. Lee (Editors)

interactive activities, the program translates empirical research findings on parent–child attachment, parent and child self-regulation, and children's neurobiological, emotional, and cognitive development into a form that parents can process, reflect upon, and apply in their everyday interactions with their children. PDEP is informed by attributional, cognitive–developmental, constructivist, epigenetic, social information processing, neurorelational, and social learning theories (Bandura & Walters, 1963; Bretherton & Mulholland, 1999; Milner, 2000; Montes, de Paúl, & Milner, 2001; Piaget, 1928; Siegel, 2001; Vygotsky, 1978; Weiner, 2010).

PDEP's theory of change posits three sets of parental outcomes. *Short-term outcomes* are the cognitive and affective shifts expected to occur as the program unfolds, namely, reductions in (a) attributions for typical child behavior to intentional "misbehavior," (b) anger in response to conflict, and (c) approval of physical and emotional punishment. These outcomes are theorized to be mediated by increases in parents' knowledge of child development, perspective taking, and emotion-regulation skills. *Medium-term outcomes* are the confidence and skills expected to be gained by the end of the program, specifically with regard to problem solving and scaffolding children's learning. These outcomes are theorized to be mediated by parents' growing ability to identify and understand the underlying causes of children's behavior and to generate nonpunitive responses. *Long-term outcomes* are expected to emerge following parents' completion of the program, namely, (a) ongoing reductions in physical and emotional punishment and in parenting stress and (b) ongoing increases in sensitive responding, problem solving, and parenting satisfaction.

Main Goals of the Intervention

The aim of PDEP is not to change children's behavior but to change the way that parents understand and respond to children's behavior, shifting their orientation away from punishment and toward respectful conflict resolution. Program activities take parents into the minds of their children to view conflict through children's eyes and to understand that children's behavior is a way of communicating their emotions and needs. The overarching aim is to help parents view their children as active learners and approach them as mentors, scaffolding their learning rather than punishing them, and engaging them as participants in the problem-solving process.

Brief Description of the Intervention

The PDEP program is delivered to groups of caregivers once weekly for 8 weeks. Caregivers meet in groups for 2 hours each week. A follow-up session 2 weeks after the program ends is strongly recommended. PDEP is delivered by trained program facilitators. Typically, they are staff of community agencies, schools, child care centers, or other nonprofit organizations who deliver the program to parents as part of their job. Each program facilitator must have a facilitator's manual, a set of materials needed to conduct the program activities, and a set of visual teaching aids. Program facilitators receive these materials when they are trained. Each parent receives an individual copy of the parent book (Durrant, 2016) and a binder containing program exercises, which program facilitators prepare.

Content Relevant to Spanking or Physical Punishment

Physical and emotional punishment are explicitly addressed throughout the program. The PDEP approach is not didactic but rather takes parents through a series of activities and guided discussions designed to encourage reflection, insight, and perspective taking. As parents increasingly view conflict from children's perspectives, they realize that punitive responses are counterproductive and potentially damaging to their relationships with their children.

Implementation of the Intervention

To date, at least 7,097 caregivers of children of all ages have taken the program. These caregivers include parents, grandparents, foster parents, and others who care for children. This figure represents only those caregivers for whom pre-/postquestionnaires have been submitted by program facilitators. The actual number of caregivers who have taken the program is unknown.

PDEP has been successfully delivered to caregivers from a wide range of cultural backgrounds, faiths, socioeconomic circumstances, literacy levels, and languages. It has been delivered in countries throughout the world, including Albania, Australia, Bangladesh, Canada, China, Colombia, Ethiopia, Fiji, Gaza and the West Bank, Gambia, Georgia, Guatemala, Indonesia, Japan, Kenya, Kosovo, Mongolia, Nepal, Papua New Guinea, Paraguay, Philippines, Solomon Islands, South Korea, Sri Lanka, Tanzania, and Venezuela. In addition to English, PDEP has been delivered in Albanian, Amharic, Arabic, Bahasa, Bengali, Cantonese, French, Hindi, Japanese, Karen, Khmer, Kinyarwanda, Kirundi, Korean, Kurdish, Mandarin, Mongolian, Punjabi, Somali, Spanish, Swahili, Tagalog, Thai, Tigrigna, Urdu, and Vietnamese. It is designed to be appropriate for all caregivers, whether or not their children live with them. PDEP has been delivered in a wide range of settings, including large urban centers, rural towns, remote villages, indigenous communities, conflict and postconflict zones, postdisaster zones, urban slums, brothel areas, refugee camps, and prisons. PDEP is not intended to be mandated by child protective services; it is intended as a nontargeted, prevention program. However, it is delivered to parents involved in the child protection system in Canada and other countries.

Evidence That Training of Program Staff Was Successful

For a parent program aimed at shifting parents' attitudes toward physical punishment to be successful, it is important that program facilitators have undergone that shift themselves. It also is important that they feel adequately prepared to deliver the program to parents. Therefore, two of our measures of training success are (a) changes in program facilitators' attitudes toward physical punishment and (b) their confidence in delivering PDEP to parents.

A study was conducted of all PDEP program facilitators ($n = 430$) who were trained in three Canadian provinces: 94% were female; 51% were between 20 and 40 years of age; 65% had worked directly with parents for more than 4 years; and 76% held either an undergraduate or postgraduate degree (Durrant et al., 2018). Each participant completed standardized pre- and post-training questionnaires from which a five-item Approval of Physical Punishment (APP) Scale was constructed ($\alpha = .75$ in this sample). Participants' scores on the APP Scale decreased significantly from pre- to posttest ($p < .001$); thus, their approval of physical punishment declined over the course of the program. At posttest, 92% reported that, since taking the training, they believed more strongly that adults should not physically punish children. These program facilitators were also asked to rate their confidence as facilitators before and after participating in the PDEP facilitator training. At pretest, 60% believed they could help parents solve most discipline challenges, and 78% believed they had the skills needed to be good facilitators. By posttest, these proportions rose to 81% and 96%, respectively.

In 2017, 96 program facilitators in Canada participated in an online survey (Durrant et al., 2018). Participants were asked how strongly they approved of physical and nonphysical punishment before and after taking the PDEP facilitator training. Although a majority (88%) stated that they "largely" or "strongly" disapproved of physical punishment before taking the training, this proportion increased to 100% through the course of the program.

Evidence That Staff Had Buy-In and Like the Program

In the study of 430 program facilitators described above (Durrant et al., 2018), participants were asked how useful they believed PDEP would be in their work with parents. Large majorities "mostly" or "strongly" agreed that PDEP will be useful in helping parents to reduce their use of physical punishment (82%), reduce their yelling (81%), understand children's development (93%), understand children's feelings (88%), control their anger (79%), communicate better with their children (88%), and build stronger relationships with their children (91%).

In an open-ended question, participants were asked what they had learned from taking the PDEP facilitator training. Their responses were typified by the following comments:

- "How you respond to a child teaches them about the world and sets an example of what a kind, empathetic, patient person looks like."
- "To see children as little people, not chattel."
- "I love this program. It has become an essential part of who I am and how I relate to others—at home and in the workplace. I have seen the light come on in parents' eyes when they understand a new concept, and I have heard over and over again how this program has deeply impacted the way they parent their children. These things keep me energized and invested in continuing to offer this program to families."

Evidence That Families Enjoy or Appreciate the Program

A study was conducted in Canada of 516 parents who completed standardized pre- and postprogram parent questionnaires (PPPQs; Durrant et al., 2018). At posttest, they were asked several questions about the impact they believed PDEP would have on their parenting. Large majorities "mostly" or "strongly" agreed that PDEP would help them to use less physical punishment (80%), control their anger (80%), communicate better with their children (90%), build stronger relationships with their children (95%), understand their children's development (91%), and understand their children's feelings (90%).

The relevance of PDEP to parents was assessed in countries at different levels of social development (Durrant, Plateau, et al., 2017). On the basis of their Inequality-Adjusted Human Development Indices (IHDI), 13 countries were classified into high ($n = 201$), medium ($n = 166$), or low ($n = 158$) development categories. Across all IHDI categories, almost all parents were "mostly" or "very" satisfied with the overall program (98%), the PDEP parent book (98%), and the program activities (98%). Across all IHDI categories, substantial majorities "mostly" or "strongly" agreed that the program would help them to use less physical punishment (82%), understand their children's development (92%), communicate better with their children (93%), understand their children's feelings (94%), control their anger (87%), and build stronger relationships with their children (96%).

In a 3-month pilot follow-up study of parents who took PDEP in Canada ($n = 23$), 95% reported that they felt "fairly" or "very" confident about using the PDEP approach with their children. Of this sample, 81% had recommended PDEP to others. The reasons they gave for recommending it were typified by the following comments:

- "It is helpful, effective, and practical."
- "It is very useful, easy to understand and to put in practice immediately in everyday parenting. It shows positive results and helps all the family to approach problems in a very positive and constructive way."
- "It is very helpful for every parent who has immigrated to [a new country], especially if the country they're immigrating from has different parenting approaches, rights, and culture."

Evidence of Effectiveness From Outcome Evaluations

Since 2007, PDEP has grown from an idea to a program implemented on a global level. During that period, the first edition of the parent book (Durrant, 2007) was published; an accompanying parent program was created and piloted in highly diverse settings around the world; a facilitator training was created (Durrant, 2008), piloted in wide-ranging settings, and adapted for low-literacy and underresourced contexts (Durrant, Plateau, & Barker, 2012); a training model was developed, tested, revised, and implemented; and the foundations were created for scaling up the program in all regions of the world. By 2012, the program team had sufficient confidence in the consistency of program delivery to begin formal monitoring. An international interdisciplinary evaluation team was established to create, pilot, and finalize pre- and post-PPPQs that could be administered to parents by facilitators. A workshop in ethical and standardized administration became part of the facilitator training program. A central data hub was established, and procedures for processing the data were developed. At present, the global data set represents more than 7,000 caregivers and more than 2,000 trained program facilitators. The research team has drawn on these data to determine whether there is any indication of change that would warrant the design and implementation of randomized controlled trials (RCTs).

The PPPQ contains an APP Scale that assesses change in parents' attitudes toward physical punishment over the course of the program (α ranges from .80 to .82 across samples). The findings have been consistent across countries. For example, parents' APP scores declined significantly ($p < .001$) among samples of 77 parents living in Japan, 678 parents living in Canada's prairie provinces, and 321 parents living in 14 cities across Canada (Durrant et al., 2014; Mori, Mochizuki, & Stewart-Tufescu, 2016; Stewart-Tufescu, Ateah, Barker, & Tinling, 2016). An abbreviated version of the PPPQ has been administered to parents with low literacy levels in Gaza and the West Bank and Bangladesh. This version contains two items measuring approval of physical punishment ("Spanking is fine as long as the parent is not angry" and "Parents should have the right to decide whether to spank their children"). Significant declines in agreement were found on both of these items ($p < .001$) among samples of 150 fathers in Gaza and the West Bank and 105 parents in very poor areas of Bangladesh (Durrant, Haj Ahmad, Ahmed, Stewart-Tufescu, & Jones, 2017; Khondkar, Ateah, & Milon, 2016).

At posttest, consistently large majorities of parents "mostly" or "strongly" agree that they have come to believe more strongly that parents should not use physical punishment: 90% in Kosovo, 94% in Japan, and 90% in Canada, for example (Ademi-Shala, Hoxha, & Ateah, 2016; Mori et al., 2016; Stewart-Tufescu et al., 2016). Recently, my colleagues and I have been piloting measures of parental behavior in situations of conflict with their children. For example, in a 3-month pilot follow-up study of parents in Canada ($n = 23$), 43% reported that they had used physical punishment in the year prior to the survey, whereas 19% reported that they had done so since taking PDEP. Of those who reported that they had physically punished their children since taking PDEP, 67% reported that they had done so less often than they did before taking the program.

Limitations

To date, an RCT has not been completed. However, on the strength of the pre–post findings, independent research teams have designed RCTs of PDEP to evaluate change in parents' attitudes toward and use of physical punishment. In Canada, parents are being randomly assigned to PDEP or wait-list control groups; data collection will continue until 2021. In Indonesia, villages were randomly assigned to PDEP or control groups (Ruiz-Casares et al., 2019). The findings of this study are not yet available.

SUGGESTED FUTURE USE OF THE PROGRAM

How Clinicians Can Use the Intervention

Clinicians can be fully trained in the PDEP approach to better help them advise parents regarding respectful discipline. In some locations, public health professionals and pediatricians have received a brief orientation to the approach so they can integrate the concepts into their interactions with caregivers.

How Community Practitioners Can Use the Intervention

Community practitioners, once trained as program facilitators, can deliver the program directly to parents through their agencies. Those who deliver it are expected to submit pre-/postquestionnaire data to the data-processing hub. They receive a user-friendly data summary in return, which provides feedback to the facilitators regarding the impact of their programs.

How Policymakers Can Use the Intervention

PDEP is a helpful program to support prohibition of physical punishment in countries around the world, which is based on human rights standards. It complements initiatives to implement the United Nations Convention on the Rights of the Child. PDEP's core concepts have been integrated into a population-level public education initiative in Alberta, Canada. Policymakers can invest in the systematic evaluation of this program.

INFORMATION ON OBTAINING THE PROGRAM

The PDEP website (http://www.positivedisciplineeveryday.com) provides information about the program and training model. The parent book can be downloaded at no cost from the website. Accompanying program materials may be obtained only through official PDEP facilitator trainings. Parents can take the program through local agencies with trained program facilitators on staff.

The PDEP training and mentorship ladder was designed to optimize program integrity, facilitator fidelity, and program sustainability in communities and countries. PDEP program facilitators are staff of family-serving agencies in local communities who deliver the program to caregivers. They are (a) trained over 4 full days by master trainers, certified country trainers, and/or country trainer mentees and (b) mentored as they deliver their first two parent programs. If they are successful, they can then deliver PDEP parent programs independently. Program facilitators must agree to deliver parent programs as part of their jobs, not for personal profit.

Experienced program facilitators may be invited to become country trainer mentees. Those who accept will cotrain a new group of program facilitators with a master trainer and be mentored as they subsequently deliver their first two facilitator trainings on their own. At that point, they are eligible for certification as country trainers, which qualifies them to train new program facilitators independently.

Full translations of all program materials have been carried out in Arabic, Bahasa, Bengali, French, Japanese, Korean, Mongolian, Spanish, Thai, and Vietnamese.

Positive Discipline in Everyday Life is a not-for-profit organization that coordinates PDEP training, delivery, program development, and data processing (posdiseveryday@gmail.com). Positive Discipline in Everyday Life is a formal partner of Save the Children Sweden, which provides global oversight of PDEP and has supported its development since 2006. Information about PDEP is provided at http://www.positivedisciplineeveryday.com.

REFERENCES

Ademi-Shala, R., Hoxha, L., & Ateah, C. (2016, August). *Delivering Kosovo's first parenting program: Challenges, strategies and outcomes.* Paper presented at the conference of the International Society for Prevention of Child Abuse and Neglect, Calgary, Alberta, Canada.

Bandura, A., & Walters, R. H. (1963). *Social learning and personality development.* New York, NY: Holt, Rinehart, & Winston.

Bretherton, I., & Mulholland, K. A. (1999). Internal working models in attachment relationships: A construct revisited. In J. Cassidy & P. R. Shaver (Eds.), *Handbook of attachment theory, research and clinical applications* (pp. 89–114). New York, NY: Guilford Press.

Durrant, J. E. (2007). *Positive discipline: What it is and how to do it.* Bangkok, Thailand: Save the Children Sweden, Southeast Asia and Pacific Region.

Durrant, J. E. (2008). *Positive discipline: What it is and how to do it. A manual for facilitators, educators and trainers.* Bangkok, Thailand: Save the Children Sweden, Southeast Asia and Pacific Region.

Durrant, J. E. (2016). *Positive discipline in everyday parenting* (4th ed.). Stockholm, Sweden: Save the Children Sweden.

Durrant, J. E. (2017). The global movement to end all corporal punishment of children. In G. Lenzer (Ed.), *Ending violence against children: Making human rights real* (pp. 64–85). New York, NY: Routledge. http://dx.doi.org/10.4324/9781351248433-4

Durrant, J. E., Barker, L., Jones, A. D., Cavers, V., Shanks, T., & Roloff, L. (2018, June). *Preventing punitive violence against children: A three-province evaluation of a primary prevention program.* Final report to the Prairie Action Foundation. Winnipeg, Manitoba: Mosaic Newcomer Family Resource Network, Saskatchewan Prevention Institute, & Alberta Home Visitation Network Association.

Durrant, J. E., Haj Ahmad, M., Ahmed, A., Stewart-Tufescu, A., & Jones, A. (2017, March). *"If I take one thing from this program, it is how I give love to my children": Engaging fathers in Positive Discipline in Everyday Parenting.* Paper presented at the Canadian National Fatherhood Conference, Winnipeg, Manitoba, Canada.

Durrant, J. E., Plateau, D. P., Ateah, C., Holden, G., Barker, L., Stewart-Tufescu, A., . . . Ahmed, R. (2017). Parents' views of the relevance of a violence prevention program in high, medium, and low human development contexts. *International Journal of Behavioral Development, 41*, 523–531. http://dx.doi.org/10.1177/0165025416687415

Durrant, J. E., Plateau, D. P., Ateah, C., Stewart-Tufescu, A., Jones, A., Ly, G., . . . Tapanya, S. (2014). Preventing punitive violence: Preliminary data on the Positive Discipline in Everyday Parenting (PDEP) program. *Canadian Journal of Community Mental Health, 33*(2), 109–125. http://dx.doi.org/10.7870/cjcmh-2014-018

Durrant, J. E., Plateau, D. P., & Barker, L. (2012). *Positive Discipline: What it is and how to do it. A manual for parent program facilitators*. Stockholm, Sweden: Save the Children Sweden.

Durrant, J. E., & Stewart-Tufescu, A. (2017). What is 'discipline' in the age of children's rights? *International Journal of Children's Rights, 25*, 359–379. http://dx.doi.org/10.1163/15718182-02502007

Khondkar, L., Ateah, C., & Milon, F. I. (2016, August). *Implementing 'Positive Discipline in Everyday Parenting' among ethnic minorities, urban slums, and brothel areas of Bangladesh*. Paper presented at the Conference of the International Society for Prevention of Child Abuse and Neglect, Calgary, Alberta, Canada.

Milner, J. S. (2000). Social information processing and child physical abuse: Theory and research. In D. J. Hansen (Ed.), *Nebraska symposium on motivation: Vol. 46. Motivation and child physical maltreatment* (pp. 39–84). Lincoln: University of Nebraska Press.

Montes, M. P., de Paúl, J., & Milner, J. S. (2001). Evaluations, attributions, affect, and disciplinary choices in mothers at high and low risk for child physical abuse. *Child Abuse & Neglect: The International Journal, 25*, 1015–1036. http://dx.doi.org/10.1016/S0145-2134(01)00254-X

Mori, I., Mochizuki, R., & Stewart-Tufescu, A. (2016, August). *Transforming parents' beliefs about physical punishment through 'Positive Discipline in Everyday Parenting' in Japan*. Paper presented at the Conference of the International Society for Prevention of Child Abuse and Neglect, Calgary, Alberta, Canada.

Piaget, J. (1928). *The child's conception of the world*. London, England: Routledge and Kegan Paul.

Pinheiro, S. P. (2006). *World report on violence against children*. New York, NY: United Nations.

Ruiz-Casares, M., Lilley, S., Thombs, B. D., Platt, R. W., Scott, S., Isdijoso, W., . . . Mayo, N. (2019). Protocol for a cluster randomised controlled trial evaluating a parenting with home visitation programme to prevent physical and emotional abuse of children in Indonesia: The Families First Programme. *BMJ Open, 9*, e021751. http://dx.doi.org/10.1136/bmjopen-2018-021751

Siegel, D. J. (2001). Toward an interpersonal neurobiology of the developing mind: Attachment relationships, "mindsight," and neural integration. *Infant Mental Health Journal, 22*, 67–94. http://dx.doi.org/10.1002/1097-0355(200101/04)22:1<67::AID-IMHJ3>3.0.CO;2-G

Stewart-Tufescu, A., Ateah, C., Barker, L., & Tinling, J. (2016, August). *Shifting attitudes toward physical punishment in a multicultural context: The case of Canada*. Paper presented at the Conference of the International Society for Prevention of Child Abuse and Neglect, Calgary, Alberta, Canada.

Vygotsky, L. S. (1978). *Mind in society: The development of higher psychological processes*. London, England: Harvard University Press.

Weiner, B. (2010). The development of an attribution-based theory of motivation: A history of ideas. *Educational Psychologist, 45*, 28–36. http://dx.doi.org/10.1080/00461520903433596

10

The ACT Raising Safe Kids Program

Michele Knox and Morgan Dynes

THE INTERVENTION

The Violence Prevention Office of the American Psychological Association, under the leadership of Julia da Silva, developed the ACT Raising Safe Kids Program (ACT). The ACT program is designed to be universal prevention available to all families, regardless of their history or level of risk.

Background and Theory of Change

The ACT program is grounded in research that demonstrates that the basic social–emotional skills children can learn early in life are critical to their development and have long-term positive effects on their lives (Goodman, Joshi, Nasim, & Tyler, 2015; Hawkins, Kosterman, Catalano, Hill, & Abbott, 2005). Furthermore, research has shown that exposure to adverse childhood experiences, such as maltreatment, can have deleterious and enduring consequences on a child's health and well-being (Anda et al., 2006; Corso, Edwards, Fang, & Mercy, 2008; Taylor, Lerner, Sage, Lehman, & Seeman, 2004). Last, it is well established that parents and caregivers serve a crucial role in teaching, modeling, protecting, and advocating for their children (Kaminski, Valle, Filene, & Boyles, 2008; Piquero et al., 2016).

Based on social learning theory (Bandura, 1978), ACT recognizes that the aggressive and violent behaviors that contribute to youth violence are often

http://dx.doi.org/10.1037/0000162-011
Ending the Physical Punishment of Children: A Guide for Clinicians and Practitioners, E. T. Gershoff and S. J. Lee (Editors)

learned in early childhood and that parents are in a unique position to limit children's early exposure to violence and other factors that contribute to later youth violence. ACT teaches parents how to model adaptive behavior and avoid exposing children to violent and other maladaptive behavior, which they may imitate (Knox, Burkhart, & Howe, 2011). For example, in one interactive activity parents are reminded that children learn from observing and imitating the behavior of those around them. Then, parents are asked what children learn when they are spanked. Facilitators emphasize responses indicating that modeling violence increases the likelihood of child aggression. Furthermore, parents are explicitly taught methods to handle anger effectively and to solve interpersonal conflicts. Parents are supported in developing strategies to teach these skills to their children in developmentally appropriate ways and through modeling. Similarly, parents are guided in identifying ways to protect children from exposure to media violence.

ACT also utilizes aspects of motivational interviewing (MI; Miller & Rose, 2009) to support parents' behavioral changes. The program helps parents identify personal goals for their children and the parenting behaviors they want to adopt to support their children in reaching those goals. ACT activities that were informed by MI strategies address parents' resistance to change and ambivalence about their parenting styles to help them learn positive ways to discipline.

Drawing from attachment theory (Ainsworth, 1978), ACT also promotes parental nurturing behavior. In addition to emphasizing the importance of parental warmth and nurturing, parents in the program are encouraged to consider the degree of nurturing in their own childhoods and to plan for a nurturing environment for their own children. In addition to these theoretical underpinnings, participants in the ACT program are provided with information on the neuroscience of brain development as a rationale supporting the use of ACT methods and anticipated positive outcomes.

Main Goals of the Intervention

The ACT program developers sought to end cycles of violence that result in child maltreatment, community violence, and youth violence. The strategy was informed by the Centers for Disease Control and Prevention's Best Practices of Youth Violence Prevention (Thornton et al., 2002). Violence is viewed largely as an acquired behavior, resulting in part from aggressive, coercive behavior that is modeled by adults and imitated by children. Cycles of violence also are understood to result from subjecting children to violence, resulting in a higher likelihood of the victimized child engaging in violence, then later becoming a violent adolescent, a parent who uses harsh and coercive techniques, and so on. Thus, the ACT program focuses on anger management and social problem-solving skills for both parent and child and the promotion of attitudes and beliefs in line with nonviolence. The Centers for Disease Control and Prevention's recommendations also called for parent- and family-based interventions that consist of training in parenting skills, education on child development, education on prevention of factors that increase children's risk of engaging in violence, and activities to improve effective parent–child communication (Thornton et al., 2002). In line with these suggestions, the ACT program curriculum uses didactic instruction paired with modeling and role playing. The sessions are highly interactive and employ strategies such as role plays and use of art and other materials to encourage expression of ideas and emotions and to engage adults to learn, retain, and use information effectively.

The main goal of the ACT program is to teach parents and caregivers how to use positive parenting practices to create safe and nurturing environments and relationships that protect children from adverse experiences. ACT uses a number of proven strategies such as MI and interactive group psychoeducation to teach parents about child development, the development and consequences of violence, anger management for adults, anger management for children, social problem solving, positive discipline, and the negative effects of media violence (Silva, 2011). The program supports parents in learning how to use nonviolent discipline techniques, such as positive reinforcement, age-appropriate consequences, and consistent limit setting (Silva, 2011). The program directly addresses the issue of physical punishment and informs parents about the potential harmful effects of physical punishment. ACT also supports parents in adopting effective, nonphysical options for discipline. ACT engages parents through collaboration with community-based and family-serving organizations. Professionals delivering the program are trained in how to use adult learning strategies, such as small-group discussions and role plays. The program also enhances participant engagement by training facilitators to deliver the program content in a nonjudgmental way.

Brief Description of the Intervention

The ACT program is a group-based universal program that consists of nine sessions that are about 1.5 to 2 hours each. ACT facilitators are preferably professionals with a minimum of a bachelor's degree. ACT facilitators include social workers, nurses, early childhood educators, psychologists, teachers, and counselors. ACT is fully manualized and is available in English, Spanish, Greek, Portuguese, Japanese, Croatian, Mandarin, and Romanian (Silva, 2011). Facilitator training consists of a 2-day workshop conducted by an ACT master trainer. The facilitator manual offers detailed, step-by-step instructions for each session. Trained facilitators receive a facilitator kit that includes all needed materials.

Content Relevant to Spanking or Physical Punishment

ACT teaches participants how to distinguish between discipline and punishment. Participants are engaged in activities to help them identify their own parenting styles. After learning about parenting styles and their outcomes, participants engage in reflection and discussion about the way they were parented by their caregivers and about their own ideal parenting style. Participants then generate ideas about why parents use physical punishment techniques. Parents learn about the results of research studies that have identified the negative outcomes of physical punishment. Facilitators urge participants to discuss how physical punishment may contribute to or deter from the goals and wishes they have for their children. Facilitators guide activities that emphasize the differences between reacting out of frustration and anger and responding to children's behaviors in more calm and rational ways. Parents learn specific techniques to recognize and deal constructively with their own anger.

Throughout the program, facilitators help parents learn how to conceptualize children's misbehaviors as mistakes rather than as intentional, manipulative, or vengeful acts. Parents are encouraged to model nonviolent behavior for their children. ACT activities place emphasis on modeling nonviolent responses to children's misbehavior. Parents complete homework between sessions that involves identifying children's problematic behavior, as perceived by the parent, and the parent identifying their response to the behavior as discipline or punishment. Parents are guided in mastering nurturing behaviors, such as using praise immediately and frequently and reinforcing positive child behaviors with contingencies. Participants learn positive discipline strategies including limit setting, time-out, distraction, giving choices, natural and logical consequences, and removal of privileges.

Implementation of the Intervention

The ACT program has been successfully implemented in multiple regions of the United States and 14 other countries with parents of children 0 to 8 years old. Approximately 17,000 families have been served to date. Parents from a variety of cultures and ethnicities, such as African American, Asian American, Native American, and Latino/a American backgrounds, have completed the ACT program. The ACT program has been delivered in English, Spanish, Greek, Portuguese, Japanese, Croatian, Bosnian, Mandarin, and Romanian. Multiple sites in the United States have offered ACT for parents and foster parents mandated by child protective services.

Evidence That Families Enjoy or Appreciate the Program

Among a sample of incarcerated women in Brazil (Howe et al., 2017), all of the participants rated the program and the team as excellent. In a qualitative study conducted in Japan, 91% of the Japanese parents reported that they would recommend the program to others, and 70% reported that they learned helpful techniques to improve their parenting (Nishizawa, 2014). Video testimonies by parents show that they praise the program for leading them to change their parenting behaviors such as by discontinuing yelling and spanking, creating a happier family, and having better communication with their children. Parents also expressed great appreciation for the work of the program facilitators.

Evidence of Effectiveness From Outcome Evaluations

Research studies conducted on the ACT program have provided an extensive base of evidence demonstrating the program's effectiveness. The major outcomes of these studies include reducing physical punishment; improving positive parenting skills; increasing positive, nurturing parenting; increasing parental control and regulation of their emotions; and reducing children's conduct problems and bullying (Knox & Burkhart, 2014; Knox, Burkhart, & Cromly, 2013; Knox, Burkhart, & Hunter, 2011; Porter & Howe, 2008; Portwood, Lambert, Abrams, & Nelson, 2011). In one study, for example, all parents involved in the program reported terminating the use of physical punishment (Porter & Howe, 2008).

The first published study on the ACT program (Porter & Howe, 2008) was conducted on a sample of 18 voluntary and mandated parents and caregivers derived from child welfare services and a parenting center using a pre–post design with a 3-month follow-up evaluation. There was no control group. Results indicated significantly reduced maladaptive beliefs about spanking as measured using the ACT Against Violence Parents Raising Safe Kids Scale (Porter & Howe, 2008). Physical punishment, measured using the Humboldt State University Parenting Survey (Porter & Howe, 2008), was reduced significantly (medium effect), to the point where all parents/caregivers involved in the study reported terminating the use of physical punishment 3 months after the end of the program (Porter & Howe, 2008).

A second U.S. study (Knox, Burkhart, & Hunter, 2011) was conducted using a sample of 92 voluntary and mandated parents/caregivers from a mental health agency for children, an urban community center, and a court of common pleas. Intervention and wait-list comparison groups were recruited sequentially. The first 50 participants were assigned to the intervention group and the next 42 to the comparison group. Participants reported both how often they spanked their child and how often they hit their child with an object, and results included reductions in both for the ACT group (small to medium effects).

Another study (Knox & Burkhart, 2014) used a pre–post design (no comparison group) and a sample of 60 voluntary parents/caregivers of children age 9 and under. The study took place at seven community-based sites in the United States. Results indicated significantly decreased negative discipline (Parent Behavior Checklist; Fox, 1994) and decreased harsh parenting (Parent–Child Conflict Tactics Scale; Straus & Hamby, 1997; Straus, Hamby, Finkelhor, Moore, & Runyan, 1998). Results indicated more robust child behavior outcomes for families that had high initial rates of harsh parenting prior to engaging in the program.

The first randomized controlled trial (RCT) of the ACT program (Portwood et al., 2011) involved a voluntary sample of 162 intervention and 109 comparison participants drawn from seven social service and parent program sites in the United States. Pre–post and 3-month follow-up evaluations demonstrated increased effective parenting, including a reduction in the use of harsh verbal and physical punishment (medium effects; Parent Behavior Checklist—Short

Form; Fox, 1994) at postintervention and 3-month follow-up. Qualitative focus group data indicated that parents reported benefits in discipline strategies.

A second multisite RCT (Knox et al., 2013) was conducted with 84 voluntary, Spanish- and English-speaking parents/caregivers at community health centers in the United States. Results collected at pre–post intervention and 3-month follow-up indicated significantly increased use of nonviolent discipline techniques and lower rates of physically aggressive behavior toward children compared with the control group.

A third RCT was conducted with 40 mothers in an ACT group and 41 mothers in a wait-list control group who participated voluntarily at a health center and two schools (Altafim & Linhares, 2019). Large effects were identified in "emotional and behavioral regulation" (mothers' reactions including spanking, hitting, and yelling as well as managing anger and calming down), showing positive changes for mothers in the ACT group relative to mothers in the wait-list control group. These improvements were maintained in the intervention group at the 3- to 4-month follow-up.

In one qualitative study in Japan, 80% of parents who used physical punishment reported that they decreased the frequency of physical punishment by the end of the program (Nishizawa, 2014).

Clearinghouse Registries

ACT is listed in the following registries:

- *California Evidence-Based Clearinghouse for Child Welfare.* ACT has been given the rating of "promising research evidence," the third highest rating. http://www.cebc4cw.org/program/safe-environment-for-every-kid-seek-model/detailed

- *Canadian Best Practices Portal, Public Health Agency of Canada.* ACT has been rated as a "promising practice." http://cbpp-pcpe.phac-aspc.gc.ca

- *Clearinghouse for Military Family Readiness,* Penn State and the U.S. Department of Defense. ACT has been given an "unclear +" rating. https://lion.militaryfamilies.psu.edu/about-us

- *Implementing Child Maltreatment Prevention Programmes: What the Experts Say,* World Health Organization. ACT is listed as an example program; no ratings or programs are provided. http://www.euro.who.int/__data/assets/pdf_file/0009/289602/Maltreatment_web.pdf?ua=1

- *Preventing Child Abuse and Neglect: A Technical Package for Policy, Norm, and Programmatic Activities,* Centers for Disease Control and Prevention. ACT is listed under the category of "parenting skill and family relationship approaches." No ratings are provided. https://www.cdc.gov/violenceprevention/pdf/can-prevention-technical-package.pdf

- *Results First Clearinghouse Database,* Pew Charitable Trusts: ACT has been given the "second-highest rated program" designation. https://

www.pewtrusts.org/pt/research-and-analysis/data-visualizations/2015/results-first-clearinghouse-database

Limitations

A few limitations to the research on the ACT program are worthy of mention. First, to date, follow-up evaluation of the outcomes of the ACT program has lasted a maximum of 3 to 4 months. To identify lasting changes and to capture changes in growth trajectories, longer-term follow-up studies are needed. Second, cost–benefit analyses would be necessary to determine if the benefits of the program outweigh the costs. Last, evaluations of the ACT program have not included moderator and mediator analyses. Therefore, research has not yet determined who benefits most from the ACT program and under what contexts and circumstances. These analyses would help direct program dissemination and allow those implementing the program to utilize scarce prevention resources in the most productive ways.

SUGGESTED FUTURE USE OF THE PROGRAM

How Clinicians Can Use the Intervention

Clinicians and other professionals trained as ACT facilitators may implement the program as a group program with their patients. Families experiencing all levels of risk are appropriate to participate in the ACT program. ACT facilitators typically conduct the nine sessions of the program over 9 weeks, with one session per week.

How Community Practitioners Can Use the Intervention

Similarly, community practitioners who are trained as ACT facilitators may implement the program with expecting parents as well as with parents and caregivers of children from birth to 8 years. Trained facilitators can deliver the program in a variety of settings, including social service locations, health and mental health organizations/agencies, Head Start centers, correctional facilities, child advocacy centers, military bases, residential facilities, child-care centers, schools, shelters, community centers, and faith-based organizations. The timing of the sessions can be adapted based on needs, such as more frequent sessions for parents living short-term in shelters.

How Policymakers Can Use the Intervention

Policymakers can support and help to disseminate the program as a component of effective initiatives designed to prevent children's exposure to maltreatment, create nurturing families, prevent community violence, build family resiliency, and secure positive outcomes for children.

INFORMATION ON OBTAINING THE PROGRAM

The 2-day facilitator training, which includes the ACT kit, costs from $250 to $380. For more information about how to obtain the program and participate in training sessions, visit the ACT website at http://www.apa.org/act. Resources are available at http://www.apa.org/act/resources/index.aspx. For more information, contact Julia Silva, Director, Office of Violence Prevention, American Psychological Association (jsilva@apa.org).

REFERENCES

Ainsworth, M. D. S. (1978). The Bowlby-Ainsworth attachment theory. *Behavioral and Brain Sciences, 1,* 436–438. http://dx.doi.org/10.1017/S0140525X00075828

Altafim, E. R. P., & Linhares, M. B. M. (2019). Preventive intervention for strengthening effective parenting practices: A randomized controlled trial. *Journal of Applied Developmental Psychology, 62,* 160–172. http://dx.doi.org/10.1016/j.appdev.2019.03.003

Anda, R. F., Felitti, V. J., Bremner, J. D., Walker, J. D., Whitfield, C., Perry, B. D., . . . Giles, W. H. (2006). The enduring effects of abuse and related adverse experiences of childhood. *European Archives of Psychiatry and Clinical Neuroscience, 256,* 174–186. http://dx.doi.org/10.1007/s00406-005-0624-4

Bandura, A. (1978). Social learning theory of aggression. *Journal of Communication, 28,* 12–29. http://dx.doi.org/10.1111/j.1460-2466.1978.tb01621.x

Corso, P. S., Edwards, V. J., Fang, X., & Mercy, J. A. (2008). Health-related quality of life among adults who experienced maltreatment during childhood. *American Journal of Public Health, 98,* 1094–1100. http://dx.doi.org/10.2105/AJPH.2007.119826

Fox, R. A. (1994). *Parent behavior checklist.* Austin, TX: ProEd.

Goodman, A., Joshi, H., Nasim, B., & Tyler, C. (2015). *Social and emotional skills in childhood and their long-term effects on adult life.* London, England: Institute of Education.

Hawkins, J. D., Kosterman, R., Catalano, R. F., Hill, K. G., & Abbott, R. D. (2005). Promoting positive adult functioning through social development intervention in childhood: Long-term effects from the Seattle Social Development Project. *Archives of Pediatrics and Adolescent Medicine, 159*(1), 25–31. http://dx.doi.org/10.1001/archpedi.159.1.25

Howe, T. R., Knox, M., Altafim, E. R. P., Linhares, M. B. M., Nishizawa, N., Fu, T. J., . . . Pereira, A. I. (2017). International child abuse prevention: Insights from ACT Raising Safe Kids. *Child and Adolescent Mental Health, 22,* 194–200. http://dx.doi.org/10.1111/camh.12238

Kaminski, J. W., Valle, L. A., Filene, J. H., & Boyles, C. L. (2008). A meta-analytic review of components associated with parent training program effectiveness. *Journal of Abnormal Child Psychology, 36,* 567–589. http://dx.doi.org/10.1007/s10802-007-9201-9

Knox, M., & Burkhart, K. (2014). A multi-site study of the ACT Raising Safe Kids Program: Predictors of outcomes and attrition. *Children and Youth Services Review, 39,* 20–24. http://dx.doi.org/10.1016/j.childyouth.2014.01.006

Knox, M., Burkhart, K., & Cromly, A. (2013). Supporting positive parenting in community health centers: The ACT Raising Safe Kids Program. *Journal of Community Psychology, 41,* 395–407. http://dx.doi.org/10.1002/jcop.21543

Knox, M., Burkhart, K., & Howe, T. (2011). Effects of the ACT Raising Safe Kids parenting program on children's externalizing problems. *Family Relations, 60,* 491–503. http://dx.doi.org/10.1111/j.1741-3729.2011.00662.x

Knox, M., Burkhart, K., & Hunter, K. E. (2011). ACT Against Violence Parents Raising Safe Kids Program: Effects on maltreatment-related parenting behaviors and beliefs. *Journal of Family Issues, 32,* 55–74. http://dx.doi.org/10.1177/0192513X10370112

Miller, W. R., & Rose, G. S. (2009). Toward a theory of motivational interviewing. *American Psychologist, 64,* 527–537. http://dx.doi.org/10.1037/a0016830

Nishizawa, N. (2014). *Adults and Children Together Against Violence Japanese translation project: Results from the second pilot program in Japan.* Unpublished manuscript.

Piquero, A. R., Jennings, W. G., Diamond, B., Farrington, D. P., Tremblay, R. E., Welsh, B. C., & Gonzalez, J. M. R. (2016). A meta-analysis update on the effects of early family/parent training programs on antisocial behavior and delinquency. *Journal of Experimental Criminology, 12,* 229–248. http://dx.doi.org/10.1007/s11292-016-9256-0

Porter, B. E., & Howe, T. R. (2008). Pilot evaluation of the ACT Parents Raising Safe Kids violence prevention program. *Journal of Child & Adolescent Trauma, 1,* 193–206. http://dx.doi.org/10.1080/19361520802279158

Portwood, S. G., Lambert, R. G., Abrams, L. P., & Nelson, E. B. (2011). An evaluation of the Adults and Children Together (ACT) Against Violence Parents Raising Safe Kids program. *The Journal of Primary Prevention, 32,* 147–160. http://dx.doi.org/10.1007/s10935-011-0249-5

Silva, J. (2011). *ACT facilitator manual: ACT Raising Safe Kids Program.* Washington, DC: American Psychological Association.

Straus, M. A., & Hamby, S. L. (1997). Measuring physical and psychological maltreatment of children with the Conflict Tactics Scales. In G. Kaufman Kantor & J. L. Jasinski (Eds.), *Out of the darkness: Contemporary perspectives on family violence* (pp. 119–135). Thousand Oaks, CA: Sage. http://dx.doi.org/10.4135/9781483328058.n1

Straus, M. A., Hamby, S. L., Finkelhor, D., Moore, D. W., & Runyan, D. (1998). Identification of child maltreatment with the Parent-Child Conflict Tactics Scales: Development and psychometric data for a national sample of American parents. *Child Abuse & Neglect: The International Journal, 22,* 249–270. http://dx.doi.org/10.1016/S0145-2134(97)00174-9

Taylor, S. E., Lerner, J. S., Sage, R. M., Lehman, B. J., & Seeman, T. E. (2004). Early environment, emotions, responses to stress, and health. *Journal of Personality, 72,* 1365–1394. http://dx.doi.org/10.1111/j.1467-6494.2004.00300.x

Thornton, T. N., Craft, C. A., Dahlberg, L. L., Lynch, B. S., & Baer, K. (2002). *Best practices of youth violence prevention: A sourcebook for community action* (Rev. ed.). Atlanta, GA: Centers for Disease Control and Prevention, National Center for Injury Prevention and Control. Retrieved from https://www.cdc.gov/violenceprevention/communicationresources/pub

11

The Chicago Parent Program

Susan M. Breitenstein, Deborah Gross, and Amie F. Bettencourt

THE INTERVENTION

The Chicago Parent Program (CPP) was developed by Deborah Gross, DNSc, RN, FAAN, of the Johns Hopkins University School of Nursing; Christine Garvey, PhD, RN, of Rush University College of Nursing; and Wrenetha Julion, PhD, RN, FAAN, of Rush University College of Nursing. The CPP's tablet-based companion program *ez*Parent was developed by Susan Breitenstein, PhD, RN, FAAN, of The Ohio State University College of Nursing and the three developers of CPP (Deborah Gross, Christine Garvey, and Wrenetha Julion). CPP and *ez*Parent can be used as a *universal* program for all parents, but they can also be used in a *selective* fashion for parents at risk for harsh parenting.

Background and Theory of Change

A large evidence base demonstrates the effectiveness of parent-focused interventions for improving parenting and child behavior in community and clinic settings (Comer, Chow, Chan, Cooper-Vince, & Wilson, 2013; Epstein, Fonnesbeck, Potter, Rizzone, & McPheeters, 2015; Furlong et al., 2012). However, most evidence-based programs for strengthening parenting skills and confidence were originally developed and tested on White, middle-class, well-educated parents (Forehand & Kotchick, 2016; Gross, Garvey, Julion, & Fogg, 2007). As a result, these programs may lack relevance for families living

http://dx.doi.org/10.1037/0000162-012
Ending the Physical Punishment of Children: A Guide for Clinicians and Practitioners,
E. T. Gershoff and S. J. Lee (Editors)

in poverty, many of whom have limited education and resources, and for families of color. The CPP was designed in collaboration with parents to address the needs of racially and ethnically diverse families raising young children in low-income communities.

The CPP is grounded in social learning theory (Bandura, 1997) and the coercive process model (Patterson, 1982), which posit that parents are powerful models and reinforcers of their children's behavior (both positive and negative behavior). CPP also incorporates attachment theory (Bowlby, 1982), which emphasizes the importance of young children having stable, responsive, and nurturing adults in their lives. In a manner consistent with social learning theory, parents learn vicariously by watching and critiquing vignettes depicting a range of common parenting situations, practicing skills using role play during group sessions, and applying the skills via standardized at-home practice assignments. Consistent with attachment theory, the CPP provides opportunities for parents to clarify their parenting values and goals and to apply strategies that create a positive, consistent, responsive, and nurturing environment to support their children's growth and learning.

The basic assumption underlying the CPP is that parents can learn how to be the change agents for promoting their children's strengths, managing challenging behavior, and nurturing their growth and development. The CPP helps parents clarify their goals for their children and learn how to apply a range of strategies for supporting those goals.

Main Goals of the Intervention

The CPP was designed for parents of children ages 2 to 5 years old because the preschool years are (a) a period of rapid emotional and behavioral change and (b) a critical period for parents to shape child behavior before behaviors become entrenched and difficult to change (Briggs-Gowan, Carter, Bosson-Heenan, Guyer, & Horwitz, 2006; Campbell, 2006; Humphries & Keenan, 2006). Therefore, the main goals of the CPP are to help parents (a) become clearer about their childrearing values and goals, (b) be more consistent with their parenting strategies, (c) feel more confident as parents, (d) replace physical or harsh discipline with positive discipline, (e) strengthen and promote interactions and relationships with their children, (f) promote child social–emotional development, and (g) decrease child misbehavior and behavior problems.

The *ez*Parent (online tablet version of the CPP) was adapted using the systematic method as described by Card, Solomon, and Cunningham (2011) to maintain consistency with the theoretical base and main goals of the CPP. Three key stakeholder groups (parents, the original program developers, and multimedia specialists) engaged in the process of identification of the core components of the CPP, development of the delivery model, assessment of and resolution of any discrepancies from CPP delivery, and full adaptation of the original program delivery strategy (Breitenstein, Shane, Julion, & Gross,

2015). The six-module *ez*Parent program contains the same core components, video vignettes, activities, and parenting strategies as does the group-based CPP.

Brief Description of the Intervention

The CPP consists of 11 weekly 2-hour sessions plus a 12th session held 4 to 6 weeks after the 11th session. The 11th session is a review of all material from weeks 1 through 10, and the 12th session is a booster session (Gross et al., 2007). The CPP is conducted in groups of up to 15 parents led by two trained group leaders. The following materials are required to implement CPP groups: the CPP group leader manual that supports group leader facilitation and parent handouts; videos for all sessions and a TV monitor/DVD or computer with projector; a room for 12 to 20 adults with chairs that can be moved to form a circle for discussion; a whiteboard, chalkboard, or large sheet of paper for making lists during group discussions; a meal or refreshments; and child care.

The *ez*Parent has six self-administered modules. The modules were developed to require no more than 1 hour each to complete; on average, parents spend 37.2 minutes per *ez*Parent module (Breitenstein, Brager, Ocampo, & Fogg, 2017). The *ez*Parent is an application that is accessed by parents via a phone or tablet running an Android operating system. To implement the *ez*Parent, users need an Android tablet or smartphone and the *ez*Parent application. The *ez*Parent is currently not formatted for iOS. A Wi-Fi connection is required to download *ez*Parent, but once it is on the device, parents can access the program without Wi-Fi access. In our current research projects, we provide tablets to parents to access the *ez*Parent and are testing the cost-effectiveness of this delivery method (Breitenstein, Schoeny, Risser, & Johnson, 2016).

Content Relevant to Spanking or Physical Punishment

The content of the CPP helps parents develop positive and effective parenting skills that either directly or indirectly assist them in decreasing their reliance on spanking and/or physical punishment. This is consistent with programs focused on reducing parents' use of physical punishment by guiding them to learn and apply positive parenting approaches to change their behavior (Gershoff, Lee, & Durrant, 2017; Kaminski, Valle, Filene, & Boyle, 2008).

The CPP was developed in collaboration with a parent advisory group of 12 low-income, African American and Latinx parents to ensure its cultural and contextual relevance for ethnic minority and low-income parents (Gross et al., 2009). The advisory group provided important guidance on how to optimally frame parenting strategies in a manner congruent with their values, lifestyle, and culture (Gross et al., 2007). The group advised that if program messaging took a hard line on the use of physical punishment (e.g., spanking), they believed parents would be less likely to disclose the type of discipline they use and might not engage in the program. Instead, they counseled that providing multiple alternative strategies and supporting and respecting parents' ideas and values were key to improving parenting practices and decreasing physical punishment. Therefore, the discussions facilitated by trained group leaders in the CPP and the activities in the *ez*Parent are integral to helping parents select, modify, and use the strategies in ways that make sense to each parent and tailor strategies to fit with their parenting values and goals. As parents used these new strategies and find them to be effective, program developers expected that the new strategies would replace physical punishment and parents' use of the latter would decrease over time.

A main guide to managing misbehavior taught in the CPP is the "8 Keys to Effective Discipline" (Gross et al., 2007). These keys were developed in collaboration with the parent advisory group and represent qualities parents need to keep in mind whenever they are disciplining their child, regardless of the strategy, and they help clarify the purposes of discipline, which is to teach, versus punishment, which is to inflict a penalty. For example, one key is that the discipline should be tied to a specific behavior (e.g., children need to know the specific thing they did wrong and what needs to change), and another key is that the discipline should be predictable (e.g., the discipline should happen whenever the misbehavior happens, not just when parents have had a bad day). The primary message of the 8 Keys to Effective Discipline is that by adopting these discipline approaches, parents are teaching children their expectations for behavior and family values in a safe and loving way.

Implementation of the Intervention

Since 2008, we have trained more than 700 CPP group leaders from the United States (nine states) and Canada. We estimate that more than 7,000 families have received the CPP. This includes parents in the community and those participating in research and evaluation studies of the CPP. Since 2015, the *ez*Parent has been received by 235 parents as part of research trials.

The CPP was developed to meet the needs of low-income African American and Latinx parents in the United States raising young children in urban communities. It has been adopted primarily in the Midwest, Northeast, and Mid-Atlantic regions of the United States. The CPP and the *ez*Parent have been used with culturally and socioeconomically diverse populations including African American, Latinx, White, Asian, and mixed-race families. Parents and agencies have used the CPP to meet requirements for parent training for child protective services in Illinois, Maryland, and Washington, DC.

The CPP has been implemented broadly in community agencies, outpatient mental health clinics, Head Start, Early Head Start, elementary schools, and preK programs. The *ez*Parent program has been delivered from pediatric primary care clinics and community-based agencies where parents are first introduced and given access to the *ez*Parent and then can complete the program at their convenience.

Evidence That Training of Program Staff Was Successful

All CPP groups are facilitated, in both professional and community-based settings, by two group leaders who complete the mandatory CPP group leader training. To date, more than 600 individuals have attended group leader training. At the end of each day of training, participants complete training evaluations. The majority of participants indicate an understanding of the CPP strategies and principles (99%), the role of the group leader (100%), how the different parts of the program work (99.7%), how to effectively lead groups (98.9%), and how to effectively use role play in the context of groups (99.6%), and they also feel confident that they could do a good job leading CPP groups (94.7%).

Evidence That Staff Had Buy-In and Like the Program

In 2015, we conducted a survey of group leaders who participated in CPP trainings between 2006 and 2015. Approximately 16% (n = 69/433) of trained group leaders responded to this survey. Sixty-three percent of respondents had run at least one CPP group at the time of the survey, and 97% of those who had led a group reported being satisfied (56%) or very satisfied (41%) with the CPP. In addition, respondents indicated using the CPP concepts in a variety of ways outside of the 12-session group format, including in their professional work with parents (75%), in interactions with coworkers (23%), in their personal lives to help their friends (34%), and in their own parenting (30%). Respondents shared positive qualitative feedback about the program. For example, one respondent noted that "the program is invaluable in providing examples for positive parenting techniques. The videos lead to very participatory discussions and brainstorming of what parents can do to manage misbehavior." Another respondent noted, "The program gives parents and leaders opportunities to self-reflect and then incorporate new tools and strategies for themselves and their families."

Evidence That Families Enjoy or Appreciate the Program

Between 2002 and 2018, the program was implemented as part of four research studies with low-income, predominantly African American and Latinx families whose children were attending child care centers, schools, and mental health clinics in Chicago and Baltimore. Parents who participated completed an end-of-program evaluation and reported high levels of satisfaction with the program (see Table 11.1). Specifically, a majority (78%–96%) of parents reported that their children's behaviors were better or much better than before they began the CPP (Bettencourt, Gross, & Breitenstein, 2018; Gross, Belcher, Budhathoki, Ofonedu, & Uveges, 2018; Gross et al., 2007). In addition, 95% of parents reported feeling more confident in managing their children's behaviors at home. Finally, 100% of parents who participated in CPP groups reported feeling satisfied or very satisfied with the CPP and would

TABLE 11.1. Parent Satisfaction With Chicago Parent Program Groups

Satisfaction variable[a]	Gross et al., 2007 (*N* = 135) Chicago	Breitenstein et al., 2012 (*N* = 267) Chicago	Bettencourt et al., 2018 (*N* = 288) Baltimore	Gross et al., 2018 (*N* = 79) Baltimore
Satisfied/very satisfied with CPP	NR	100%	99.7%	100%
Child behavior better/ much better than before	96%	NR	94.8%	78.3%
More/much more confident in managing child behavior	NR	NR	94.8%	NR
Recommend/highly recommend CPP to another parent	100%	100%	NR	100%

Note. CPP = Chicago Parent Program; NR = not reported.
[a]Parent report

recommend or highly recommend the program to another parent (Bettencourt et al., 2018; Breitenstein et al., 2012; Gross et al., 2018).

Evidence of Effectiveness From Outcome Evaluations

A pooled data set (n = 504) from two cluster randomized controlled trials (RCTs) conducted in Chicago child care centers from 2002 to 2011 was used to examine effects of the CPP (Breitenstein et al., 2012). In both RCTs, child care centers were purposively sampled for study inclusion and randomly assigned to either the CPP intervention or the control group. Parent self-report surveys and observational parent and child behavior assessments were completed at baseline, postintervention (3 months postbaseline), and follow-up at 6 months and 1 year postintervention. In addition, the child's teacher completed measures of child behavior in the classroom at each of the data collection time points.

In this analysis, only parents who self-reported as African American or Latinx were included, and they accounted for 94% (n = 504/538) of the total participant group across the two studies. Of these parents, 57.7% were African American and 42.3% were Latinx. Participants primarily identified as mothers (90%) and unmarried (74%). Mean parent age was 30.9 years (SD = 7.53 years). Fifty-four percent of the children were male, and their mean age was 2.81 years (SD = 0.73 years). Sixty percent of the sample reported an annual income of less than $20,000 and 31% an income of $20,000 to $40,000 a year.

Results of a multivariate repeated measures analysis of variance were significant, indicating overall treatment improvement in the intervention condition compared with the control (Breitenstein et al., 2012). Compared with controls, intervention parents showed significant improvements in parenting self-efficacy ($p < .01$), a decline in the use of physical punishment ($p < .01$), and more consistent discipline ($p < .05$). Significant effects were found from baseline to postintervention ($p < .05$), indicating a short-term improvement in parents' use of praise for the intervention group (Breitenstein et al., 2012).

Parents in the intervention group reported a reduction in their children's behavior problems based on the Intensity scale ($p < .05$) of the Eyberg Child Behavior Inventory but not on the Problem scale. At 1-year postintervention, children's teachers reported reductions in externalizing ($p < .01$) and internalizing ($p < .05$) behavior problems on the Caregiver–Teacher Report Form.

We tested the *ez*Parent in a small ($N = 79$) RCT with a sample of primarily single, low-income, ethnic minority (African American or Latinx) mothers of young children in Chicago (Breitenstein, Fogg, Ocampo, Acosta, & Gross, 2016). Parents receiving the intervention had significant improvements in parenting warmth compared with the control group. In addition, we examined the between-group effect-size magnitude for intervention group improvements in parenting warmth, use of physical punishment, follow through, parenting stress, and intensity of child behavior problems. Effect sizes for *ez*Parent were comparable to the group-based CPP and ranged from small to medium from baseline to 6 months postbaseline (Breitenstein, Fogg, et al., 2016).

Taken together, these results suggest that parents who receive the CPP content show improved use of effective and supportive discipline techniques and decrease their use of physical punishment. Indeed, these findings align with social learning theory such that as parents apply the new skills and strategies, their parenting self-efficacy improves, which in turn promotes continued use of positive parenting strategies. As parents become more consistent and confident in the use of strategies learned in the program and observe positive responses from their children, they engage in fewer negative responses to their children's misbehavior (yelling and physical punishment), which promotes child social and emotional development and strengthens parent–child relationships.

Clearinghouse Registries

The CPP is listed in the following registries:

- *California Evidence-Based Clearinghouse for Child Welfare (CEBC).* CPP has been given the rating of "supported by research evidence," the second highest rating. http://www.cebc4cw.org/program/chicago-parent-program
- *Clearinghouse for Military Family Readiness.* CPP has been given the rating of "promising," the second highest rating on their continuum of evidence. https://lion.militaryfamilies.psu.edu/programs/chicago-parent-program-cpp
- *Results First,* Pew Charitable Trusts. The CPP was designated as "highest rated" for promoting mental health. https://www.pewtrusts.org/pt/research-and-analysis/data-visualizations/2015/results-first-clearinghouse-database

Limitations

The CPP was originally designed to address the needs of parents of children ages 2 to 5 years old. To date, the CPP has not been validated for use with parents of infants under 2 years. Age-appropriate portions of CPP have been pilot tested with parents of infants with promising results.

SUGGESTED FUTURE USE OF THE PROGRAM

How Practitioners Can Use the Intervention

The CPP was developed as a 12-session, group-based parent management training intervention. Results of randomized trials and implementation studies have provided evidence of its effectiveness as a standalone program in public child care centers, schools, and community mental health agencies. The CPP research team is exploring ways to expand its use in community and health care settings and testing dissemination of the CPP through primary care via *ez*Parent. Efforts are also under way to integrate the use of *ez*Parent into home-visiting interventions. It is recommended that future work explore the impact of implementing the CPP in tandem with other evidence-based programs (e.g., behavior management training for teachers, social-skills groups for children) as part of a system-of-care approach to supporting families of young children.

Although they have not been formally tested, there are also multiple options for adapting the program for use by a variety of providers in their work one-on-one with families. For example, mental health clinicians can use the video vignettes, discussion questions, and role-play opportunities built into the program as tools to introduce and model the strategies for parents in the context of family therapy sessions before encouraging them to try the skills with their children. In addition, the concepts covered in the CPP may also be useful in training the early childhood workforce (e.g., providers in day care, child care, and preschool settings) in use of effective behavior management strategies.

How Policymakers Can Use the Intervention

Efforts are under way in many states to make evidence-based parent training interventions reimbursable through Medicaid. In light of the evidence base, policymakers are encouraged to seek similar approval for the CPP and integrate it into systems where families of young children receive services (e.g., universal preK, Head Start).

INFORMATION ON OBTAINING THE PROGRAM

Information on purchasing the CPP materials and *ez*Parent program or participating in the group leader training program can be found at http://www.chicagoparentprogram.org or by email at CPPinfo@chicagoparentprogram.org. Participation in the group leader training program is required to purchase CPP program materials. CPP curriculum costs include $699 for the CPP videos, $100 for the group leader manual, and $20/packet for session handouts (session handouts are available for all trained group leaders). Materials are available in English and Spanish.

Qualifications to be a CPP group leader include at least a high school diploma, excellent interpersonal skills, and experience working with adults and families. A mental health background is preferred but not required. Required training for CPP group leaders comprises two 8-hour training days. Training workshops are currently conducted in Chicago and Baltimore, and there is an option for on-site training. The group leader training workshops are facilitated by two certified CPP group leaders trained to run CPP workshops. The training includes a review of the theory underlying the CPP; instruction in the core strategies taught across the group sessions; instruction on group discussion, role-play activities, and the CPP group facilitation model; in vivo practice of group facilitation; and a posttest evaluation of training (trainees must achieve > 80% on this evaluation to complete training).

CPP group leaders can become certified group leaders. Certification is conducted through the CPP office and provides group leaders with expert feedback on group leading skills and documentation that group leaders have the essential skills for leading groups. To obtain certification, group leaders must facilitate at least two 12-session CPP groups and receive a minimum of three independent fidelity ratings meeting certification criteria. Feedback is provided using the Fidelity Checklist to assess group leader competence and adherence (Breitenstein et al., 2010). Independent raters who have been trained to reliability complete the fidelity assessments. To date, 30 group leaders have become certified. A half-day training is available to individuals who are interested in using and supporting parent use of the *ez*Parent program in their sites. The training includes a review of the theory underlying the CPP, core strategies in the program, and how the *ez*Parent program works. Additional information about CPP can be obtained from Deborah Gross, DNSc, RN, FAAN (debgross@jhu.edu or CPPinfo@chicagoparentprogram.org). Additional information and purchasing information about the CPP and *ez*Parent can be obtained from Susan M. Breitenstein, PhD, RN, FAAN (breitenstein.5@osu.edu or CPPinfo@chicagoparentprogram.org).

REFERENCES

Bandura, A. (1997). *Self-efficacy: The exercise of control*. New York, NY: W. H. Freeman/Times Books/Henry Holt.

Bettencourt, A. F., Gross, D., & Breitenstein, S. (2018). Evaluating implementation fidelity of a school-based parenting program for low-income families. *The Journal of School Nursing*. Advance online publication. http://dx.doi.org/10.1177/1059840518786995

Bowlby, J. (1982). *Attachment and loss: Vol. 1. Attachment* (2nd ed.). New York, NY: Basic Books.

Breitenstein, S. M., Brager, J., Ocampo, E. V., & Fogg, L. (2017). Engagement and adherence with *ez*Parent, an mHealth parent-training program promoting child well-being. *Child Maltreatment, 22*, 295–304. http://dx.doi.org/10.1177/1077559517725402

Breitenstein, S. M., Fogg, L., Garvey, C., Hill, C., Resnick, B., & Gross, D. (2010). Measuring implementation fidelity in a community-based parenting intervention. *Nursing Research, 59*, 158–165. http://dx.doi.org/10.1097/NNR.0b013e3181dbb2e2

Breitenstein, S. M., Fogg, L., Ocampo, E. V., Acosta, D. I., & Gross, D. (2016). Parent use and efficacy of a self-administered, tablet-based parent training intervention: A randomized controlled trial. *JMIR mHealth and uHealth, 4*(2), e36. http://dx.doi.org/10.2196/mhealth.5202

Breitenstein, S. M., Gross, D., Fogg, L., Ridge, A., Garvey, C., Julion, W., & Tucker, S. (2012). The Chicago Parent Program: Comparing 1-year outcomes for African American and Latino parents of young children. *Research in Nursing & Health, 35,* 475–489. http://dx.doi.org/10.1002/nur.21489

Breitenstein, S. M., Schoeny, M., Risser, H., & Johnson, T. (2016). A study protocol testing the implementation, efficacy, and cost effectiveness of the ezParent program in pediatric primary care. *Contemporary Clinical Trials, 50,* 229–237. http://dx.doi.org/10.1016/j.cct.2016.08.017

Breitenstein, S. M., Shane, J., Julion, W., & Gross, D. (2015). Developing the *e*CPP: Adapting an evidence-based parent training program for digital delivery in primary care settings. *Worldviews on Evidence-Based Nursing, 12*(1), 31–40. http://dx.doi.org/10.1111/wvn.12074

Briggs-Gowan, M. J., Carter, A. S., Bosson-Heenan, J., Guyer, A. E., & Horwitz, S. M. (2006). Are infant-toddler social-emotional and behavioral problems transient? *Journal of the American Academy of Child & Adolescent Psychiatry, 45,* 849–858. http://dx.doi.org/10.1097/01.chi.0000220849.48650.59

Campbell, S. B. (2006). *Behavior problems in preschool children: Clinical and developmental issues* (2nd ed.). New York, NY: Guilford Press.

Card, J. J., Solomon, J., & Cunningham, S. D. (2011). How to adapt effective programs for use in new contexts. *Health Promotion Practice, 12*(1), 25–35. http://dx.doi.org/10.1177/1524839909348592

Comer, J. S., Chow, C., Chan, P. T., Cooper-Vince, C., & Wilson, L. A. S. (2013). Psychosocial treatment efficacy for disruptive behavior problems in very young children: A meta-analytic examination. *Journal of the American Academy of Child & Adolescent Psychiatry, 52*(1), 26–36. http://dx.doi.org/10.1016/j.jaac.2012.10.001

Epstein, R. A., Fonnesbeck, C., Potter, S., Rizzone, K. H., & McPheeters, M. (2015). Psychosocial interventions for child disruptive behaviors: A meta-analysis. *Pediatrics, 136,* 947–960. http://dx.doi.org/10.1542/peds.2015-2577

Forehand, R., & Kotchick, B. A. (2016). Cultural diversity: A wake-up call for parent training—republished article. *Behavior Therapy, 47,* 981–992. http://dx.doi.org/10.1016/j.beth.2016.11.010

Furlong, M., McGilloway, S., Bywater, T., Hutchings, J., Smith, S. M., & Donnelly, M. (2012, February 15). Behavioural and cognitive-behavioural group-based parenting programmes for early-onset conduct problems in children aged 3 to 12 years. *Cochrane Database of Systematic Reviews, 2012*(2), CD008225. http://dx.doi.org/10.1002/14651858.CD008225.pub2

Gershoff, E. T., Lee, S. J., & Durrant, J. E. (2017). Promising intervention strategies to reduce parents' use of physical punishment. *Child Abuse & Neglect: The International Journal, 71,* 9–23. http://dx.doi.org/10.1016/j.chiabu.2017.01.017

Gross, D., Belcher, H. M. E., Budhathoki, C., Ofonedu, M. E., & Uveges, M. K. (2018). Does parent training format affect treatment engagement? A randomized study of families at social risk. *Journal of Child and Family Studies, 27,* 1579–1593. http://dx.doi.org/10.1007/s10826-017-0984-1

Gross, D., Garvey, C., Julion, W., & Fogg, L. (2007). Preventive parent training with low-income ethnic minority parents of preschoolers. In J. M. Briesmeister & C. E. Schaefer (Eds.), *Handbook of parent training: Helping parents prevent and solve problem behaviors* (3rd ed., pp. 5–24). New York, NY: John Wiley & Sons.

Gross, D., Garvey, C., Julion, W., Fogg, L., Tucker, S., & Mokros, H. (2009). Efficacy of the Chicago parent program with low-income African American and Latino parents of young children. *Prevention Science, 10*(1), 54–65. http://dx.doi.org/10.1007/s11121-008-0116-7

Humphries, M. L., & Keenan, K. E. (2006). Theoretical, developmental & cultural orientations of school-based prevention programs for preschoolers. *Clinical Child and Family Psychology Review, 9*, 135–148. http://dx.doi.org/10.1007/s10567-006-0005-1

Kaminski, J. W., Valle, L. A., Filene, J. H., & Boyle, C. L. (2008). A meta-analytic review of components associated with parent training program effectiveness. *Journal of Abnormal Child Psychology, 36*, 567–589. http://dx.doi.org/10.1007/s10802-007-9201-9

Patterson, G. R. (1982). *Coercive family process*. Eugene, OR: Castalia.

12

The Moms' Empowerment Program

Andrew Grogan-Kaylor, Kathryn H. Howell, Maria M. Galano, and Sandra A. Graham-Bermann

THE INTERVENTION

The Moms' Empowerment Program (MEP) is a 10-session brief intervention and support program for women who have experienced intimate partner violence (IPV). It was created by Sandra A. Graham-Bermann, PhD, of the University of Michigan. MEP is an *indicated* program because it targets women who have already been victims of IPV.

Background and Theory of Change

IPV is defined as physical assault, sexual assault, stalking, psychological aggression, and threats of serious harm or death engaged in by one intimate partner against another (Breiding, Basile, Smith, Black, & Mahendra, 2015). Millions of women in the United States experience IPV. Specifically, one in three women experience IPV in their lifetime, with approximately 7 million women experiencing IPV each year (Black et al., 2011). Racial and ethnic disparities in IPV victimization have been documented, with 54% of multiracial women, 44% of Black women, and 37% of Hispanic women reporting lifetime IPV exposure, compared with 35% of White women (Black et al., 2011).

The development and evaluation of the Moms' Empowerment Program has been supported by grants from the Centers for Disease Control and Prevention and the Blue Cross and Blue Shield of Michigan Foundation.

http://dx.doi.org/10.1037/0000162-013
Ending the Physical Punishment of Children: A Guide for Clinicians and Practitioners,
E. T. Gershoff and S. J. Lee (Editors)

The effects of IPV are numerous and, without intervention, are enduring. For example, women who have experienced IPV are at high risk for depression, anxiety, traumatic stress, posttraumatic stress disorder, and physical health difficulties (Bonomi et al., 2006; Clark, Grogan-Kaylor, Galano, Stein, & Graham-Bermann, 2018; Lagdon, Armour, & Stringer, 2014). Researchers have noted that survivors of IPV have lower self-esteem, higher overall distress, and less access to social support that mediates the negative effects of exposure to violence (Beeble, Bybee, Sullivan, & Adams, 2009; Bonomi et al., 2006). Studies also show 2 to 3 times higher rates of major depression for this population than for nonabused women, which is indicative of low mood, exhaustion, sadness, and hopelessness (Beydoun, Beydoun, Kaufman, Lo, & Zonderman, 2012).

Traumatic stress symptoms are widespread in women who have experienced IPV. Several studies show rates of posttraumatic stress disorder from 33% to 85%, with virtually all women reporting some symptoms of posttraumatic stress (Graham-Bermann & Miller, 2013; Mignone, Papagni, Mahadeo, Klostermann, & Jones, 2017). Symptoms of traumatic stress can interfere with daily living and include having nightmares or other intrusive reminders of the violence, being hypervigilant or on guard, having negative mood and cognitions, and avoiding feelings or places associated with the violence (American Psychiatric Association, 2013). Among the physical health challenges faced by women who experience IPV are being less healthy overall and having more chronic health disorders, as well as gynecological problems associated with sexual assaults (Dillon, Hussain, Loxton, & Rahman, 2013). Other researchers have associated chronic exposure to distress (e.g., IPV) with compromised immune functioning that can contribute to developing asthma, arthritis, and high blood pressure (Wang et al., 2017). In addition to all the health problems faced by women who experience IPV are the costs for mental and physical health care as well as the estimated US$8 billion a year in lost wages (Centers for Disease Control and Prevention, 2003; Max, Rice, Finkelstein, Bardwell, & Leadbetter, 2004).

The consequences of IPV exposure are pronounced among women who are also parenting children amidst this violence (Ahlfs-Dunn & Huth-Bocks, 2016), with each of the effects of IPV impinging on mothers' efforts to parent effectively (Levendosky & Graham-Bermann, 2001). Approximately 40% of children who are exposed to IPV are in the clinical range on adjustment problems—including anxiety, depression, and conduct disorder or delinquency—and the task of parenting under the stress of IPV becomes extremely difficult (Graham-Bermann, Gruber, Howell, & Girz, 2009; Grogan-Kaylor et al., 2019). Although the need for safety, connection to resources, and financial support are paramount, women who have experienced IPV commonly request help with the challenges they face in parenting their children.

MEP is based on an empowerment model (Cattaneo & Goodman, 2015) with a focus on both the process of change and the outcome of change. Elements of empowerment are emphasized throughout the intervention, with the MEP aiming to enhance social and instrumental supports, coping skills, and caregiving knowledge (Graham-Bermann, 2018). By providing psychoeducation, teaching problem solving and conflict resolution skills, and assisting women in clarifying and attaining their goals, participants in the MEP may become more hopeful and empowered. By observing their progress toward goals, receiving support and feedback from other members of the group, and recognizing and sharing the changes they have made, women can evaluate and track their success. In addition to enhancing empowerment, women's mental health is also targeted for improvement via intervention participation. Specifically, women are guided through the process of naming problems in their lives, describing the effects of IPV on themselves and their children, and making plans to obtain resources and to address life stressors. Elements of the MEP that focus on parenting are designed to assist women in learning new parenting and disciplinary skills or building upon existing skills to better manage and reduce their child's psychosocial and behavioral problems. The effects are transactional, such that successful parenting reduces children's adjustment problems while also enhancing mother's well-being and increasing her self-efficacy (Miller, Howell, & Graham-Bermann, 2014).

Main Goals of the Intervention

The MEP was designed to provide support for women to talk about and process the effects of IPV on themselves and their children and to address parenting issues in the context of a supportive group of women with similar experiences (Graham-Bermann, 2011). The program aims to reduce women's exposure to violence, to enhance their mental health, and to improve their parenting practices in order to reduce their children's adjustment problems.

Brief Description of the Intervention

The MEP is delivered as a group-based intervention with 10 sessions, each lasting 1 hour. Group leaders are trained in implementing the program and are service providers at agencies, licensed professionals, or graduate students in psychology or social work. The materials that are needed for the intervention are the training DVD and the training manual. The latter includes handouts that can be copied to give to the group members concerning safety planning, defining IPV, child discipline, stress reduction, and information about community resources.

Content Relevant to Spanking and Physical Punishment

Three MEP sessions were specifically designed to address parenting in terms of the women's (a) parenting fears and worries, (b) parenting in their family of origin, and (c) current management of child behavior. In general, women in the MEP express many fears about their children as well as experience many difficulties in effectively managing their children's behavior. Because women in the groups tend to have many concerns in this area, disciplining children and utilizing physical punishment are always discussed as part of the MEP. This topic often emerges during the family-of-origin session, as many of the women who have participated in the group share that they experienced physical punishment as children. The topic of physical punishment is then directly addressed in a later session of the MEP when disciplining children is discussed.

Women endorse using a range of disciplinary strategies, from taking away privileges to giving extra chores to time-out, yelling, and spanking. Women in the groups have a range of responses to the topic of physical punishment. Some of the women who have participated in the MEP express the belief that spanking is an effective form of managing problem behaviors and use it as one of their primary forms of discipline. Often, these same mothers will state that they really do not know any other strategies for disciplining problem behavior. Other mothers state that they believe spanking should be used as a last resort or in response to really bad behavior—for example, one woman stated that she spanked her child after that child was arrested for shoplifting at age 12. Finally, some women in the group state that they actively avoid using any form of physical punishment out of fear that they will lose control and hurt their children or because they do not want to add to the level of hitting and violence their children already witness related to the IPV. Regardless of where they fall in this spectrum, the group members are always provided with evidence demonstrating that physical punishment is not an effective form of discipline. Women in the group are generally open to hearing this psychoeducation and are often willing to learn and practice alternative forms of discipline, like time-out or having a constructive talk with their child.

Implementation of the Intervention

The MEP has been implemented successfully in shelters for abused women and their children, at Catholic Social Services in Michigan, at community centers, and at mental health clinics. It has also been used in conjunction with child protective services in Windsor, Ontario, Canada. The MEP intervention has served more than 2,000 families in a number of states, including Alaska, and in Sweden, Australia, and Canada. Participants to date have included mothers of children ages 3 to 13 years, and the program is appropriate for mothers with school-age children. The MEP is available in English and Spanish and has been used with families from a range of cultural backgrounds, including African American, biracial, White, Latina, Native American/Alaskan Indian, and Swedish.

Evidence of Feasibility From Process Evaluations

In the randomized controlled trial evaluation of the program, women were asked an open-ended question as to what they considered to be the benefits of participating in the MEP. Their most common response was the support received from the other women in the group. They also appreciated the support of the group leaders and group-level discussions. The ability to consult with the group leaders, particularly around issues related to parenting, was mentioned frequently. The women felt that the group leaders were helpful and knowledgeable. Finally, they remarked on their gains in self-confidence as a great benefit of this program.

Evidence of Effectiveness From Outcome Evaluations

Research has suggested that the MEP is associated with reductions in parental use of physical punishment. In a study of the MEP conducted in 2016, Grogan-Kaylor and colleagues (2019) used multilevel modeling to examine the trajectory of mothers' use of physical punishment. Mothers' use of physical punishment was assessed at a pretest, a posttest immediately following the 10 sessions, and a long-term follow-up collected 6 to 8 months after the intervention had concluded. These authors found that participation in the MEP was associated with reductions in the use of physical punishment at posttest (immediately following the 10 intervention sessions). These reductions in use of physical punishment were maintained at the 6- to 8-month follow-up. Mothers in the control group did not reduce their use of physical punishment over time.

The effectiveness of the MEP in enhancing broader positive parenting practices was first evaluated in a sample of 181 women from diverse ethnoracial groups who experienced IPV and who had school-age children (Graham-Bermann & Miller-Graff, 2015). They were randomly assigned to treatment and comparison groups. Their parenting and mental health were assessed with standardized measures before and after the intervention period, then 8 months later. Women who participated in the MEP showed the greatest improvement over time in both positive parenting and depression. It is notable that parenting grew worse over time for the comparison-group women.

A second study evaluated 120 mothers of preschool-age children who experienced recent and severe IPV, half of whom were randomly assigned to receive the MEP intervention and half of whom were randomly assigned to a wait-list control condition (Howell et al., 2015). Mothers participating in MEP were interviewed at baseline and immediately following the intervention. Their parenting abilities were compared with women in a wait-list control group who did not receive services. After mother age, child age, child sex, IPV severity, mental health, and baseline parenting abilities were controlled for, group assignment was a significant predictor of change in positive parenting scores from baseline to follow-up. Women showed significantly more change in their positive parenting scores if they were in the MEP. This study indicated that the MEP was successful in strengthening positive parenting practices, which include consistency, use of positive reinforcement, parental involvement, and consistent monitoring, among women who have experienced IPV.

Clearinghouse Registries

MEP is listed in the following registries:

- *The California Evidence-Based Clearinghouse for Child Welfare*. MEP has been given the rating of "promising research evidence." http://www.cebc4cw.org/program/kids-club-moms-empowerment
- *Results First Clearinghouse Database*, Pew Charitable Trusts. MEP has been given the "second highest rated program" designation. https://www.pewtrusts.org/pt/research-and-analysis/data-visualizations/2015/results-first-clearinghouse-database

Limitations

MEP research is mostly driven by measures that are collected via self-report from the mothers. Therefore, responses may be influenced to some degree by considerations of social desirability.

SUGGESTED FUTURE USE OF THE PROGRAM

How Clinicians Can Use the Intervention

MEP addresses the numerous issues that women exposed to IPV face and highlights that many factors lead to the use of physical punishment in the context of IPV. In working with parents who have experienced IPV and are attempting to change their disciplinary strategies, it is likely important for clinicians to address the way that parents were raised and disciplined. As was the case for many of the women who have participated in the intervention, it may be that the use of physical punishment was normalized as a result of their childhood experiences of discipline. It is also important for clinicians to recognize that parents who experience IPV often struggle with depression, trauma, and other mental health problems. In cases when children's behaviors act as a trigger for traumatic stress symptoms, which is especially true when children act aggressively or hit, women have to actively down-regulate their own intense emotions while also trying to effectively parent. These intense emotions may then lead a parent to react by yelling or hitting. Thus, a clinician may have to spend more time on emotion regulation as a part of the parenting intervention when working with an abused parent than they typically would with a nonabused parent.

How Community Practitioners Can Use the Intervention

The information in the MEP can be used in community settings to provide important parenting resources and support to abused women. It is especially important to share resources around parenting and the use of nonphysical disciplinary strategies. Furthermore, this program is designed to be implemented in community settings by community providers, given that they have received training in the intervention and are being supervised by someone who has experience with the program. Thus, community practitioners can incorporate this program into the current services that they have for women who experience IPV—for example, this program could be part of the support a woman receives while staying in a domestic violence shelter.

How Policymakers Can Use the Intervention

The MEP is an evidence-based intervention for women who experience IPV that improves parenting behaviors and reduces women's mental health problems as a result of IPV. Because this is a brief intervention delivered to groups of women in community settings, the MEP is also a cost-effective way of supporting women and children who are victims of domestic violence. Thus, policymakers should consider the broad implementation of this program into domestic violence shelters and community organizations that support abused women as a way of simultaneously addressing two important public health problems: IPV and physical punishment.

INFORMATION ON OBTAINING THE PROGRAM

Information on obtaining the program is available at http://grahambermann.simplesite.com. Implementation of the program requires in-person training for the group leaders. There are now several trainers certified by the program developer in the United States and in Sweden. For further information or to arrange a training, contact the project developer, Dr. Sandra Graham-Bermann (sandragb@umich.edu).

REFERENCES

Ahlfs-Dunn, S. M., & Huth-Bocks, A. C. (2016). Intimate partner violence involving children and the parenting role: Associations with maternal outcomes. *Journal of Family Violence, 31*, 387–399. http://dx.doi.org/10.1007/s10896-015-9791-x

American Psychiatric Association. (2013). *Diagnostic and statistical manual of mental disorders* (5th ed.). Washington, DC: Author.

Beeble, M. L., Bybee, D., Sullivan, C. M., & Adams, A. E. (2009). Main, mediating, and moderating effects of social support on the well-being of survivors of intimate partner violence across 2 years. *Journal of Consulting and Clinical Psychology, 77*, 718–729. http://dx.doi.org/10.1037/a0016140

Beydoun, H. A., Beydoun, M. A., Kaufman, J. S., Lo, B., & Zonderman, A. B. (2012). Intimate partner violence against adult women and its association with major depressive disorder, depressive symptoms and postpartum depression: A systematic review and meta-analysis. *Social Science & Medicine, 75*, 959–975. http://dx.doi.org/10.1016/j.socscimed.2012.04.025

Black, M. C., Basile, K. C., Breiding, M. J., Smith, S. G., Walters, M. L., Merrick, M. T., . . . Stevens, M. R. (2011). *The National Intimate Partner and Sexual Violence*

Survey (NISVS): 2010 Summary Report. Atlanta, GA: National Center for Injury Prevention and Control, Centers for Disease Control and Prevention.

Bonomi, A. E., Thompson, R. S., Anderson, M., Reid, R. J., Carrell, D., Dimer, J. A., & Rivara, F. P. (2006). Intimate partner violence and women's physical, mental, and social functioning. *American Journal of Preventive Medicine, 30,* 458–466. http://dx.doi.org/10.1016/j.amepre.2006.01.015

Breiding, M. J., Basile, K. C., Smith, S. G., Black, M. C., & Mahendra, R. R. (2015). *Intimate partner violence surveillance: Uniform definitions and recommended data elements, Version 2.0.* Atlanta, GA: National Center for Injury Prevention and Control, Centers for Disease Control and Prevention.

Cattaneo, L. B., & Goodman, L. A. (2015). What is empowerment anyway? A model for domestic violence practice, research, and evaluation. *Psychology of Violence, 5*(1), 84–94. http://dx.doi.org/10.1037/a0035137

Centers for Disease Control and Prevention. (2003). *Costs of intimate partner violence against women in the United States.* Atlanta, GA: National Center for Injury Prevention and Control.

Clark, H. M., Grogan-Kaylor, A. C., Galano, M. M., Stein, S. F., & Graham-Bermann, S. A. (2018). Moms' empowerment program participation associated with improved physical health among Latinas experiencing intimate partner violence. *Revista Panamericana de Salud Pública/Pan American Journal of Public Health, 42,* e39. http://dx.doi.org/10.26633/RPSP.2018.39

Dillon, G., Hussain, R., Loxton, D., & Rahman, S. (2013). Mental and physical health and intimate partner violence against women: A review of the literature. *International Journal of Family Medicine, 2013,* 313909. http://dx.doi.org/10.1155/2013/313909

Graham-Bermann, S. A. (2011). *The Moms' Empowerment Program: A training manual.* Ann Arbor: Department of Psychology, University of Michigan.

Graham-Bermann, S. A. (Ed.). (2018). *Cultural considerations in intervention with women and children exposed to intimate partner violence.* Hauppauge, NY: Nova Science.

Graham-Bermann, S. A., Gruber, G., Howell, K. H., & Girz, L. (2009). Factors discriminating among profiles of resilience and psychopathology in children exposed to intimate partner violence (IPV). *Child Abuse & Neglect: The International Journal, 33,* 648–660. http://dx.doi.org/10.1016/j.chiabu.2009.01.002

Graham-Bermann, S. A., & Miller, L. E. (2013). Intervention to reduce traumatic stress following intimate partner violence: An efficacy trial of the Moms' Empowerment Program (MEP). *Psychodynamic Psychiatry, 41,* 329–349. http://dx.doi.org/10.1521/pdps.2013.41.2.329

Graham-Bermann, S. A., & Miller-Graff, L. (2015). Community-based intervention for women exposed to intimate partner violence: A randomized control trial. *Journal of Family Psychology, 29,* 537–547. http://dx.doi.org/10.1037/fam0000091

Grogan-Kaylor, A. C., Galano, M., Howell, K. H., Miller-Graff, L. E., & Graham-Bermann, S. A. (2019). Reductions in parental use of corporal punishment on pre-school children following participation in the Moms' Empowerment Program. *Journal of Interpersonal Violence, 34,* 1563–1582. http://dx.doi.org/10.1177/0886260516651627

Howell, K. H., Miller, L. E., Lilly, M. M., Burlaka, V., Grogan-Kaylor, A. C., & Graham-Bermann, S. A. (2015). Strengthening positive parenting through intervention: Evaluating the Moms' Empowerment Program for women experiencing intimate partner violence. *Journal of Interpersonal Violence, 30,* 232–252. http://dx.doi.org/10.1177/0886260514533155

Lagdon, S., Armour, C., & Stringer, M. (2014). Adult experience of mental health outcomes as a result of intimate partner violence victimisation: A systematic review. *European Journal of Psychotraumatology, 5*(1), 24794. http://dx.doi.org/10.3402/ejpt.v5.24794

Levendosky, A. A., & Graham-Bermann, S. A. (2001). Parenting in battered women: The effects of domestic violence on women and children. *Journal of Family Violence, 16,* 171–192. http://dx.doi.org/10.1023/A:1011111003373

Max, W., Rice, D. P., Finkelstein, E., Bardwell, R. A., & Leadbetter, S. (2004). The economic toll of intimate partner violence against women in the United States. *Violence and Victims, 19,* 259–272. http://dx.doi.org/10.1891/vivi.19.3.259.65767

Mignone, T., Papagni, E., Mahadeo, M., Klostermann, K., & Jones, R. A. (2017). PTSD and intimate partner violence: Clinical considerations and treatment options. *Journal of Addiction Medicine and Therapeutic Science, 3*(1), 001–006. http://dx.doi.org/10.17352/2455-3484.000018

Miller, L. E., Howell, K. H., & Graham-Bermann, S. A. (2014). The effect of an evidence-based intervention on women's exposure to intimate partner violence. *American Journal of Orthopsychiatry, 84,* 321–328. http://dx.doi.org/10.1037/h0099840

Wang, L., Chernov, C., Nolan, V., Perlman, S., Relyea, G., Mzayek, F., & Gwynn, C. (2017). Predictors of high allostatic load in New York City residents, NYC HANES 2013–14. *Annals of Epidemiology, 27,* 510. http://dx.doi.org/10.1016/j.annepidem.2017.07.077

IV

MULTILEVEL OR UNIVERSAL INTERVENTIONS

13

Triple P—Positive Parenting Program

Ronald J. Prinz

THE INTERVENTION

Over multiple decades, Matthew R. Sanders, PhD, from the University of Queensland, developed the Triple P—Positive Parenting Program. The full Triple P system is a blend of universal, selective, and indicated preventive interventions. The system itself is designed for universal access by the general population of parents, but there are programs within the system that are more targeted. For example, Stepping Stones Triple P is a *selective* intervention for parents of a child with developmental disabilities. The more intensive Triple P interventions (Levels 4 and 5) are more likely to be oriented toward indicated populations (e.g., families with children who have elevated behavior problems).

Background and Theory of Change

The Triple P—Positive Parenting Program is a multifaceted and multitiered system of programs for parenting and family support (Sanders, 2008, 2012). An optimal approach to implementation involves deployment of the entire

---

The author has received funding on family-based interventions including Triple P from the Centers for Disease Control and Prevention and the National Institutes of Health. He has been a consultant to Triple P International, which is the joint-venture entity of the University of Queensland responsible for the dissemination of the Triple P system of interventions.

http://dx.doi.org/10.1037/0000162-014
Ending the Physical Punishment of Children: A Guide for Clinicians and Practitioners,
E. T. Gershoff and S. J. Lee (Editors)

Triple P system to achieve universal population impact, which is being undertaken in some communities and jurisdictions. But it is also possible to implement specific programs from the system without adopting the entire system. Triple P has multiple levels, delivery formats, and specialized variants. The Triple P system is organized into five levels of increasing intensity, from Level 1, which is a communitywide media and communication strategy, to Level 5, which involves intensive family intervention. Another dimension of Triple P programs is delivery format, which provides flexibility and choice for parents. Triple P variants for specialized populations include

- Family Transitions Triple P for parents going through separation or divorce;
- Lifestyle Triple P for parents of children of overweight or obese status;
- Pathways Triple P for parents who have engaged in, or are at high risk to engage in, child maltreatment; and
- Stepping Stones Triple P for parents of children with developmental disabilities.

All of the programs in the Triple P system share a unifying theoretical framework, are grounded in the same guiding principles of positive parenting, and draw from a common pool of specific parenting techniques and strategies.

Triple P focuses on fostering positive parenting for the promotion of children's optimal development. The intervention strategies found in Triple P belong to a broader class of interventions that emerged in the 1970s. Prior to that, the prevailing paradigm for mental health treatment based on psychoanalytic conceptualizations was beginning to be replaced by a new paradigm emphasizing the impact of the social environment. Child mental health experienced this shift more quickly than did adult mental health, in part because the impact of the family environment on children was readily apparent. A key tenet of the approach was that parents were well positioned to influence the social–environmental conditions at home and elsewhere to improve their children's lives (Kazdin, 2008; Patterson, 1976; Wahler, 1969). Accordingly, Triple P began as a coaching model with parents in the home, making use of principles from applied behavior analysis. Triple P evolved to become a transtheoretical model that integrates empirically supported principles of behavioral, cognitive, and affective change at a population level, further informed by research on self-regulation, attachment, family systems, and public health strategy (Sanders & Prinz, 2018).

There are several rationales for adopting a population approach to parenting support such as Triple P. Many parents are uncertain or lack confidence to address childrearing challenges they encounter at various points in their children's development. At the adverse end of the parenting continuum, problematic parenting practices bordering on abuse are much more common than official child protective services records reflect (Theodore et al., 2005). Adopting a population approach to parenting support potentially avoids the stigma that might arise from singling out parents as high-risk. Finally, a population approach increases the likelihood that several problem areas can be impacted by the same parenting support intervention, such as prevention of child maltreatment; promotion of positive adjustment at school entry; prevention of social, emotional, and behavioral problems; and risk reduction for adolescent delinquency, substance abuse, and school dropout.

Triple P programs are guided by five core principles of positive parenting: (a) ensuring a safe, engaging, and healthy environment for children; (b) having a positive learning environment; (c) using assertive, consistent, and nonviolent discipline; (d) having reasonable expectations of children and oneself as a parent; and (e) taking care of oneself. These principles are somewhat elastic, but all are deemed important if parents are to succeed in promoting children's development by imparting the social and emotional skills they need to thrive.

Parents are often looking for practical guidance and specific actions to solve childrearing challenges, and that can be obtained through Triple P without committing to a long and intensive program. Some parents might be seeking more extensive parenting support. In either instance, Triple P taps into self-regulatory processes that empower parents by emphasizing collaborative goal setting, parental selection of parenting strategies, facilitating parental access to additional resources for self-help, and avoiding long-term parental dependence on professional assistance (Sanders & Mazzucchelli, 2013). With respect to processes for change, Triple P makes use of modeling, self-monitoring, and constructive self-evaluation; coaching and feedback; provision of detailed information in a wide menu of specific parenting strategies; and normalization of parenting experiences (Sanders & Mazzucchelli, 2018).

Main Goals of the Intervention

The main goals of Triple P can be described at two levels—the first in terms of intervention at the family level and the second in terms of the system as a public health strategy at the population level. The Triple P goals for family-level intervention contribute to, and inform, the goals for population-level implementation.

At the family level, the main goals of Triple P are to support parents (a) in their efforts to create or further enhance a nurturing environment that will allow children to grow up healthy and well-adjusted, (b) in establishing or maintaining a warm and responsive relationship with their children, and (c) in acquiring the knowledge, skills, and confidence necessary to promote children's optimal development. These goals are guided by the five principles of positive parenting articulated earlier.

The main goals of the Triple P system as a public health and population approach, as articulated by Sanders and Prinz (2018), are as follows:

1. To increase the number of parents who have the necessary knowledge, skills, and confident to parent their children and adolescents well by increasing the number of parents who complete an evidence-based, culturally appropriate parenting support program.

2. To increase the number of children and adolescents who are thriving socially, emotionally, and academically.
3. To decrease the number of children and adolescents who develop serious social, emotional, and behavioral problems.
4. To decrease the number of children and adolescents who are maltreated or at risk of being maltreated by their parents. (Sanders & Prinz, 2018, p. 34)

Brief Description of the Intervention

The full Triple P system is designed for universal access by the general population of parents, but there are programs within the system that are more targeted. Because Triple P is a multitiered system, the term *levels* has an additional meaning. Triple P has five levels of increasing program intensity: Level 1, media and communication strategy; Level 2, brief parenting advice; Level 3, narrow-focus parenting support; Level 4, broad-focus parenting support; and Level 5, intensive family intervention. Triple P is delivered to parents by a broad array of professionals including but not limited to social workers, psychologists, counselors, primary care practitioners (nurses, physicians, clinically trained assistants), parent educators in schools, trained home-visitation specialists, and preschool directors.

The lengths of intervention with Triple P vary across levels and formats. In general, Levels 2 and 3 Triple P tend to be briefer, whereas Levels 4 and 5 Triple P are longer. For example, parenting seminars (Level 2 Triple P) are single 2-hour sessions, Brief Primary Care Triple P (also Level 2) involves one or two 30-minute consultation sessions, Primary Care Triple P (Level 3) involves up to four 30-minute consultation sessions, Standard Triple P (Level 4) consists of 10 sessions delivered over a 3-month period, and Enhanced Triple P (Level 5) involves 14 sessions over approximately a 4-month period. These delivery lengths do not include follow-up sessions, which are at the discretion of the practitioner.

Triple P has several modes of delivery. The in-person modes include brief consultation with an individual parent (or couple), intervention delivered to a parent (or couple) over 10 to 14 sessions, a large-group seminar delivered to many parents (eight–100), discussion groups for parents on specific topics, and intervention delivered to a group of eight to 10 parents/couples over a 2-month period. Triple P Online is delivered through a tailored Web-based platform. A self-help workbook version of Triple P is available offline. Finally, evidence-informed parenting information is delivered to the community at large through the Level 1 Triple P media and communication strategy.

Each of the different Triple P programs has implementation materials tailored to the particular level, format, and, where relevant, the variant. For example, the brief consultation formats in Levels 2 and 3 draw on a collection of evidence-informed tip sheets addressing a range of child issues, organized by developmental period: infants and toddlers, preschoolers, elementary-school-age children, and teenagers. These tip sheets allow a practitioner to tailor them to each parent using annotations to specify parent-generated details and to highlight the most critical points. The individual and group programs in Levels 4 and 5 each have parent workbooks.

For the practitioner, there is a unique manual for each program, videos for most of the programs, and presentation slides for the group-based programs. Triple P trained practitioners also have access to additional resources and support through the web-based Triple P provider network. Communities and agencies implementing the Level 1 media and communication strategy can make use of *Stay Positive*, a web-based platform tailorable to local jurisdictions.

Content Relevant to Spanking and Other Physical Punishment

In any given family, a parent's use of spanking and other forms of physical aggression and punishment can occur for multiple reasons and in varying contexts. Three of the more common contexts are discussed here in terms of how Triple P interventions are relevant to each. First, parents might believe that responsible parenting requires physical punishment as a disciplinary practice. Second, parents commonly find themselves enmeshed in escalating cycles of coercive interactions in which both physical and verbal aggression are more likely to occur. And third, child behavior and environmental events can trigger in some parents an out-of-proportion emotional response by which a parent physically lashes out at their child.

The first reason, the belief that responsible parenting requires physical punishment, is addressed by introducing a set of disciplinary strategies that help parents achieve their goals without the use of physical punishment. The principle of assertive discipline assumes that children need to learn to accept responsibility for their behavior, to develop self-control, and to take into account the needs of others. Triple P includes a range of behavior change procedures that help parents to be consistent, to respond quickly and decisively to child misbehavior, and to show children how to behave in acceptable ways. The specific parenting procedures relate to parents selecting and presenting situation-specific ground rules; using directed discussion and planned ignoring; giving clear, calm, age-appropriate directions backed up by logical consequences; using quiet time (nonexclusionary time-out) and time-out; and reinforcing positive child behaviors incompatible with the target misbehaviors. Overall, by helping parents acquire a more comprehensive and effective repertoire for addressing or preventing misbehavior, reliance on physical punishment can be reduced. When parents become more knowledgeable and skilled in noncoercive discipline methods, they might find less stress and more satisfaction in not spanking.

The second reason, pertaining to escalation of coercive interactions, is addressed in part by the acquisition of the aforementioned assertive discipline approach. In addition, Triple P exposes parents to practical concepts about the causes of behavior. In particular, parents learn about the "criticism trap" in which a parent's criticism, spanking, or other negative response can result in a child's immediate cessation of misbehavior, which reinforces the parent's aversive response but paradoxically leads to an increase in future occurrences of the misbehavior. Armed with an understanding of this common trap and with a stronger repertoire of parenting procedures, parents are often able to extricate themselves from the recurring coercive cycles.

Finally, the third reason for physical aggression, namely triggered emotional reactions, is addressed in some of the Triple P programs (Pickering & Sanders, 2016). One intervention strategy in Triple P aims to help parents alter their unhelpful attributions and manage anger more effectively through a series of steps:

1. Parents learn to identify the effects of negative or harsh discipline practices on children and the possible cause of their own negative behaviors toward their child including physical punishment.
2. To prevent anger escalation and negative parenting practices, parents receive coaching in how to identify, challenge, and dispute irrational attributions (e.g., "My 2-year-old spilled their milk because they are out to get me") and replace these with more rational and less inflammatory attributions (e.g., "My child mishandled their milk cup").
3. Parents acquire a better understanding of their own anger emotions that arise in parenting situations.
4. With coaching, parents learn and then practice a sequence of parenting practices that involves catching unhelpful thoughts/attributions, developing alternative coping statements in arousing situations to challenge thoughts that lead to physically and verbally lashing out, applying coping plans to manage anger in the specific situations, and then addressing the child behavioral situation with one or more of the already acquired positive parenting methods.

In general, when delivered appropriately, Triple P interventions are not about moralizing or shaming parents into not spanking. Rather, the focus is on collaborative problem solving by parent and practitioner to acquire or expand effective strategies that are satisfying and devoid of adverse side effects. Triple P's approach to helping parents to reduce reliance on physical punishment and other coercive parenting practices is founded on (a) a better understanding of the causes of child behavior and parent reactions, (b) personalized assessment of specific parent–child situations followed by planned actions, (c) replacement strategies that are more effective and less harmful than physical and coercive punishment, and (d) support for parents in their efforts to foster their children's development.

Implementation of the Intervention

To date, Triple P is being delivered to varying degrees in 28 countries and in more than 30 states in the United States. In terms of the number of families involved with Triple P programs (i.e., Levels 2–5, not counting the Level 1 media and communication strategy) over the past 20 years worldwide, a general estimate is that more than 2 million parents have participated in Triple P, although a more precise count is not available. In addition, Triple P–served families come from many racial, ethnic, and country-of-origin groups (including indigenous peoples in the United States, Canada, Australia, and New Zealand), socioeconomic strata (including families residing in low- and middle-income countries), and community demographics (rural, semiurban, and urban). Participating families have included biological, step, foster, and adoptive parents, as well as grandparents and other relatives. The children in the participating families range in age from infants to teenagers.

Evidence of Feasibility From Process Evaluations

There is considerable evidence to indicate successful training of professionals to use the Triple P system. Data from 2,961 Triple P professional training courses conducted between 2012 and 2016, representing more than 50,000 practitioners, provided evaluative information about parent consultation skills and practitioner satisfaction (Ralph & Dittman, 2018). Across program levels, formats, and variants, practitioners who received training in Triple P reflected significant and substantial increases over pretraining levels with respect to adequacy, confidence, and skill acquisition on the self-reported Parent Consultation Skills Checklist at posttraining and follow-up. Practitioner satisfaction with training was high and averaged 6.5 on a 7-point scale.

Evidence of Effectiveness From Outcome Evaluations

The evidentiary database on Triple P spanning multiple decades is large and continually growing. As of spring 2018, a total of 298 studies on Triple P have been conducted, including 151 randomized controlled trials. Most of the studies tested specific programs or components of Triple P, but a small number of studies tested the population impact of the Triple P system. Most of the outcome studies on Triple P have assessed impact on parenting practices, although some of the studies have addressed additional outcomes (e.g., parental adjustment, child behavior). A meta-analysis published in 2014 summarized 101 Triple P studies (including both published and unpublished studies) with respect to several outcome domains. Of particular relevance here, the review reported an average effect size (Cohen's *d*) of 0.47 for parenting practices, which includes reduction of coercive parenting. The review also reported an average effect size of 0.52 for parental satisfaction and self-efficacy (Sanders, Kirby, Tellegen, & Day, 2014).

A randomized population trial of the Triple P system demonstrated positive impact on the prevalence rates of three indicators related to child maltreatment (Prinz, 2017; Prinz, Sanders, Shapiro, Whitaker, & Lutzker, 2009, 2016). Two of these indicators—child maltreatment cases and hospital-treated maltreatment injuries—have direct relevance to prevention of physical punishment and coercive parenting. The study involved randomization of 18 midsize counties in South Carolina, none of which had any prior exposure to either the Triple P system or services as usual. In the nine Triple P system counties, more than 600 practitioners in several service sectors received training in the delivery of Triple P for the level or levels suitable to the particular setting and their professional background. Archival records from the child protective services system, the foster care system, and hospitals were systematically analyzed, controlling for the 5 years of baseline leading up to the initiation of the Triple P interventions. The intervention and control counties were equivalent at baseline. On the basis of 2.5 years of exposure to Triple P, the Triple P system counties were significantly lower than control counties with respect to prevalence rates of child maltreatment cases (including physical abuse), hospital-treated child maltreatment injuries, and child out-of-home placements.

Cost–Benefit Analyses

The Washington State Institute for Public Policy (2018) evaluated the costs and savings/benefits of Triple P. They determined that the Triple P system, with an estimated cost of $152/parent, yielded $3.36 in benefits for every $1.00 invested. They also reported that Level 4 Standard Triple P (delivered individually to families), with an estimated cost of $992/family, yielded $9.29 in benefits for every $1.00 invested.

Clearinghouse Registries

Triple P has been identified on several U.S. and international clearinghouse registries as an evidence-based program. Examples from U.S. clearinghouses include the following:

- *Blueprints for Healthy Youth Development.* Triple P was rated as a promising program. http://blueprintsprograms.com
- *California Evidence-Based Clearinghouse for Child Welfare.* The overall Triple P system is rated as "supported by research evidence"; Triple P Level 4 is rated as "well-supported by research evidence." http://www.cebc4cw.org
- *Canadian Best Practices Portal,* Public Health Agency of Canada. Triple P has been rated as a "best practice." http://cbpp-pcpe.phac-aspc.gc.ca
- *Clearinghouse for Military Family Readiness,* Penn State and the U.S. Department of Defense. Triple P has been given a "promising" rating. https://lion.militaryfamilies.psu.edu/about-us
- *Evidence-Based Prevention and Intervention Support Center* (EPISCenter) is a listing of rigorously evaluated, evidence-based prevention and intervention programs for families approved for use in the state of Pennsylvania. Triple P is the only program in this book included in EPISCenter. http://www.episcenter.psu.edu/ebp

- *Implementing Child Maltreatment Prevention Programmes: What the Experts Say*, World Health Organization. Triple P is listed as an example program; no ratings or programs are provided. http://www.euro.who.int/__data/assets/pdf_file/0009/289602/Maltreatment_web.pdf?ua=1
- *Results First Clearinghouse Database*, Pew Charitable Trusts. Triple P has been given the "highest rated program" designation. https://www.pewtrusts.org/pt/research-and-analysis/data-visualizations/2015/results-first-clearinghouse-database

Limitations

The impact of Triple P on parents and children depends heavily on the quality of actual implementation. This observation applies to all evidence-based programs but is more complex as it pertains to the full Triple P system. To yield positive effects at a population level, Triple P implementation needs to effectively address (a) initial assessment of organizational program fit and readiness; (b) specification of, and commitment to, key goals, program choices, leadership teams, community partnerships, and training parameters; (c) planning for detailed internal support of delivery personnel and for sustainability and expansion; (d) systematic training and accreditation; and (e) adoption of best practices in maintenance of quality implementation (Prinz, 2019). It is conceivable that organizations and a community could fulfill most of these needs and yet not achieve substantial population gains because the program reached low numbers of parents—which is why it is essential for communities to commit fully to an optimal implementation framework.

SUGGESTED FUTURE USE OF THE PROGRAM

How Clinicians and Community Practitioners Can Use the Intervention

Many of the clinicians who could be delivering Triple P often have multiple responsibilities and deliver a range of services. Triple P can be added to their toolboxes of programming. For example, counselors treating families in which a parent has a substance-use problem can also make use of Triple P to provide parenting support. Similarly, individuals in community organizations who interface with parents, such as child care/preschool directors and health-clinic workers, can add Triple P to their activities. More generally, the workforce that delivers Triple P can integrate it into their set of services to meet the needs of children and families in multiple ways.

How Policymakers Can Use the Intervention

The Triple P system is designed for broad, scaled-up utilization. Consequently, it is especially germane when policymakers are looking to knit together multiple service sectors to achieve multiple concurrent goals (Prinz, 2019).

By using a multipurpose system such as Triple P, community and organizational leaders can avoid having one parenting program to prevent child maltreatment, another program to reduce children's behavioral health problems, yet another to serve high-stress parents, and so on. Triple P provides a better policy fit when communities seek an alliance of agencies and organizations rather than a more siloed configuration.

INFORMATION ON OBTAINING THE INTERVENTION

Information about professional training and program adoption can be obtained by contacting Triple P America by email (contact.us@triplep.net) or telephone (803-451-2278). Additional information is available at http://www.triplep.net. For a recent detailed compendium on the content, underpinnings, variants, implementation developments, and research about the Triple P system, the reader is referred to the 2018 Oxford University Press book edited by Matthew R. Sanders and Trevor G. Mazzucchelli entitled *The Power of Positive Parenting: Transforming the Lives of Children, Parents, and Communities Using the Triple P System*. Furthermore, a comprehensive database of more than 700 studies and conceptual articles pertinent to Triple P can be found at https://pfsc-evidence.psy.uq.edu.au.

REFERENCES

Kazdin, A. E. (2008). *Parent management training: Treatment for oppositional, aggressive and antisocial behavior in children and adolescents.* New York, NY: Oxford University Press. http://dx.doi.org/10.1093/med:psych/9780195386004.001.0001

Patterson, G. R. (1976). The aggressive child: Victim and architect of a coercive system. In L. A. Hammerlynck, L. C. Handy, & E. J. Mash (Eds.), *Behavior modification and families: Theory and research* (Vol. 1, pp. 267–316). New York, NY: Brunner/Mazel.

Pickering, J. A., & Sanders, M. R. (2016). Reducing child maltreatment by making parenting programs available to all parents: A case example using the Triple P—Positive Parenting Program. *Trauma, Violence, & Abuse, 17,* 398–407. http://dx.doi.org/10.1177/1524838016658876

Prinz, R. J. (2017). Assessing child maltreatment prevention via administrative data systems: A case example of reproducibility. *Child Abuse & Neglect: The International Journal, 64,* 13–18. http://dx.doi.org/10.1016/j.chiabu.2016.12.005

Prinz, R. J. (2019). A population approach to parenting support and prevention: The Triple P system. *The Future of Children, 29*(1), 123–143.

Prinz, R. J., Sanders, M. R., Shapiro, C. J., Whitaker, D. J., & Lutzker, J. R. (2009). Population-based prevention of child maltreatment: The U.S. Triple P system population trial. *Prevention Science, 10,* 1–12. http://dx.doi.org/10.1007/s11121-009-0123-3

Prinz, R. J., Sanders, M. R., Shapiro, C. J., Whitaker, D. J., & Lutzker, J. R. (2016). Addendum to "Population-based prevention of child maltreatment: The U.S. Triple P system population trial." *Prevention Science, 17,* 410–416. http://dx.doi.org/10.1007/s11121-016-0631-x

Ralph, A., & Dittman, C. K. (2018). Training a workforce to implement evidence-based parenting programs. In M. R. Sanders & T. G. Mazzucchelli (Eds.), *The power of positive parenting: Transforming the lives of children, parents, and communities using the Triple P system* (pp. 371–382). New York, NY: Oxford University Press.

Sanders, M. R. (2008). Triple P-Positive Parenting Program as a public health approach to strengthening parenting. *Journal of Family Psychology, 22,* 506–517. http://dx.doi.org/10.1037/0893-3200.22.3.506

Sanders, M. R. (2012). Development, evaluation, and multinational dissemination of the Triple P-Positive Parenting Program. *Annual Review of Clinical Psychology, 8,* 345–379. http://dx.doi.org/10.1146/annurev-clinpsy-032511-143104

Sanders, M. R., Kirby, J. N., Tellegen, C. L., & Day, J. J. (2014). The Triple P-Positive Parenting Program: A systematic review and meta-analysis of a multi-level system of parenting support. *Clinical Psychology Review, 34,* 337–357. http://dx.doi.org/10.1016/j.cpr.2014.04.003

Sanders, M. R., & Mazzucchelli, T. G. (2013). The promotion of self-regulation through parenting interventions. *Clinical Child and Family Psychology Review, 16,* 1–17. http://dx.doi.org/10.1007/s10567-013-0129-z

Sanders, M. R., & Mazzucchelli, T. G. (2018). Core principles and techniques of positive parenting. In M. R. Sanders & T. G. Mazzucchelli (Eds.), *The power of positive parenting: Transforming the lives of children, parents, and communities using the Triple P system* (pp. 63–78). New York, NY: Oxford University Press.

Sanders, M. R., & Prinz, R. J. (2018). Emergence of a population approach to evidence-based parenting support. In M. R. Sanders & T. G. Mazzucchelli (Eds.), *The power of positive parenting: Transforming the lives of children, parents, and communities using the Triple P system* (pp. 32–62). New York, NY: Oxford University Press.

Theodore, A. D., Chang, J. J., Runyan, D. K., Hunter, W. M., Bangdiwala, S. I., & Agans, R. (2005). Epidemiologic features of the physical and sexual maltreatment of children in the Carolinas. *Pediatrics, 115,* e331–e337. http://dx.doi.org/10.1542/peds.2004-1033

Wahler, R. G. (1969). Oppositional children: A quest for parental reinforcement control. *Journal of Applied Behavior Analysis, 2,* 159–170. http://dx.doi.org/10.1901/jaba.1969.2-159

Washington State Institute for Public Policy. (2018, December). *Benefit-cost report.* Olympia, WA: Author.

14

No Hit Zones

Elizabeth T. Gershoff

THE INTERVENTION

The first No Hit Zone intervention was developed by Lolita McDavid, MD, at Rainbow Babies and Children's Hospital in Cleveland, OH. Originally designed as a universal intervention for a hospital, No Hit Zones have been created in a range of nonmedical settings.

Background and Theory of Change

Over the past several decades, the medical community has become increasingly concerned about the potential harm to children associated with physical punishment. A large and consistent body of research has linked parents' use of physical punishment to increases in children's aggression, behavior problems, mental health problems, and academic problems (Gershoff & Grogan-Kaylor, 2016). Parents' use of physical punishment increases the risk that they will physically abuse their children (Lee, Grogan-Kaylor, & Berger, 2014) and is linked with the same harmful outcomes as is physical abuse (Afifi et al., 2017; Gershoff & Grogan-Kaylor, 2016).

As a result of this accumulation of research and of a growing acceptance of professional responsibility, the American Academy of Pediatrics Committee on Psychosocial Aspects of Child and Family Health (1998), the American Academy of Pediatrics (2014), the Canadian Paediatric Society

http://dx.doi.org/10.1037/0000162-015
Ending the Physical Punishment of Children: A Guide for Clinicians and Practitioners,
E. T. Gershoff and S. J. Lee (Editors)

(Durrant, Ensom, & Coalition on Physical Punishment of Children and Youth, 2004), the National Association of Pediatric Nurse Practitioners (2011), and the American Academy of Child and Adolescent Psychiatry (2012) have issued statements about physical punishment. In these statements, the organizations assert that physical punishment is harmful to children, that parents should avoid using it, and that their members have an obligation to educate parents about physical punishment and alternatives to it. Medical professionals are ideal conduits for such messages because parents often ask medical professionals for advice about discipline and rate them as highly trustworthy when it comes to giving such advice (Taylor, Moeller, Hamvas, & Rice, 2013).

Medical settings are also important spaces for intervening and educating parents around physical punishment because the hitting of children by parents is a relatively common experience in them. A study of two medical centers in the Midwest found that half of physicians and a quarter of nurses reported that they had witnessed a parent hitting a child in the medical center in the past year (Font et al., 2016). When asked if they responded to such incidents, two thirds of direct-care staff took action, such as talking with the parent or calling security, but only slightly more than a third of non–direct-care staff (e.g., receptionists, custodians) took any action (Font et al., 2016).

Taken together, the research, the positions of professional organizations, and the prevalence of physical punishment in medical settings point to a clear need for an intervention that involves training medical staff both why and how they should intervene if they witness parents hitting their children. No Hit Zones (NHZs) are just such an intervention. An NHZ is a universal policy adopted by an organization that states explicitly that no forms of hitting will be tolerated, including parents hitting children.

The theoretical basis for NHZs is Darley and Latané's (1968) theory of bystander intervention, in which they observed that the bystander must notice the concerning behavior, interpret it as a situation needing intervention, feel it is their responsibility to intervene, and know how to intervene effectively. Because NHZ is a bystander intervention, its foundation is training staff how to recognize when parents are hitting or about to hit their children, why they should be concerned about their behavior, why they should intervene, and how to intervene.

The first NHZ was created by Lolita McDavid, MD, at Rainbow Children's Hospital in Cleveland, Ohio. Minimal efforts were made to spread the idea of NHZs until Norton Health System (previously Kosair Children's Hospital) in Lexington, Kentucky, adopted an NHZ and made their materials available to other institutions. The two pediatricians who led the NHZ effort at Norton—Erin Frazier, MD, and Kelly Dauk, MD—brought more attention to NHZs by publishing an academic article discussing their experiences developing and implementing the NHZ at their medical center (Frazier, Liu, & Dauk, 2014). The job of disseminating NHZ materials was then assumed by the Center for Effective Discipline at Gundersen Health System in La Crosse, Wisconsin, after the latter implemented its NHZ in 2014.

As of August 2019, 15 hospitals or medical centers had instituted NHZ policies (see Table 14.1). In recent years, NHZs have expanded beyond non-medical settings to include mental and behavioral health clinics and city and county offices and facilities (see Table 14.2).

Main Goals of the Intervention

The primary goal of the NHZ is to create a safe and healthy environment for the children, families, staff, and visitors of the organization by preventing or ending incidents of parent-to-child hitting (Frazier et al., 2014). A secondary goal is to momentarily disrupt parents' reliance on physical punishment and encourage them to try nonphysical forms of discipline instead.

Brief Description of the Intervention

An NHZ begins with the establishment of an institutional policy that no hitting of any kind will be accepted and that institutional staff have an obligation to intervene, deescalate, and educate individuals who are hitting or about to hit someone else, including their own children. Next, all staff in the institution are trained via an online or in-person presentation explaining the rationale for the NHZ and outlining staff's responsibilities under the new policy to intervene if they see hitting or hear hitting being threatened. The training typically includes scenarios to illustrate how staff might intervene in various scenarios. The NHZ policy is then communicated to all visitors using posters and pamphlets placed around the institution. The trainings can be conducted by any employee of the organization who has familiarity with the research on the harms associated with physical punishment and who understands and is committed to the notion of an NHZ.

Content Relevant to Spanking or Physical Punishment

An NHZ has four main content components, each of which includes information about physical punishment. First, staff training, in the form of a slide presentation, includes research about the harms linked with physical punishment, the fact that physical punishment is a form of hitting, the organization's decision to not allow any hitting including physical punishment, and staff responsibility to intervene. Second, posters are put up around the organization that announce the NHZ to both staff and visitors and that state explicitly that all forms of hitting, including physical punishment, are not allowed to protect the safety of everyone at the organization. Third, pamphlets are typically made available to parents that summarize the harms linked with physical punishment and that suggest alternative forms of discipline. Fourth, staff can intervene directly with parents who are hitting or about to hit their children and educate them about the NHZ and possibly about physical punishment, although their actions will likely be focused on defusing the immediate situation and helping the parent calm themselves.

TABLE 14.1. Hospitals and Medical Centers With No Hit Zone Policies

Launched	Institution	City	No Hit Zone website
2005	Rainbow Babies and Children's Hospital	Cleveland, OH	No Hit Zone is currently inactive.
2012	Norton Children's Hospital	Louisville, KY	Not on website, but described in Frazier et al. (2014)
2014	Gundersen Medical Center	La Crosse, WI	http://www.gundersenhealth.org/health-wellness/publications/gundersen-magazine/spring-2017/positive-parenting-pays-off http://www.thisisanohitzone.com
2014	Children's Mercy Hospital	Kansas City, MO	https://www.youtube.com/watch?v=y3LbEUzjm5I https://www.kansascity.com/living/family/article2182555.html
2016	Greenville Health System Children's Hospital, Center for Pediatric Medicine	Greenville, SC	http://www.ghschildrens.org/pediatric-primary-care/center-pediatric-medicine
2016	University of Minnesota Masonic Children's Hospital	Minneapolis, MN	https://www.youtube.com/watch?v=q_QQ2_OIG70
2016	University of Wisconsin, American Family Children's Hospital	Madison, WI	https://www.uwhealthkids.org/news-and-events/hitting-hurts-no-hit-zone/49408
2017	Children's Hospital of New Orleans	New Orleans, LA	http://nocac.net/no-hit-zone

2017	General Academic Pediatrics Office, Children's Hospital of The King's Daughters	Norfolk, VA	http://www.championsforchildrenhr.org/no-hit-zone-launches https://www.youtube.com/watch?v=JJAmErXj75o
2017	Lehigh Valley Health Network	Allentown, PA	https://news.lvhn.org/no-hit-zone
2017	Mother Baby Unit and Emergency Department of Chesapeake Regional Healthcare	Chesapeake, VA	http://www.championsforchildrenhr.org/no-hit-zone-launches/#1526475341800-cb4297ff-7cf8
2017	Nationwide Children's Hospital	Columbus, OH	https://www.nationwidechildrens.org/family-resources-education/health-wellness-and-safety-resources/resources-for-parents-and-kids/hitting-harms-hugging-helps
2017	Peyton Manning Children's Hospital	Indianapolis, IN	http://www.peytonmanningch.org/child-protection-team
2018	Montefiore Medical Center and Children's Hospital at Montefiore	Bronx, NY	http://www.cham.org/programs-centers/je-and-zb-butler-center-for-children-and-families/no-hitting-zone
2018	University of Rochester Medical Center Golisano Children's Hospital	Rochester, NY	https://www.urmc.rochester.edu/childrens-hospital/no-hit-zone.aspx
2018	Wolfson Children's Hospital, University of Florida	Jacksonville, FL	https://www.wolfsonchildrens.com/about/positive-parenting

TABLE 14.2. Nonhospital Public and Private Settings With No Hit Zone Policies

Launched	Institution	City	No Hit Zone Website
2014	Dane County District Attorney's Office	Madison, WI	https://da.countyofdane.com/nohit.aspx
2014	Kansas City Public Libraries	Kansas City, MO	https://www.youtube.com/watch?v=8egU_QxD-QM
2017	Chesapeake Health Department	Hampton Roads, VA	http://www.championsforchildrenhr.org/no-hit-zone-launches/#1526475340400-cf34b06a-10e0
2017	Chesapeake Department of Human Services	Hampton Roads, VA	http://www.championsforchildrenhr.org/no-hit-zone-launches/#1526475341100-8c42c6d2-c61c
2017	City of Stoughton, all city facilities (e.g., police department, library, public parks)	Stoughton, WI	https://www.youtube.com/watch?v=4WbYWTdYX9o http://www.unifiednewsgroup.com/stoughton_courier_hub/news/council-adopts-no-hit-zone-policy/article_46fec33c-4685-561d-acb1-8e29c9abcd24.html https://www.stoughtonpubliclibrary.org/no-hit-zone
2017	Family & Children's Center	La Crosse, WI	https://www.fcconline.org/community-partners/no-hit-zone
2017	Jefferson Family Court	Frankfort, KY	https://www.youtube.com/watch?v=1hZ5W4YHd_s
2018	City of Madison Heights, all city facilities	Madison Heights, MI	https://www.wthr.com/article/community-starts-no-spanking-zones
2018	Harbor Point Behavioral Health Center	Portsmouth, VA	https://harborpointbhc.com/news/harbor-point-bhc-is-pleased-to-announce-its-certification-as-no-hit-zone-partnership-with-champions-for-children-prevent-child-abuse-hampton-roads http://www.championsforchildrenhr.org/no-hit-zone-launches
2018	Shiloh Baptist Church	Trenton, NJ	http://www.shilohtrenton.org/bulletins/Bulletin%202018%20Second%20Sunday%20June%2010%20FNL.pdf

Implementation of the Intervention

To date, NHZs have been implemented primarily in the Midwest, Southeast, and Northeast regions of the United States. NHZs began in hospitals (see Table 14.1) but have expanded to city- and county-level government offices, public libraries, mental health facilities, and at least one church (see Table 14.2). Exactly how many families have been exposed to the NHZ intervention is unknown, given its universal nature. Because an average children's hospital sees 229,814 inpatient, outpatient, and emergency department visits per year (Children's Hospital Association, 2018), it is likely that hundreds of thousands of families have been exposed to NHZs across hospitals and other institutions around the United States. NHZs are targeted to parents of all ages of children and to families of all cultural backgrounds.

Evidence of Feasibility From Process Evaluations

Only one NHZ implemented by Gundersen Health System in La Crosse, Wisconsin, has been evaluated to date (Gershoff et al., 2018). The evaluation used a pre–post design with anonymous respondents of staff and parents at each wave; thus, within-individual change could not be assessed. For the staff pretest (n = 3,000) and posttest (n = 623) surveys, both sets of respondents were primarily female, White, and parents. Half of each set of staff respondents (54%) was involved in direct care of patients (nurses, therapists, social workers, physicians), and the remaining respondents were non–direct-care staff (e.g., technicians, support staff, medical records staff). For the parent surveys, 225 parents participated in the pretest and 180 in the posttest; the parent sample was also primarily female and White. Staff completed online surveys; parents completed paper surveys while in pediatric outpatient clinics in the medical center.

Evidence That Training of Program Staff Was Successful

Immediately after their online training about the NHZ, the majority of staff agreed that the policy was clear (96%), that they understood their responsibilities to act (93%), and that they had been provided strategies in the training that they could use to intervene if they saw a parent hitting their child (94%; Gershoff et al., 2018).

Evidence That Staff Had Buy-In and Like the Program

In the posttest survey, which occurred 10 months after the NHZ was introduced, a majority of staff agreed that the NHZ was a good idea for the medical center, believed in its goals, and agreed that it had a positive impact on the families at the center. This was true across both direct-care and non–direct-care staff (Gershoff et al., 2018).

Evidence That Families Enjoy or Appreciate the Program

Among parents in the posttest survey who had seen the NHZ materials, a fifth agreed that the NHZ had changed their beliefs about discipline and spanking and more than a quarter agreed that there are better ways to discipline. Parents who spank their children reported more change in their attitudes about spanking than did parents who did not spank (Gershoff et al., 2018).

Evidence of Effectiveness From Outcome Evaluations

After the NHZ had been in place for 10 months, staff were more supportive of the notion that staff should intervene in parent-to-child hitting and were more knowledgeable about the best ways to intervene when parents hit children. Staff surveyed after the NHZ were less likely to say their coworkers were in favor of spanking than were staff surveyed pre-NHZ. However, staff's own attitudes about spanking were equivalent pre- and post-NHZ (Gershoff et al., 2018).

Among the parents surveyed, the evaluation revealed no difference in support for or use of spanking between the pretest and posttest groups, although the pretest reported that rates of spanking were already low (mean = 2.22 on a 1–5 scale, equivalent to "less than once per month"). The only significant change for parents was a decrease in whether they believed their pediatricians had positive attitudes about spanking (Gershoff et al., 2018).

Limitations

NHZs are proliferating throughout the country but without a standard plan for implementation or a standard set of materials to be used across sites. Developing a set of such materials is an important and necessary step for further dissemination of NHZs. Regarding the evidence for NHZs, only one pre–post evaluation of an NHZ has been completed and published. Further evidence is needed from a variety of other hospitals or settings and from randomized controlled trial studies that can establish that NHZs are the cause of changes in staff and visitor attitudes about and use of physical punishment.

SUGGESTED FUTURE USE OF THE PROGRAM

How Clinicians Can Use the Intervention

Clinicians can make their offices into NHZs and use the materials as opportunities to talk with parents about alternatives to physical punishment.

How Community Practitioners Can Use the Intervention

Practitioners can implement NHZs anywhere families and children will be. To date, NHZs have been instituted in settings that are public (e.g., public parks, libraries), governmental (e.g., courts, public services buildings), and private (e.g., hospitals, behavioral clinics). NHZs could also be implemented in public and private schools, in stores, and at sports fields.

How Policymakers Can Use the Intervention

NHZs are consistent with public health goals to prevent physical, mental, and behavioral harm to children. The city of Stoughton, Wisconsin, has led the way in becoming the first city in the United States to institute a citywide NHZ. Policymakers at city, county, and state levels could implement NHZs across their jurisdictions such that NHZs could take effect in all public buildings and facilities. Much like no-smoking areas led to a decrease in both the incidence and acceptance of smoking, NHZs could do the same regarding the hitting of children.

INFORMATION ON OBTAINING THE PROGRAM

The Center for Effective Discipline, based at Gundersen Health System, is currently the hub for information about NHZs (see http://www.thisisanohitzone.org). Organizations can access a free Readiness Assessment flyer to determine their readiness to implement NHZs, as well as an implementation plan and a program evaluation tool to guide them once they have decided to proceed. Organizations that register with the center can receive a set of presentation slides for training staff as well as technical assistance. Posters, pamphlets, and stickers can be purchased through the website.

Some of the organizations that have implemented NHZs make some of their materials available to the public for free. For example, the New Orleans Children's Advocacy Center at the Children's Hospital of New Orleans includes the hospital's approved policies and procedures regarding its NHZ, a flyer about NHZs, and discipline guidance for parents with children at four developmental stages on its website (http://nocac.net/no-hit-zone). Although these materials are branded with the hospital's logo, other institutions are free to model their own materials after these.

REFERENCES

Afifi, T. O., Ford, D., Gershoff, E. T., Merrick, M., Grogan-Kaylor, A., Ports, K. A., . . . Peters Bennett, R. (2017). Spanking and adult mental health impairment: The case for the designation of spanking as an adverse childhood experience. *Child Abuse & Neglect: The International Journal, 71,* 24–31. http://dx.doi.org/10.1016/j.chiabu.2017.01.014

American Academy of Child and Adolescent Psychiatry. (2012, July 30). *Corporal punishment.* Retrieved from http://www.aacap.org/aacap/policy_statements/2012/Policy_Statement_on_Corporal_Punishment.aspx

American Academy of Pediatrics. (2014). AAP publications reaffirmed or retired. *Pediatrics, 134,* e1520. http://dx.doi.org/10.1542/peds.2014-2679

American Academy of Pediatrics Committee on Psychosocial Aspects of Child and Family Health. (1998). Guidance for effective discipline. *Pediatrics, 101*(4 Pt. 1), 723–728.

Children's Hospital Association. (2018). *About children's hospitals*. Retrieved from https://www.childrenshospitals.org/About-Us/About-Childrens-Hospitals

Darley, J. M., & Latané, B. (1968). Bystander intervention in emergencies: Diffusion of responsibility. *Journal of Personality and Social Psychology, 8*(4 Pt. 1), 377–383. http://dx.doi.org/10.1037/h0025589

Durrant, J. E., Ensom, R., & Coalition on Physical Punishment of Children and Youth. (2004). *Joint statement on physical punishment of children and youth*. Retrieved from http://www.cheo.on.ca/en/physicalpunishment

Font, S. A., Gershoff, E. T., Taylor, C. A., Terreros, A., Nielsen-Parker, M., Spector, L., . . . Olson-Dorff, D. (2016). Staff responses when parents hit children in a hospital setting. *Journal of Developmental and Behavioral Pediatrics, 37*, 730–736. http://dx.doi.org/10.1097/DBP.0000000000000343

Frazier, E. R., Liu, G. C., & Dauk, K. L. (2014). Creating a safe place for pediatric care: A no hit zone. *Hospital Pediatrics, 4*, 247–250. http://dx.doi.org/10.1542/hpeds.2013-0106

Gershoff, E. T., Font, S. A., Taylor, C. A., Garza, A. B., Olson-Dorff, D., & Foster, R. H. (2018). A short-term evaluation of a hospital no hit zone policy to increase bystander intervention in cases of parent-to-child violence. *Children and Youth Services Review, 94*, 155–162. http://dx.doi.org/10.1016/j.childyouth.2018.09.040

Gershoff, E. T., & Grogan-Kaylor, A. (2016). Spanking and child outcomes: Old controversies and new meta-analyses. *Journal of Family Psychology, 30*, 453–469. http://dx.doi.org/10.1037/fam0000191

Lee, S. J., Grogan-Kaylor, A., & Berger, L. M. (2014). Parental spanking of 1-year-old children and subsequent child protective services involvement. *Child Abuse & Neglect: The International Journal, 38*, 875–883. http://dx.doi.org/10.1016/j.chiabu.2014.01.018

National Association of Pediatric Nurse Practitioners. (2011). NAPNAP position statement on corporal punishment. *Journal of Pediatric Health Care, 25*, e31–e32. http://dx.doi.org/10.1016/j.pedhc.2011.07.003

Taylor, C. A., Moeller, W., Hamvas, L., & Rice, J. C. (2013). Parents' professional sources of advice regarding child discipline and their use of corporal punishment. *Clinical Pediatrics, 52*, 147–155. http://dx.doi.org/10.1177/0009922812465944

15

Legal Prohibitions of Physical Punishment

Elizabeth T. Gershoff and Joan E. Durrant

THE INTERVENTION

The government of Sweden was the first to institute a ban on all physical punishment of children, including by parents, in 1979. Many countries have truly *universal* legal prohibitions of physical punishment that apply to all parents, caregivers, and teachers. The majority of countries have limited legal prohibitions on physical punishment in certain settings (e.g., child-care centers, schools, juvenile detention centers); however, the current chapter does not consider such partial bans and instead focuses on complete bans on physical punishment. To date, no country has reversed a complete ban on physical punishment.

Background and Theory of Change

Physical punishment of children remains prevalent worldwide. A global survey found that 63% of 2- to 4-year-old children had experienced physical punishment in the previous month (UNICEF, 2017). Caregivers continue to use physical punishment despite evidence that it is ineffective at changing children's behavior and that it is linked with a range of negative cognitive and social–emotional outcomes (Gershoff & Grogan-Kaylor, 2016), including a heightened risk for increasingly severe violence (Lee, Grogan-Kaylor, & Berger, 2014).

http://dx.doi.org/10.1037/0000162-016
Ending the Physical Punishment of Children: A Guide for Clinicians and Practitioners,
E. T. Gershoff and S. J. Lee (Editors)

There are also human rights arguments against physical punishment. The United Nations Committee on the Rights of the Child (UN CRC, 2007) has stated that physical punishment violates children's rights to protection from violence under Article 19 of the UN Convention on the Rights of the Child (United Nations, 1989). The CRC has stated that physical punishment is a form of violence and has called on all states parties (i.e., UN member states that have ratified the Convention on the Rights of the Child) "to move quickly to prohibit and eliminate all corporal punishment" (UN CRC, 2007, §1.2). (Note: Outside the United States, the term *corporal punishment* is more common than *physical punishment.*) States parties are monitored through reports that they submit every 5 years to the CRC. The CRC reviews those reports and issues concluding observations to each country, recommending legal and policy changes that will better comply with the standards of the Convention. The CRC regularly recommends that countries ban all physical punishment of children. For example, in its 2016 Concluding Observations to France, the CRC stated "that no violence against children is justifiable and that corporal punishment is a form of violence," and that it "reiterates its recommendation to the State party to explicitly prohibit corporal punishment in all settings, including in the family, in schools, in childcare settings and in alternative care" (UN CRC, 2016, §III.D.44). The UN (2017) has targeted the elimination of all forms of violence against children in its Sustainable Development Goals for 2030. One of three indicators that will measure progress toward this target is the proportion of children who experience physical punishment by caregivers.

Main Goals of the Intervention

The goals of bans are as follows:

- to reduce and ultimately eliminate all physical punishment of children,
- to raise public awareness of violence against children and reduce societal tolerance of it, and
- to allow earlier supportive intervention into situations where children are experiencing violence and thereby reduce its risk of escalation.

Mode of Delivery

In most countries, children lack a political voice, and thus legislative action must be taken by adults on their behalf. A typical first step is for advocacy groups to mount campaigns to raise legislators' awareness of research findings on physical punishment as well as of children's inherent rights to equal protection under the law.

Physical punishment is considered fully prohibited when a government passes a bill into law. In some cases, a high court has ruled that physical punishment is not permissible, and that ruling has subsequently been confirmed in legislation (e.g., Israel). In other cases, high court decisions have not yet been confirmed in legislation (e.g., Italy). Only in the former cases would physical punishment be considered banned.

To have optimal impact, bans must be accompanied by public education and effective supports for parents, teachers, and others who care for children. In some countries (e.g., Sweden, Germany), legislation has been followed by a media public education campaign to raise awareness of the law, the risks associated with physical punishment, and alternative approaches to teaching and guiding children. When professionals in a country with a ban are aware of the legislation, they can inform parents and support them in ending their use of physical punishment.

Content Relevant to Spanking or Physical Punishment

In most countries, assault of a person is a crime. However, many countries have legal defenses available to adults who assault children if the force is intended to be corrective (i.e., physical punishment). In countries that have introduced physical punishment bans, that defense is no longer available (Durrant, 2019). Thus, an assault of a child is legally equivalent to a similar assault against an adult. In addition, these countries have added explicit prohibitions of physical punishment to their legal statutes. Although in a few countries these prohibitions have been added to penal codes and carry penalties (e.g., New Zealand, Portugal), in most cases they have been added to civil codes and thus do not carry penalties beyond those already in place for assault. The aim is to ensure that children and adults have equal legal protection from assault, removing any gray zone of legalized violence against children (Durrant, 2019).

Sweden was the first country to prohibit all physical punishment of children. Its civil code law states the following:

> Children are entitled to care, security and a good upbringing. Children shall be treated with respect for their person and individuality and may not be subjected to corporal punishment or any other humiliating treatment. (Children and Parents Code, art. 6.1, 1979, as cited in Global Initiative to End All Corporal Punishment of Children, 2018c)

Nepal is a country that quite recently prohibited all physical punishment of children:

> Each child has a right to be protected against all types of physical or mental violence and punishment, neglect, inhumane behaviour, gender based or discriminatory abuse, sexual abuse and exploitation committed by his/her father, mother, other family members or guardian, teacher or any other person. (Act Relating to Children 2018, Section 7(5), as cited in Global Initiative to End All Corporal Punishment of Children, 2018a)

Paraguay's ban specifies children's rights to protection and dignity and makes clear that adults are responsible for upholding those rights:

> All children and adolescents have the right to good treatment and for their physical, psychological and emotional integrity to be respected. This right includes the protection of their image, their identity, their autonomy, their thoughts,

> their feelings, their dignity and their values. Corporal punishment and humiliating treatment of children and adolescents is prohibited as a form of correction or discipline, especially when it is imparted by parents, tutors, guardians or anyone responsible for their education, care, guidance, or treatment of any kind. Children and adolescents are especially entitled to receive guidance, education, care and discipline by implementing guidelines for positive parenting. ("Promotion of Good Treatment, Positive Parenting and Protection of Children and Adolescents against Corporal Punishment or Any Type of Violence as a Method of Correction or Discipline," 2016, as cited in Global Initiative to End All Corporal Punishment of Children, 2018b)

South Sudan prohibited all physical punishment of children in its first constitution as an independent country:

> Every child has the right: . . . (f) to be free from corporal punishment and cruel and inhuman treatment by any person including parents, school administrations and other institutions. . . . (Transitional Constitution of the Republic of South Sudan, 2011, article 17(1), as cited in Global Initiative to End All Corporal Punishment of Children, 2017)

Regardless of its wording, each prohibition affirms children's fundamental rights and explicitly identifies physical punishment as a form of maltreatment.

Implementation of the Intervention

Full prohibitions of physical punishment are now in place in 56 countries, which include most of Central and South America, most of Europe, several countries in Africa and central Asia, and New Zealand. See Table 15.1 for a complete list of these countries. Together, these 56 countries with legal prohibitions account for 10% of the world's population of children (Global Initiative to End All Corporal Punishment of Children, 2019). This means that as many as 200,000,000 of the world's 2 billion children are protected by law from physical punishment.

Evidence of Feasibility From Process Evaluations

There has been concern in some countries that a ban would lead to a surge in reports to police or child protection agencies, overtaxing these public safety institutions. To assess the impact of prohibition on law enforcement in New Zealand, the police monitored the number of reports involving physical punishment for the first 5 years following the ban. The majority (74%) of reports made during that period involved injurious assaults (New Zealand Police, 2009). The number of "smacking" reports increased over the 5-year period, but the proportion that were prosecuted declined. Of the eight "smacking" cases that were prosecuted over the 5 years, all involved hard and/or multiple slaps or resulted in injuries to the child. The police concluded that the ban did not lead to undue burden on law enforcement. Similarly, in Sweden, reports of child assault increased following the ban, but the rate of prosecution remained steady (Durrant, 1999). In New Zealand, reports to child protective services increased following the ban, but the substantiation rate of maltreatment

TABLE 15.1 Countries That Have Implemented Legal Bans on Physical Punishment, by Year of Ban

Country (Year)	Country (Year)	Country (Year)
1. Sweden (1979)	20. Portugal (2007)	39. Argentina (2014)
2. Finland (1983)	21. Spain (2007)	40. Bolivia (2014)
3. Norway (1987)	22. Togo (2007)	41. Brazil (2014)
4. Austria (1989)	23. Uruguay (2007)	42. Estonia (2014)
5. Cyprus (1994)	24. Venezuela (2007)	43. Malta (2014)
6. Denmark (1997)	25. Costa Rica (2008)	44. Nicaragua (2014)
7. Latvia (1998)	26. Liechtenstein (2008)	45. San Marino (2014)
8. Croatia (1999)	27. Luxembourg (2008)	46. Benin (2015)
9. Bulgaria (2000)	28. Republic of Moldova (2008)	47. Ireland (2015)
10. Germany (2000)	29. Albania (2010)	48. Peru (2015)
11. Israel (2000)	30. Congo, Republic of (2010)	49. Mongolia (2016)
12. Turkmenistan (2002)	31. Kenya (2010)	50. Montenegro (2016)
13. Iceland (2003)	32. Poland (2010)	51. Paraguay (2016)
14. Romania (2004)	33. Tunisia (2010)	52. Slovenia (2016)
15. Ukraine (2004)	34. South Sudan (2011)	53. Lithuania (2017)
16. Hungary (2005)	35. Cabo Verde (2013)	54. Nepal (2018)
17. Greece (2006)	36. Honduras (2013)	55. Republic of Kosovo (2019)
18. Netherlands (2007)	37. TFYR Macedonia (2013)	56. France (2019)
19. New Zealand (2007)	38. Andorra (2014)	

Note. Data from Global Initiative to End All Corporal Punishment of Children (2019).

remained stable from 2001 to 2009 (Hughes, 2009). Together, these findings suggest that bans can raise public awareness of and willingness to report violence against children, but families are no more likely to be drawn into the criminal justice or child protection systems. One goal of physical punishment bans is to send a clear message that no violence against children is acceptable, thereby inhibiting parents' impulses to strike their children. Four years after Germany's 2000 legal ban on physical punishment, 84% of family-serving agencies reported that they informed parents about the ban, and 68% of staff at these agencies reported that telling parents about the ban made their jobs easier (Bussmann, 2011).

Few systematic surveys of citizens' opinions about bans have been conducted. A national survey carried out 1 year after the passage of New Zealand's bans found that 91% of adults were aware that physical punishment had been banned; of these, 43% were in support of the ban, 29% were neutral, and 28% were opposed (New Zealand Children's Commissioner, 2008).

Evidence of Effectiveness From Outcome Evaluations

The relationship between attitudes and laws is reciprocal; changes in laws can lead to changes in attitudes, but changes in attitudes also lead to changes in laws. In the case of physical punishment bans, there is often a lengthy public debate prior to the law's passage, which can itself influence public attitudes. As it is impossible to conduct controlled studies of legislative changes (countries cannot be assigned to legal conditions, and societal-level variables cannot be controlled), researchers have relied on comparative studies of pre- to postban attitudes toward physical punishment and of attitudes in countries with and without bans.

Sweden, the first country to institute a full physical punishment ban (in 1979), has seen approval of physical punishment drop dramatically, from 53% in 1965 to 26% in 1981 (Swedish Institute for Opinion Surveys, 1981). By 1999, only 10% of parents approved of physical punishment, decreasing to 8% by 2011 (Janson, Jernbro, & Långberg, 2011; Statistics Sweden, 1996). These attitudinal changes have translated into behavioral changes. Before the ban, virtually all children had been hit before they reached high school (Klackenberg, 1981). This rate decreased to 66% by 1995 (Statistics Sweden, 1996) and to 15% by 2011 (Janson et al., 2011).

In 1996, 72% of parents in Germany reported having ever given their children "light slaps" and 33% reported having spanked their children at some time. By 2001, a year after the ban was passed, these proportions had decreased to 59% and 25%, respectively (Bussmann, 2004). In New Zealand, support for physical punishment declined from 89% in 1981 to 40% in 2013, 6 years following the ban (D'Souza, Russell, Wood, Signal, & Elder, 2016). The proportion of parents reporting that they had physically punished their children in the previous 4 weeks was approximately 10% by 2006; this proportion decreased by almost half by 2015 (New Zealand Ministry of Health, 2016).

Large surveys were conducted in 2007 in three countries with bans (Austria, Germany, Sweden) and two without bans (France, Spain). Parents in the countries with bans reported significantly less spanking (range: 4%–17%) compared with parents in the countries without bans (range: 51%–54%; Bussmann, Erthal, & Schroth, 2011). A 2010 cross-sectional survey of parents in six European countries examined rates of physical punishment in four countries with bans (Bulgaria, Germany, Netherlands, Romania) and in two countries without bans at the time of the survey (Lithuania [which instituted a ban in 2017], Turkey). Parents in countries without bans reported an average physical punishment frequency that was 1.7 times higher than that reported by parents living in countries with bans (duRivage et al., 2015). These two European studies provide preliminary evidence that physical punishment bans are associated with decreases in physical punishment.

A third study found that bans were not consistently linked with decreases in physical punishment in countries with bans (Albania, Macedonia, Togo, Ukraine) compared with those without bans (Central African Republic, Kazakhstan, Montenegro [which passed a ban later in 2016], Sierra Leone; Lansford et al., 2017). The authors concluded that bans alone may be insufficient to have an impact on attitudes and behavior. This speculation is supported by Bussmann and colleagues' (2011) findings. They compared countries that varied based on whether they had banned physical punishment and whether they had implemented public education campaigns. They found the highest rate of physical punishment in the country with neither a prohibition nor public education (France, 92%), followed by the country with public education but not a prohibition (Spain, 50%), followed by the country with prohibition but no public education (Austria, 14%). The lowest rate of physical punishment was found in the countries with both prohibition and public education (Germany and Sweden, 9%).

Limitations

Passing laws that restrict parents' behaviors within a family can be difficult and can take a long time. When such laws are proposed, they are often met with resistance from religious groups and from parents' rights groups, who typically construe the proposed legislation as an infringement on parents' right to discipline their children rather than as an affirmation of children's human rights to equal protection under the law from violence. Legal prohibitions are most successful if they have strong advocates both in the community and in the deliberative body itself. These limitations are outweighed by the fact that, once a bill has passed, all children in a country are simultaneously granted protection from assault, including from their parents. Laws are the ultimate universal intervention.

SUGGESTED FUTURE USE OF THE PROGRAM

How Clinicians Can Use the Intervention

Clinicians can advocate for legal reform in their countries, both as individuals and through their professional organizations, which can study the research on physical punishment and formulate position statements on physical punishment.

How Community Practitioners Can Use the Intervention

Community practitioners can advocate for legal reform and educate citizens about children's rights not to be hit, about the harms of physical punishment, and about the goals of prohibition.

How Policymakers Can Use the Intervention

Policymakers are clearly the key people to implement physical punishment bans. They now have 56 examples of how this can be done and 56 examples of how legislation can be drafted. Policymakers can seek information and support from professional organizations that have developed policy statements on physical punishment and on law reform.

INFORMATION ON OBTAINING THE PROGRAM

The Global Initiative to End All Corporal Punishment of Children provides guidance on the steps to achieving full prohibition of physical punishment (https://endcorporalpunishment.org/reforming-national-laws). This organization has also compiled a list of resources to support law reform, research on countries with and without bans, texts of laws, and detailed information on each country that has achieved full prohibition (https://endcorporalpunishment.org/resources/resources-on-law-reform).

Each law has been written in the official language of the country where it was passed. English translations of all 56 bans can be found at https://endcorporalpunishment.org/countdown.

REFERENCES

Bussmann, K. D. (2004). Evaluating the subtle impact of a ban on corporal punishment of children in Germany. *Child Abuse Review, 13,* 292–311. http://dx.doi.org/10.1002/car.866

Bussmann, K. D. (2011). Germany: Background and legal consequences of the right to be reared without violence. In J. E. Durrant & A. B. Smith (Eds.), *Global pathways to abolishing physical punishment: Realizing children's rights* (pp. 134–145). New York, NY: Routledge.

Bussmann, K. D., Erthal, C., & Schroth, A. (2011). Effects of banning corporal punishment in Europe: A five-nation comparison. In J. E. Durrant & A. B. Smith (Eds.), *Global pathways to abolishing physical punishment: Realizing children's rights* (pp. 299–322). New York, NY: Routledge.

D'Souza, A. J., Russell, M., Wood, B., Signal, L., & Elder, D. (2016). Attitudes to physical punishment of children are changing. *Archives of Disease in Childhood, 101,* 690–693. http://dx.doi.org/10.1136/archdischild-2015-310119

duRivage, N., Keyes, K., Leray, E., Pez, O., Bitfoi, A., Koç, C., . . . Kovess-Masfety, V. (2015). Parental use of corporal punishment in Europe: Intersection between public health and policy. *PLoS ONE, 10*(2), e0118059. http://dx.doi.org/10.1371/journal.pone.0118059

Durrant, J. E. (1999). Evaluating the success of Sweden's corporal punishment ban. *Child Abuse & Neglect: The International Journal, 23,* 435–448. http://dx.doi.org/10.1016/S0145-2134(99)00021-6

Durrant, J. E. (2019). Corporal punishment and the law in global perspective. In J. G. Dwyer (Ed.), *Oxford handbook of children and the law.* Oxford, England: Oxford University Press. Advance online publication.

Gershoff, E. T., & Grogan-Kaylor, A. (2016). Spanking and child outcomes: Old controversies and new meta-analyses. *Journal of Family Psychology, 30,* 453–469. http://dx.doi.org/10.1037/fam0000191

Global Initiative to End All Corporal Punishment of Children. (2017). *Country report for South Sudan.* Retrieved from http://endcorporalpunishment.org/reports-on-every-state-and-territory/south-sudan

Global Initiative to End All Corporal Punishment of Children. (2018a). *Country report for Nepal.* Retrieved from https://endcorporalpunishment.org/reports-on-every-state-and-territory/nepal

Global Initiative to End All Corporal Punishment of Children. (2018b). *Country report for Paraguay.* Retrieved from http://endcorporalpunishment.org/reports-on-every-state-and-territory/paraguay

Global Initiative to End All Corporal Punishment of Children. (2018c). *Country report for Sweden.* Retrieved from http://endcorporalpunishment.org/reports-on-every-state-and-territory/sweden

Global Initiative to End All Corporal Punishment of Children. (2019). *Progress.* Retrieved from https://endcorporalpunishment.org/countdown

Hughes, P. (2009). *Report to the Minister for Social Development and Employment Pursuant to Section 7(2) of the Crimes (Substituted Section 50) Amendment Act 2007.* Wellington, New Zealand: Ministry of Social Development.

Janson, S., Jernbro, C., & Långberg, B. (2011). *Corporal punishment and other humiliating behavior towards children in Sweden*. Stockholm, Sweden: Almänna Barnhuset Foundation.

Klackenberg, G. (1981). The development of children in a Swedish urban community: A prospective longitudinal study. In S. Mednick & A. Baert (Eds.), *Prospective longitudinal research: An empirical basis for the primary prevention of psychosocial disorders* (pp. 212–215). New York, NY: Oxford University Press.

Lansford, J. E., Cappa, C., Putnick, D. L., Bornstein, M. H., Deater-Deckard, K., & Bradley, R. H. (2017). Change over time in parents' beliefs about and reported use of corporal punishment in eight countries with and without legal bans. *Child Abuse & Neglect: The International Journal, 71*(Suppl.), 44–55. http://dx.doi.org/10.1016/j.chiabu.2016.10.016

Lee, S. J., Grogan-Kaylor, A., & Berger, L. M. (2014). Parental spanking of 1-year-old children and subsequent child protective services involvement. *Child Abuse & Neglect: The International Journal, 38*, 875–883. http://dx.doi.org/10.1016/j.chiabu.2014.01.018

New Zealand Children's Commissioner. (2008). *One year on: Public attitudes and New Zealand's child discipline law*. Wellington, New Zealand: Office of the Children's Commissioner. Retrieved from http://www.occ.org.nz/assets/Publications/OCC-UMR-Research-141108.pdf

New Zealand Ministry of Health. (2016). *Annual Update of Key Results 2015/16: New Zealand Health Survey*. Wellington, New Zealand: Ministry of Health.

New Zealand Police. (2009). *Final results of 2 year review of police activity since enactment of the Crimes (substituted section 59) Amendment Act of 2007*. Retrieved from https://www.police.govt.nz/sites/default/files/publications/2-year-review-of-crimes-section-59.pdf

Statistics Sweden. (1996). Spanking and other forms of physical punishment: A study of adults' and middle school students' opinions, experience and knowledge. *Demografiska Rapporter, 1*(2).

Swedish Institute for Opinion Surveys. (1981). *Corporal punishment and child abuse*. Stockholm, Sweden: Author.

UNICEF. (2017). *A familiar face: Violence in the lives of children and adolescents*. Retrieved from https://data.unicef.org/wp-content/uploads/2017/11/VAC-Brochure-FINAL-10-31-17.pdf

United Nations. (1989, November 20). Convention on the Rights of the Child, G. A. Res. 44/25, U. N. GAOR, 44th Sess., at 3, U. N. Doc. A/RES/44/25. Retrieved from http://www.unicef.org/crc

United Nations. (2017, July 6). Work of the Statistical Commission pertaining to the 2030 Agenda for Sustainable Development, G.A. Res. 71/313, U.N. GAOR, 71st Sess., at 13 and 117, U.N. Doc A/RES/71/313. Retrieved from http://ggim.un.org/documents/A_RES_71_313.pdf

United Nations Committee on the Rights of the Child (CRC). (2007, March 2). *CRC General Comment No. 8 (2006): The Right of the Child to Protection from Corporal Punishment and Other Cruel or Degrading forms of Punishment (CRC/C/GC/8)*. Retrieved from http://www.refworld.org/docid/460bc7772.html

United Nations Committee on the Rights of the Child. (2016, February 23). *Concluding observations on the fifth periodic report of France (CRC/C/FRA/CO/5)*. Retrieved from http://undocs.org/CRC/C/FRA/CO/5

Afterword

Common Themes and Next Steps

Elizabeth T. Gershoff and Shawna J. Lee

The 15 interventions described in this book vary on a range of dimensions. Some are delivered through one-on-one intervention (e.g., Baby Books: Chapter 3, Reich & Díaz), others use a group format (e.g., Moms' Empowerment Program: Chapter 12, Grogan-Kaylor, Howell, Galano, & Graham-Bermann), and still others use universal education approaches (e.g., Legal Prohibitions: Chapter 15, Gershoff & Durrant). The format of each intervention is tied to its theory of change; for some interventions, sustainable change is realized when parent education is individualized through one-on-one sessions. For other interventions, change is effected through smaller doses to a larger audience, in the expectation that communitywide attitude shifts are necessary for sustained reductions in parents' use of physical punishment. In addition to such structural differences, the interventions vary on a few other key dimensions that we wish to highlight.

PROHIBITION OR REPLACEMENT

The interventions in this book were included because they have each demonstrated through research that they are effective at reducing physical punishment. The majority of the interventions explicitly include content about physical punishment, which typically takes the form of education about the harms to children that have been linked to parents' use of physical punishment

http://dx.doi.org/10.1037/0000162-017
Ending the Physical Punishment of Children: A Guide for Clinicians and Practitioners,
E. T. Gershoff and S. J. Lee (Editors)

(e.g., Brief Online Education; Chapter 1, Holden & Brown). Many such programs also include information about replacement strategies parents can use instead of physical punishment (e.g., Positive Discipline in Everyday Parenting (PDEP): Chapter 9, Durrant). Yet some programs rely solely on this replacement strategy to avoid confronting parents about physical punishment directly in favor of having them realize on their own that physical punishment is both ineffective and undesirable as a parenting strategy (e.g., Chicago Parent Program: Chapter 11, Breitenstein, Gross, & Bettencourt). The developers of the Chicago Parent Program explain that, for the population to be served by the program, the most effective strategy is *not* to explicitly tell parents to avoid spanking. Indeed, the program has led to significant decreases in physical punishment, illustrating that the same ultimate goal of reduced physical punishment can be achieved without directly addressing the topic, which has the potential to lead to a confrontation. Of course, including an explicit prohibition of physical punishment provides the clearest message to parents that certain behaviors are not acceptable ways of dealing with child misbehavior (e.g., Legal Prohibitions of Physical Punishment: Chapter 15, Gershoff & Durrant). However, it is clear that parents need effective strategies to discipline their children, and instruction on behaviors that can replace physical punishment is likely crucial to sustained reduction of parents' use of physical punishment.

LEVELS OF INTERVENTION AND TARGET POPULATIONS

As we noted in the introduction, interventions are typically thought of as occurring at one of three levels: indicated interventions, selective interventions, and universal interventions (Mrazek & Haggerty, 1994). The chapters of this book illustrate strategies to reduce physical punishment that have been effectively implemented at each of these levels of intervention. The Moms' Empowerment Program (Chapter 12, Grogan-Kaylor et al.) is an indicated intervention because it was designed for mothers who have been victims of intimate partner violence and, because of the resulting stress, are at risk of engaging in harsh parenting behaviors. The Alternative Biblical Interpretations Intervention (Chapter 2, Miller-Perrin & Perrin) is a selective intervention because it was designed to address the beliefs about physical punishment held by individuals with conservative Christian backgrounds. The Baby Books intervention (Chapter 3, Reich & Díaz) is targeted at parents with babies, not because they are at particular risk but because an intervention that starts before parents start disciplining children in toddlerhood can prevent physical punishment from happening in the first place. Several of the interventions in this book are universal and thus designed for all parents or even all adults, such as the Play Nicely intervention (Chapter 5, Scholer), which was designed to teach parents about effective forms of discipline, or the Brief Online Education (Chapter 1, Holden & Brown), which can be used to educate both parents and nonparents about the harms linked with physical punishment.

One intervention highlighted in this book, Triple P (Chapter 13, Prinz), is a multitiered intervention that incorporates universal, selective, and indicated components that can be implemented separately or in concert within a given community. Such an approach is necessarily time- and resource-intensive, but its comprehensive nature ensures that all members of a community receive a consistent message about the ineffectiveness of physical punishment and that those with the most immediate need to change their behaviors are provided the assistance to do so.

THEORETICAL BASIS

A successful intervention is based on the expectation that if a change in a target attitude or behavior occurs, a desired change in an outcome behavior of interest will result. Such expectations are often derived from theory or from theoretical models, and the interventions in this book are no exception.

Several of the interventions described in the book draw from social psychology or clinical psychology theories that help explain individuals' motivation to change their behavior. Motivational interviewing (MI), in which individuals are guided to think critically about their own behavior and develop their own motivation to change, is increasingly popular in clinical work (Miller & Rollnick, 2012). The MI intervention described in Chapter 4 (Holden & Holland) explicitly takes this approach, but it is also a foundation of the ACT Raising Safe Kids Program (Chapter 10, Knox & Dynes) and Safe Environment for Every Kid (SEEK; Chapter 6, Dubowitz).

A similar approach is the transtheoretical model (Prochaska & Velicer, 1997), which identifies several stages of cognitive decision making as necessarily preceding several steps of behavioral change. Underlying both SEEK (Chapter 6, Dubowitz) and Triple P (Chapter 13, Prinz) is the principle that behavior change follows attitudinal change and deliberate decisions to change. The Educational Intervention for Health Care Providers (Chapter 8, Hornor et al.) utilizes the theory of planned behavior (Fishbein & Ajzen, 2011), which has underpinnings similar to those of MI. An overarching theme is that changes in beliefs about the utility and convenience of a given behavior are necessary to change the likelihood that the behavior will recur. In the case of physical punishment, increases in beliefs that spanking is ineffective and inefficient are expected to lead to decreases in parents' reliance on physical punishment.

Another theory from social psychology, Darley and Latané's (1968) theory of bystander intervention, is the foundation of the No Hit Zone intervention (Chapter 14, Gershoff). The intervention is based on the theory's arguments that individuals will intervene in situations of danger only if they notice and recognize the situation as concerning, feel they have a responsibility to intervene, and know what they can do to effectively intervene.

Developmental theories can also provide the basis for intervention because they can identify developmentally appropriate behaviors and can highlight the processes underlying target behavior that can be the focus of intervention.

Two interventions described in this book draw from several developmental theories as the bases for the content of the interventions and the theories of change. PDEP (Chapter 9, Durrant) draws from "attributional, cognitive–developmental, constructivist, epigenetic, social information processing, neuro-relational, and social learning theories" (Chapter 9, this volume, p. 90)—clearly taking a comprehensive approach to understanding what parenting behaviors are most promotive of children's well-being. The Chicago Parent Program (Chapter 11, Breitenstein et al.) and the ACT Raising Safe Kids Program (Chapter 10, Knox & Dynes) similarly draw from several developmental theories, namely social learning theory (Bandura, 1997), the coercive family processes model (Patterson, 1982), and attachment theory (Bowlby, 1982). Because these developmental theories help explain parent–child interactions both when they are going well and when they are not, they inform intervention content by illustrating and explaining both effective and ineffective parenting behaviors.

Several other interventions in the book are centered on core principles more so than theories. The Video Interaction Project (VIP; Chapter 7, Canfield, Roby, & Mendelsohn) takes a strengths-based approach that aims to build up individuals' parenting self-efficacy as a key step toward building more reliance on positive parenting strategies. The Moms' Empowerment Program (Chapter 12, Grogan-Kaylor et al.) is designed for mothers who have been victims of intimate partner violence and thus for whom learning new parenting behaviors happens in parallel to them learning how to address their own mental health, manage stress, and resolve conflicts. The overall principle is to empower women to reduce their and their children's exposure to violence and to address mental health needs from past exposure. The key principle underlying the legal prohibitions of physical punishment (Chapter 15, Gershoff & Durrant) is that physical punishment violates children's human right to protection from violence. Just as adults have the right to protection from assault, so should children.

INTERNATIONAL REACH

All of the interventions described in this book were developed by professionals in the United States or Canada, and several have been used with a range of cultural groups across both of these countries. It is encouraging that three of the interventions have been translated and adapted to other countries as well. The ACT Raising Safe Kids Program (Chapter 10, Knox & Dynes) has been used in 14 countries, PDEP (Chapter 9, Durrant) has been used in 26 countries, and Triple P has been used in 28 countries (Chapter 13, Prinz). The reach of these programs across all regions of the world represents a significant commitment by the intervention developers to adapt and disseminate their interventions and brings these interventions closer to being universal in all senses of the word.

EXTERNAL RECOGNITION FROM CLEARINGHOUSES AND COMPENDIA

Given the growing commitment among practitioners and funders to rely on evidence-based programs, there is a growing need for reliable vetting of prevention and intervention programs. This need is being met by organizations in the United States and around the world that have created online clearinghouses that collect information about programs and rate the quality of the evidence supporting the program or that produce reports that recommend particular programs or types of intervention.

From 1997 to 2018, when it was discontinued, the most widely used of such clearinghouses was the National Registry for Evidence-Based Programs and Practices (NREPP), which had been created and maintained by the Substance Abuse and Mental Health Services Administration (SAMHSA). NREPP rated programs and was a widely respected arbiter of program quality. Unfortunately, SAMHSA ended NREPP in 2018 and replaced it with the Evidence-Based Practices Resource Center, which, despite its name, does not rate the evidence of programs but merely provides a brief description and link to the program's website.

Several clearinghouses and registries have stepped into the gap left by the demise of NREPP. We list here nine of the leading such clearinghouses, in alphabetical order, and the programs within this book that have been listed as evidence-based and recommended programs by each.

Blueprints for Healthy Youth Development (http://blueprintsprograms.org), based at the Center for the Study and Prevention of Violence at the University of Colorado Boulder, is an online registry of the evidence base of programs designed to promote positive child and youth development. According to its website, less than 5% of more than 1,500 reviewed programs have been given their top designations, which are "model" (programs with evidence of success from two experimental or one experimental and one quasiexperimental study) or "promising" (program has evidence from one experimental or two quasiexperimental evaluations; https://blueprintsprograms.org/about). Only one of the programs reviewed in this book has been included in the Blueprints registry: Triple P (Chapter 13), which was rated "promising."

The *California Evidence-Based Clearinghouse for Child Welfare (CEBC)* (http://www.cebc4cw.org) is an online resource created by the California Department of Social Services for clinicians and agencies working with families involved with the child welfare system. The CEBC provides a scientific rating for each program on a 1 to 5 scale: 1 = *well-supported by research evidence*, 2 = *supported by research evidence*, 3 = *promising research evidence*, 4 = *evidence fails to demonstrate effect*, and 5 = *concerning practice*. Five programs in this book have been reviewed and rated in the clearinghouse:

- Chapter 6, SEEK: 1 (well-supported by research evidence)
- Chapter 10, ACT Raising Safe Kids Program: 3 (promising research evidence)
- Chapter 11, Chicago Parent Program: 2 (supported by research evidence)

- Chapter 12, Moms' Empowerment Program (listed as Kids Club & Moms Empowerment): 3 (promising research evidence)
- Chapter 13, Triple P: 2 (supported by research evidence)

The *Canadian Best Practices Portal* (http://cbpp-pcpe.phac-aspc.gc.ca) is an online database of programs designed to promote public health that is run by the Public Health Agency of Canada. It rates programs that do not yet have a high level of impact as "promising practices" and rates programs that have high impact and high quality of evidence as "best practices."

- Chapter 10, ACT Raising Safe Kids Program: promising practice
- Chapter 13, Triple P: best practice

The *Clearinghouse for Military Family Readiness* (https://lion.militaryfamilies.psu.edu/about-us) is a web-based collaboration between Penn State University and the U.S. Department of Defense. The clearinghouse is designed to assist professionals who work with military families in identifying effective interventions and supports. There are seven levels of ratings (effective–RCT, effective–quasi, promising, unclear +, unclear 0, unclear –, and ineffective). Unfortunately, the clearinghouse does not define these categories on its website. Three programs from this book are listed in the clearinghouse:

- Chapter 10, ACT Raising Safe Kids Program: unclear +
- Chapter 11, Chicago Parent Program: promising
- Chapter 13, Triple P: promising

The *Evidence-Based Prevention and Intervention Support Center* (EPISCenter; http://www.episcenter.psu.edu/ebp) is a listing of evidence-based prevention and intervention programs for families approved for use in the state of Pennsylvania. The EPISCenter is a collaboration between the Pennsylvania Commission on Crime and Delinquency and the Prevention Research Center at Penn State University. Only programs judged as having undergone rigorous evaluation are included in the EPISCenter list of evidence-based programs; there is no separate quality rating. One program from this book is included: Chapter 13, Triple P.

Implementing Child Maltreatment Prevention Programmes: What the Experts Say (http://www.euro.who.int/__data/assets/pdf_file/0009/289602/Maltreatment_web.pdf?ua=1) is a guide to interventions to prevent child maltreatment compiled by the World Health Organization Regional Office for Europe (Hardcastle, Bellis, Hughes, & Sethi, 2015). No quality rating is provided, nor is the listing comprehensive; interventions are included as examples of intervention strategies. That said, three of the interventions in this book were included as illustrative child maltreatment prevention programs:

- Chapter 6, SEEK
- Chapter 10, ACT Raising Safe Kids Program
- Chapter 13, Triple P

Innovations Exchange (https://innovations.ahrq.gov/profiles/pediatrician-training-and-office-support-significantly-reduce-instances-child-maltreatment) is an online listing of programs sponsored by the Agency for Healthcare Research and Quality. Programs are rated as strong (one or more experimental evaluations), moderate (quasiexperimental evaluation), or suggestive (nonexperimental). One program from this book is included in the exchange: Chapter 6, SEEK: strong.

Preventing Child Abuse and Neglect: A Technical Package for Policy, Norm, and Programmatic Activities (https://www.cdc.gov/violenceprevention/pdf/can-prevention-technical-package.pdf) is a document created by the Centers for Disease Control and Prevention that recommends strategies and approaches that have been demonstrated to prevent child maltreatment or its precursors. Two of the interventions in this book were specifically mentioned in the technical package:

- Chapter 6, SEEK: under the category of "enhanced primary care"
- Chapter 10, ACT Raising Safe Kids Program: under the category of "parenting skill and family relationship approaches"

Results First Clearinghouse Database (https://www.pewtrusts.org/pt/research-and-analysis/data-visualizations/2015/results-first-clearinghouse-database) is an online database of programs that draws from nine existing national clearinghouses and is the result of a collaboration between Pew Charitable Trusts and the John D. and Catherine T. MacArthur Foundation. Each included program is rated on a 5-point scale (*highest rated, second-highest rated, mixed effects, no effects, negative effects*).

- Chapter 6, SEEK: highest rated
- Chapter 10, ACT Raising Safe Kids Program: second-highest rated
- Chapter 11, Chicago Parent Program: highest rated
- Chapter 12, Moms' Empowerment Program: second-highest rated
- Chapter 13, Triple P: highest rated

NEXT STEPS FOR PROFESSIONAL ENGAGEMENT

Each of the interventions described in this book presents an innovative and exciting approach that professionals can use to work with parents to reduce parents' use of physical punishment. In addition, professionals can consider other types of professional engagement to reduce physical punishment of children.

Policy and Practice Statements Against the Use of Physical Punishment

One such strategy is working within professional organizations to advocate for the implementation of policy and practice standards against the use of physical punishment. In fact, as we noted in the introduction, a number of leading professional organizations such as the American Psychological Association

(APA, 2019), American Academy of Pediatrics (AAP; Sege, Siegel, Council on Child Abuse and Neglect, & Committee on Psychosocial Aspects of Child and Family Health, 2019), Canadian Paediatric Society (Durrant, Ensom, & Coalition on Physical Punishment of Children and Youth, 2004), Canadian Psychological Association (2004), American Academy of Child and Adolescent Psychiatry (2012), and American Professional Society on the Abuse of Children (2016) have policy or practice statements that inform professionals within those organizations to advise parents against the use of physical punishment. For example, APA's (2019) *Resolution on Physical Discipline of Children by Parents* specifically calls for caregivers to "use alternative forms of discipline that are associated with more positive outcomes for children" (p. 2). The AAP policy statement on effective discipline to raise healthy children

> recommends that adults caring for children use healthy forms of discipline, such as positive reinforcement of appropriate behaviors, setting limits, redirecting, and setting future expectations. The AAP recommends that parents do not use spanking, hitting, slapping, threatening, insulting, humiliating, or shaming. (Sege et al., 2019, p. 6)

Statements such as these send a clear message to professionals who work with families and children regarding their role to provide evidence-based guidance to parents about effective discipline.

However, numerous other major professional organizations, including organizations that represent professionals who work directly with parents and abused children (e.g., the National Association of Social Workers), do not currently have similar statements. Professionals who are members of these organizations can continue policy-change advocacy efforts and use the examples provided by the APA and the AAP to advocate for policy and practice statements against the use of physical punishment.

There are a number of potential benefits to policy advocacy as a mechanism to shift behaviors and norms related to the use of physical punishment. One study of professionals in the field of child maltreatment prevention found most respondents agreed that physical punishment is harmful to children and leads to negative outcomes for children; however, in the same survey, respondents felt that their colleagues were more likely to endorse spanking than they were (Taylor, Fleckman, & Lee, 2017). In other words, many professionals perceive that their colleagues are more accepting of physical punishment than is actually the case. Thus, by establishing professional norms against the use of physical punishment, such standards may also minimize the gap between individuals' personal beliefs about physical punishment and the perceived beliefs of one's colleagues and coworkers. Policy or practice statements can also establish norms regarding what type of advice is appropriate to give to parents. Professionals can invoke those policy or practice standards to normalize the practice of addressing the topic of physical punishment with parents. As parents understand that the professionals are acting within their professional organization guidelines, they may be more willing to consider intervention and programs that help to minimize the use of physical punishment.

Public Health Messaging Campaigns As a Direction for Future Intervention

An additional strategy that has not yet been tested in the United States in the area of physical punishment but that is well vetted in other domains is the use of public health messaging. Many parents and some professionals think that spanking is effective (Taylor et al., 2016), despite research evidence to the contrary. Public health campaigns have been successfully used to establish social norms and change individual behavior in numerous domains ranging from increasing vaccination rates of young children to smoking and tobacco cessation. In the realm of child maltreatment prevention, many may be aware of the shaken baby syndrome messaging campaign sponsored by the Centers for Disease Control and Prevention (n.d.), which included messaging strategies such as reframing shaken baby syndrome as a public health problem (Poole, Seal, & Taylor, 2014). In addition, the Triple P program incorporates a universal messaging component to normalize the challenges of parenting and provide general tips to parents about effective parenting strategies (Triple P: Chapter 13, Prinz; see also Gagné, Bélanger-Gravel, Clément, & Poissant, 2018; Poole et al., 2014; Prinz, Sanders, Shapiro, Whitaker, & Lutzker, 2009).

However, to date, no public health messaging campaigns in the United States have focused specifically on the issue of reducing hitting or physical punishment of children (Poole et al., 2014). An ongoing campaign in the city of Toronto's public health department is targeted at reducing spanking through the promotion of positive discipline techniques through clear and concise messages on their website (Toronto Public Health, 2018). In the United States, given the high rates of physical punishment directed toward young children and even babies, one messaging strategy may be for pediatricians and social workers to provide anticipatory guidance to parents during well-child visits during the first year of life specifically about the dangers of spanking babies; for example, along with "don't shake your baby," parents could be directed to "never hit your baby." Another strategy could be to use a messaging campaign to counter commonly heard arguments in favor of physical punishment, such as the notions that spanking is effective and that spanking does not harm children (Taylor et al., 2016).

Bans in Schools

There has been progress toward the goal of reducing violence toward children. For example, as reviewed in Gershoff and Durrant (Chapter 15, this volume), 56 countries currently have full prohibitions of physical punishment. However, neither the United States nor Canada have instituted legal bans, and, at least in the United States, full prohibition seems unlikely in the near future. One policy step that may be feasible, however, is prohibition of corporal punishment in schools (Gershoff & Font, 2016). Corporal punishment is legal in many states in the United States but is disproportionally used against children with disabilities and racial and ethnic minority children

(Gershoff & Font, 2016). Prohibition against physical punishment of children in schools would benefit children as well as contribute to a general shift in norms away from the use of hitting children in any setting. Furthermore, working toward ending corporal punishment in schools could be an important intermediary step in establishing norms that would support full prohibition of physical punishment, including in the home.

CONCLUSION

We hope that researchers and interventionists will further refine existing interventions or develop new ones. A key gap in our existing interventions is an acknowledgment of the perspectives of children themselves. None of the interventions in this book explicitly incorporate children's experiences of what it is like to be hit by their parents. A key reason parents stop using physical punishment is their empathy for their children (Holden, Thompson, Zambarano, & Marshall, 1997), which suggests that helping parents identify with their children could be an effective way to spur parents to stop using violent discipline.

We hope clinicians, community practitioners, and policymakers take inspiration from the interventions described in this book and implement them at all levels of society. Reduction of violence at any scale is a positive outcome, particularly so when children are the targets of violent behavior.

REFERENCES

American Academy of Child and Adolescent Psychiatry. (2012, July 30). *Corporal punishment*. Retrieved from http://www.aacap.org/aacap/policy_statements/2012/Policy_Statement_on_Corporal_Punishment.aspx

American Professional Society on the Abuse of Children. (2016). *APSAC position statement on corporal punishment of children*. Retrieved from https://www.apsac.org/apsacpublications

American Psychological Association. (2019). *Resolution on physical discipline of children by parents*. Retrieved from https://www.apa.org/about/policy/physical-discipline.pdf

Bandura, A. (1997). *Self-efficacy: The exercise of control*. New York, NY: W. H. Freeman/Times Books/Henry Holt.

Bowlby, J. (1982). *Attachment and loss: Vol. 1. Attachment* (2nd ed.). New York, NY: Basic Books.

Canadian Psychological Association. (2004). *Policy statements: Physical punishment of children and youth*. Retrieved from https://cpa.ca/aboutcpa/policystatements/#physical

Centers for Disease Control and Prevention, National Center for Injury Prevention and Control. (n.d.). *Preventing shaken baby syndrome: A guide for health departments and community-based organizations*. Washington, DC: U.S. Department of Health and Human Services. Retrieved from https://stacks.cdc.gov/view/cdc/5863

Darley, J. M., & Latané, B. (1968). Bystander intervention in emergencies: Diffusion of responsibility. *Journal of Personality and Social Psychology, 8*(4, Pt. 1), 377–383. http://dx.doi.org/10.1037/h0025589

Durrant, J. E., Ensom, R., & Coalition on Physical Punishment of Children and Youth. (2004). *Joint statement on physical punishment of children and youth*. Retrieved from http://www.cheo.on.ca/en/physicalpunishment

Fishbein, M., & Ajzen, I. (2011). *Predicting and changing behavior: The reasoned action approach.* New York, NY: Taylor & Francis. http://dx.doi.org/10.4324/9780203838020

Gagné, M. H., Bélanger-Gravel, A., Clément, M. E., & Poissant, J. (2018). Recall and understanding of a communication campaign designed to promote positive parenting and prevent child maltreatment. *Preventive Medicine Reports, 12,* 191–197. http://dx.doi.org/10.1016/j.pmedr.2018.09.015

Gershoff, E. T., & Font, S. A. (2016). Corporal punishment in U.S. public schools: Prevalence, disparities in use, and status in state and federal policy. *Social Policy Report, 30*(1), 1–26. http://dx.doi.org/10.1002/j.2379-3988.2016.tb00086.x

Hardcastle, K. A., Bellis, M. A., Hughes, K., & Sethi, D. (2015). *Implementing child maltreatment prevention programmes: What the experts say.* Copenhagen, Denmark: WHO Regional Office for Europe. Retrieved from http://www.euro.who.int/__data/assets/pdf_file/0009/289602/Maltreatment_web.pdf?ua=1

Holden, G. W., Thompson, E. E., Zambarano, R. J., & Marshall, L. A. (1997). Child effects as a source of change in maternal attitudes toward corporal punishment. *Journal of Social and Personal Relationships, 14,* 481–490. http://dx.doi.org/10.1177/0265407597144004

Miller, W. R., & Rollnick, S. (2012). *Motivational interviewing: Preparing people for change* (3rd ed.). New York, NY: Guilford Press.

Mrazek, P. J., & Haggerty, R. J. (Eds.). (1994). *Reducing risks for mental disorders: Frontiers for prevention intervention research.* Washington, DC: National Academies Press.

Patterson, G. R. (1982). *Coercive family process.* Eugene, OR: Castalia.

Poole, M. K., Seal, D. W., & Taylor, C. A. (2014). A systematic review of universal campaigns targeting child physical abuse prevention. *Health Education Research, 29,* 388–432. http://dx.doi.org/10.1093/her/cyu012

Prinz, R. J., Sanders, M. R., Shapiro, C. J., Whitaker, D. J., & Lutzker, J. R. (2009). Population-based prevention of child maltreatment: The US Triple P system population trial. *Prevention Science, 10*(1), 1–12. http://dx.doi.org/10.1007/s11121-009-0123-3

Prochaska, J. O., & Velicer, W. F. (1997). The transtheoretical model of health behavior change. *American Journal of Health Promotion, 12,* 38–48. http://dx.doi.org/10.4278/0890-1171-12.1.38

Sege, R. D., Siegel, B. S., Council on Child Abuse and Neglect, & Committee on Psychosocial Aspects of Child and Family Health. (2019). Effective discipline to raise healthy children. *Pediatrics, 142*(6), e20183112. http://dx.doi.org/10.1542/peds.2018-3112

Taylor, C. A., Al-Hiyari, R., Lee, S. J., Priebe, A., Guerrero, L. W., & Bales, A. (2016). Beliefs and ideologies linked with approval of corporal punishment: A content analysis of online comments. *Health Education Research, 31,* 563–575. http://dx.doi.org/10.1093/her/cyw029

Taylor, C. A., Fleckman, J. M., & Lee, S. J. (2017). Attitudes, beliefs, and perceived norms about corporal punishment and related training needs among members of the "American Professional Society on the Abuse of Children." *Child Abuse & Neglect: The International Journal, 71,* 56–68. http://dx.doi.org/10.1016/j.chiabu.2017.04.009

Toronto Public Health. (2018). *Positive discipline.* Retrieved from https://www.toronto.ca/community-people/children-parenting/pregnancy-and-parenting/parenting/positive-discipline

INDEX

Q

R

V

W

Y

ABOUT THE EDITORS

Elizabeth T. Gershoff, PhD, is a professor of human development and family sciences and is associate director for faculty development at the Population Research Center, both at the University of Texas at Austin. She has published extensively on the topic of physical punishment and is an internationally recognized expert on the effects that physical punishment by parents or by school personnel has on children.

Shawna J. Lee, PhD, is an associate professor in the School of Social Work at the University of Michigan. Dr. Lee has published numerous articles and book chapters on early parent–child relationships, physical discipline of children, and child maltreatment prevention. She was lead author of the American Professional Society on the Abuse of Children statement against the use of physical punishment.